3PARA

PATRICK BISHOP

3 PARA

HarperPress
An Imprint of HarperCollins*Publishers*

Harper*Press*
An imprint of HarperCollins*Publishers*
77–85 Fulham Palace Road,
Hammersmith, London W6 8JB
www.harpercollins.co.uk

Published by Harper*Press* in 2007

1

Maps © HarperCollins*Publishers*
designed by HL Studios, Oxfordshire

A catalogue record for this book
is available from the British Library

HB ISBN 978-0-00-725778-2
TPB ISBN 978-0-00-725779-9

Typeset in Giovanni Book with Photina display

Printed and bound in Great Britain by Clays Ltd, St Ives plc

'The following account is based on interviews with the soldiers of the 3 PARA Battle Group. Inquests have not yet been held into many of the deaths reported in these pages. The author has made his best endeavour to report events accurately and truthfully, and any insult or injury to any of the parties described or quoted herein or to their families is unintentional. The publishers will be happy to correct any inaccuracies in later editions.

Afghan identities have been obscured in a few cases in order to protect the individuals and their families.

Contents

List of Illustrations

Private Neil Edwards, Lance Corporal Noel Brooksbank, and
Private Scott Boyle and Alistair Hartley in a Sangin sangar.
© *Private Dale Tyrer*
Lance Corporal Paul Roberts, Corporal Stuart Giles, Sergeant Brian
Reidy and Medical Officer Captain Harvey Pynn.
© *Sergeant Dan Jarvie*
Soldiers doss down on the floor at the Sangin district centre. ©
Captain Harvey Pynn

Corporal Mark Wright in the Sangin compound.
© *Captain Nick French*
Lieutenant Any Mallet leads a patrol into Sangin town centre.
© *Corporal Andrew Waddington*
Sergeant Dan Jarvie. © *Crown copyright*

Major Will Pike, OC 'A' Company. © *Crown copyright*
Captain Martin Taylor. © *Major Will Pike*
WO2 Zac Leong. © *Captain Martin Taylor*
Captain Matt Taylor. © *Lieutenant Martin Hewitt*

SECOND PLATE SECTION

Captains Alex Mackenzie and mate Piers Ashfield having a brew at
Sangin. © *Lieutenant Martin Hewitt*
Corporal Jay Jackson on stag in Sangin. © *Corporal Dave Salmon*
Regimental Sergeant Major John Hardy.
© *Lieutenant Colonel Stuart Tootal*
Lieutenant Ollie Dale gets his head down in Sangin.
© *Corporal Dave Salmon*

The Pathfinders at Musa Qaleh. © *Nick Wight-Boycott*
Company Commanders Jamie Loden and Paddy Blair on the roof
at Sangin. © *Lieutenant Colonel Stuart Tootal*
Sergeant Major Mick Bolton in front of the Sangin district centre.
© *Captain Euan Goodman*

A mortar section at Sangin fires in support of patrols on the
   ground. © *Captain Euan Goodman*
A Chinook takes off from Sangin under fire. © *Corporal Carl Tees*

Private Pete McKinley recovering from shrapnel wounds in the
   base hospital. © *Lieutenant Colonel Stuart Tootal*
Corporal Bryan Budd on patrol in Sangin. © *Captain Hugo Farmer*

Rifleman Nabin Rai after a contact with Taliban in Now Zad.
   © *Major Dan Rex*
Major Huw Williams, Captain Nick French and a signaller at Musa
   Qaleh. © *Captain Martin Taylor*
A .50-cal heavy machine gun inside a well-reinforced sangar at
   Sangin. © *Major Jamie Loden*
Lieutenant Colonel Stuart Tootal in the desert near Musa Qaleh.
   © *Captain Nick French*

Heading out to the helicopter landing site after a successful
   resupply operation at Musa Qaleh. © *Crown copyright*
'Giving the Taliban the good news'. Watching an air strike go in
   outside Musa Qaleh. © *Crown copyright*
Sergeant Christopher 'Freddie' Kruyer. © *Staff Sergeant Pete Joiner*

Dinner at Bastion. © *Crown copyright*
Major Adam Jowett, OC of Easy Company, chats with local elders.
   © *Gaz Faulkner*
Captain Hugo Farmer on patrol in Gereshk in full kit.
   © *Captain Emma Couper*

Private Dave Prosser and other members of Mortar Platoon.
   © *Sergeant Freddie Kruyer*
A *shura* in Sangin.
Brigadier Ed Butler on the day of the official battle group photo.
   © *Crown copyright*

ENDPAPERS
The 3 Para battle group. © *Crown copyright*

List of Maps

AFGHANISTAN

TURKMENISTAN

UZBEKISTA

N
W E
S

JOWZJAN

BALKH

Sheberghan   Mazar-e
Sharif

Meymaneh   Sar-e-pol

FARYAB   SAR-E POL

SAMAN

IRAN

BADGHIS
Qal eh-ye Now

BAMIAN

Bamia

Herat   Chaghcharan

HERAT

GHOWR   DAYKONDI

GHAZ

FARAH   Musa
Qaleh   ORUZGAN

Farah   *Helmand Rud*   Tarin Kowt

ZABOL

Gereshk   *Helmand Rud*   Qalat

Lashkar
Gah   Kandahar

Zaranj

NIMRUZ   KANDAHAR

Helmand Rud

HELMAND   Quetta

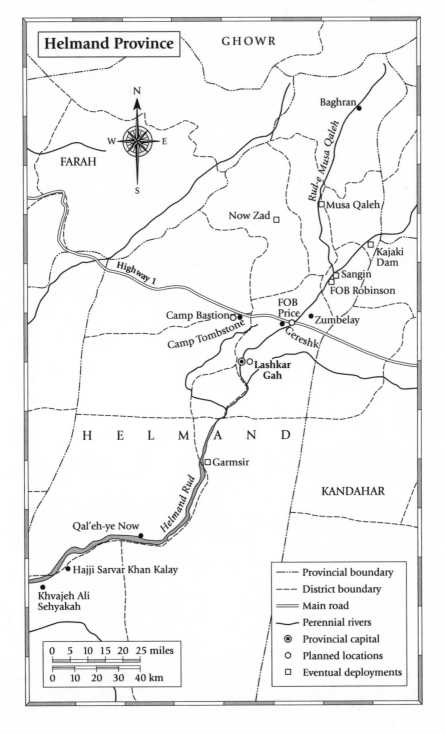

Helmand Province

GHOWR

FARAH

Baghran

Musa Qaleh

Now Zad

Kajaki Dam

Highway 1

Sangin

FOB Robinson

FOB Price

Camp Bastion

Zumbelay

Camp Tombstone

Gereshk

Lashkar Gah

HELMAND

Garmsir

KANDAHAR

Helmand Rud

Qal'eh-ye Now

Hajji Sarvar Khan Kalay

Khvajeh Ali Sehyakah

—·—·— Provincial boundary
— — — District boundary
═══ Main road
—— Perennial rivers
◉ Provincial capital
○ Planned locations
□ Eventual deployments

0   5   10 15 20 25 miles

0   10 20 30 40 km

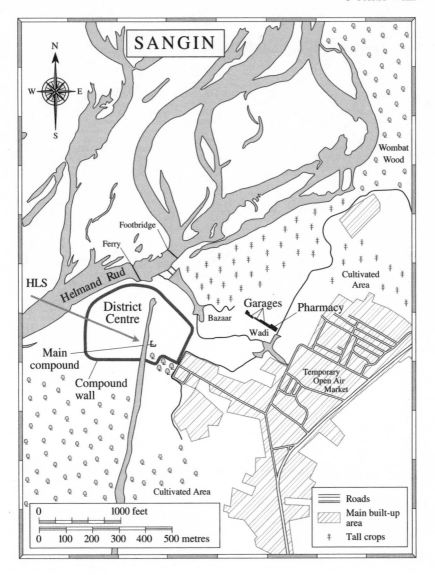

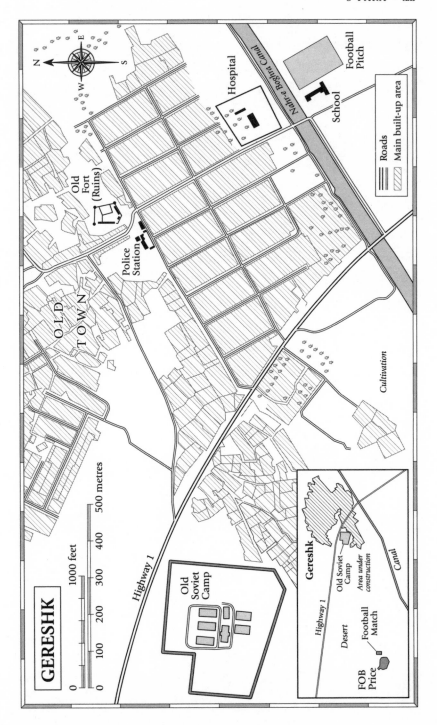

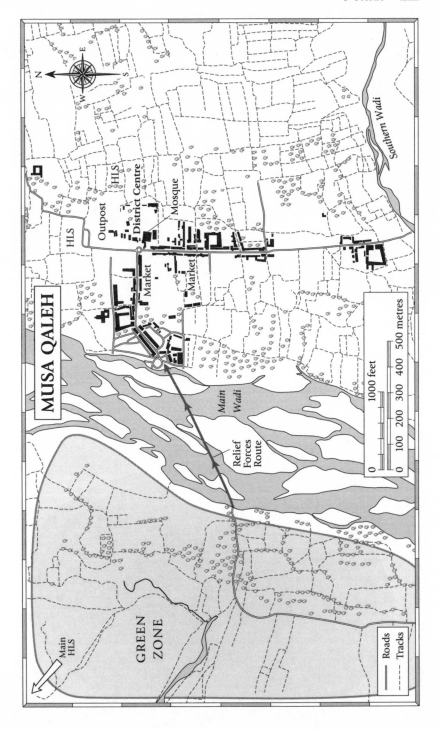

MUSA QALEH

GREEN ZONE

Main HLS

Relief Forces Route

Main Wadi

Market

Market

District Centre

Mosque

Outpost

HLS

HLS

Southern Wadi

N

Roads
Tracks

0   100   200   300   400   500 metres
0   1000 feet

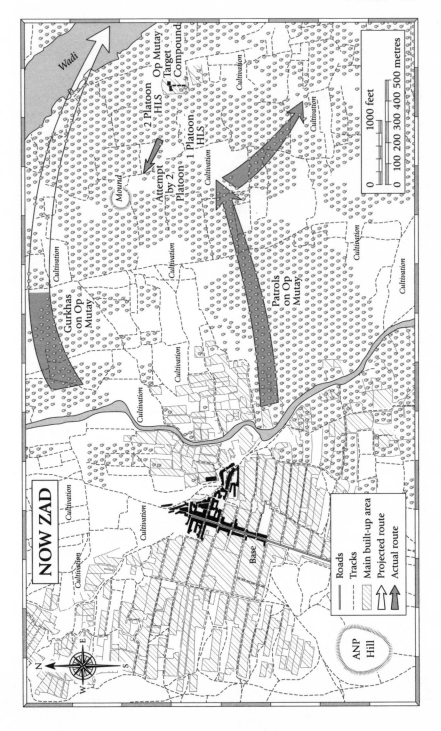

1

Day of Days

At about 8 a.m. on the morning of 6 September 2006 Lieutenant Colonel Stuart Tootal rolled out of his cot, pulled on his uniform and boots and set off along the duckboard walkway to catch up on overnight events.

The sun was already high and a pale, malevolent haze hovered over the talcum-powder dust of the Helmand desert. He reached a tent bristling with radio antennae and pushed aside the door flap. Inside it was warm and stuffy. The gloom was pricked with little nails of green and red light, winking from stacks of electronic consoles. It was quiet except for the occasional squawk from the radios. This was the Joint Operational Command, the 'JOC', where the synapses of the battle group he led came together.

Tootal was slight, wiry and driven. He was as interested in the theory of soldiering as he was in the practice, and had as many degrees as battle honours. His enthusiasm for his job was matched by his concern for his men. There would be much to be concerned about before the day was over.

The 3 Para battle group had arrived in Helmand five months earlier. Its task was to create a security zone within which development agencies could get to work on projects to develop an area barely touched by progress and lay the foundations for a future of relative prosperity.

The plan had always been aspirational. The religious warriors of the Taliban, who were struggling to reassert their power in the province, were certain to oppose the arrival of the British.

Everyone had expected some trouble, but not the relentless combat the soldiers were now immersed in. The reconstruction mission had become a memory. 3 Para and their comrades were fighting a desperate war of attrition. Most of them were besieged in bare mud-and-breeze-block government compounds – 'platoon houses', as they had become known – scattered over the north of the province, fighting off daily attacks from an enemy who, despite taking murderous losses, kept on coming. They spent their days pounded by the sun as they took their turn at 'stag', crouching in sandbagged, rooftop gun positions, or standing by to run to their posts when the shooting started. They slept on floors, washed rarely and lived off ration packs and sterilised water. They were gaunt, bony and rough looking. Their sunburned faces were fuzzed with beards, just like those of the men they were fighting.

They were on their own out there. Beyond the walls of the compound and the shattered towns lay tawny, sun-baked mountains and vast stretches of desert, ridged with dry water-courses. The mother base at Camp Bastion was far away and they were connected to it by the slimmest of links, the helicopters whose vulnerability to the insurgents' fire made every sortie heart-stoppingly tense.

The morning started calmly. The previous day, most of the fighting had been around the base at Musa Qaleh, a broken-down fortress in the middle of a ghost town, now inhabited only by men trying to kill each other. It was held by the soldiers of Easy Company, some of whom had been there for thirty-one days. In the morning, the insurgents had lobbed five mortars into the compound from concealed positions in the maze of alleyways and walled gardens that pressed against the walls of the base.

At about 7.40 that evening some of the Royal Irish Regiment soldiers with the 3 Para battle group were on a satellite phone to their comrades at their home near Inverness, discussing the 'big piss-up' that was being organised to celebrate their expected home-coming in a few weeks' time. The call was interrupted by the crash of an RPG (rocket-propelled grenade) smashing into one of the sandbagged 'sangar' defensive positions ringing the platoon house. The blast knocked the four men inside flat and sent a soldier flying down the stone steps, knocking him unconscious. The soldiers in the sangar struggled upright and got on their guns, scanned the ground in front of them for muzzle flashes, and poured fire into the darkness. Green and red tracer flowed back and forth, and the crack of rifles and the throb of machine guns shattered the air.

The Taliban attack was finally beaten off after forty minutes when British and American jets arrived to bomb and strafe the insurgents' positions. Intelligence reported 'many Taliban killed in action'. Before he grabbed some sleep, Corporal Danny Groves, one of the Royal Irish soldiers, wrote with satisfaction in his diary: 'Today was a very good day for the boys ... The Taliban had attempted to over-run us but instead they received a hell of a beating from the mismatched men of Easy Company.'

And now, another day in Helmand was dawning. At 9 a.m., Tootal's headquarters staff gathered in the JOC for the morning brief. A few incidents had trickled in over the radio net. Just before 8 a.m., four mortars had landed in the base at Now Zad. This was the most remote of the outstations, about fifty miles to the north-west as the helicopter flew from Bastion. Half an hour later, small-arms fire and RPGs were fired at the platoon house at Sangin. This was the normal back-and-forth violence, the metronome tick of aggression and counter-aggression that punctuated every day. There was nothing to distract Tootal from his usual crowded morning of meetings and briefings.

Then, just after midday, the atmosphere in the JOC changed. Reports of casualties started filtering in from Kajaki Dam. The dam was a prize target for the insurgents. The hydroelectric station there generated power for the whole region. The British troops, who lived in sweltering trenches dug out of the stony hills overlooking it, came under regular Taliban attack. But this sounded like something different. The details were sketchy at first. A sniper on his way to spy out a Taliban position had stepped on a mine and was very badly wounded.

Tootal called up his higher headquarters at Kandahar to request a Black Hawk helicopter, equipped with a winch, to lift the casualty out. He was told there would be a long delay. A CH-47 Chinook casualty evacuation helicopter was available. But it did not have lifting gear.

On a patch of barren hillside in Kajaki, a group of men stood rooted to the ground. Beside them lay Lance Corporal Stuart Hale of 3 Para Support Company. The mine had blown off his foot. Corporal Mark Wright was on his position about a mile away when he heard the explosion. He rounded up some soldiers and medics and they ran down the hill to help. They had gone to Hale's side knowing the potential danger they were in. Now they were trying to get him out. They began prodding the gritty sun-baked ground, clearing a path to a spot where the helicopter could get in, then carried Hale on a stretcher to the landing site. Corporal Stuart Pearson turned back along the cleared path. As he bent down to pick up a water container, there was another explosion. Until now, it had seemed that Hale might be the victim of a stray mine, probably left behind by the Russians who had spent years occupying Kajaki. Now the rescuers were hit by a grim realisation. 'We thought, fucking hell,' said Corporal Jay Davis, 'we are in a minefield now. They are everywhere.'

Pearson was only four or five yards away. But every step risked another explosion. He applied a tourniquet and dosed himself with morphine while they waited for the helicopter. It arrived at 1.30, and landed more than fifty yards away across ground that for all anyone knew was thick with mines. There was no question of carrying the casualties to the Chinook. As it lifted off in a cloud of muck and grit, another mine went off, blasting shrapnel into the shoulder, chest and face of Mark Wright.

A medic, Lance Corporal Paul 'Tug' Hartley, moved forward to help. He threw his medical pack on the ground in front of him to detonate any mines in his path. He reached Wright safely. But as he arrived Fusilier Andy Barlow moved back to give him room, treading on a mine that blasted shrapnel into his lower leg. The blast also blew Hartley to the ground and wounded Private Dave Prosser.

All around, men lay bleeding into the dirt. Hunched over the radios, Tootal and his staff had been listening with mounting dismay as the picture grew darker. The only way the wounded and the stranded could escape the minefield was if they were lifted out.

Tootal harassed Kandahar for updates on when the winch-equipped Black Hawk would be ready to haul his men to safety. Nearly four hours after the initial request, two Black Hawks arrived. Two American aircrew were lowered into the minefield and, one by one, winched everyone aboard.

When the casualties reached Bastion, Tootal and 3 Para's RSM (regimental sergeant major), John Hardy, were at the landing site to meet them. As the helicopter touched down, they jumped aboard. Six men were stacked across the floor. Three had stumps where one of their legs had been. One was dead. Mark Wright, who had been chatting and joking with his mates during the two and a half hours they had waited to be rescued, had bled to death on the way home. The wounded were hurried away. Hardy and Tootal zipped Wright into a body bag and carried him to an ambulance.

Tootal had been back in the JOC for fifteen minutes when another spate of emergency signals squawked over the radio. There were more wounded soldiers in two of the platoon houses. In Sangin, three soldiers had been hit by mortar shrapnel as they stood in an orchard within the walls of the base being briefed on their tasks for the evening. Mortar fire had injured two more British soldiers and two of their Afghan allies in Musa Qaleh. There was, however, only one Chinook helicopter available to mount a casualty evacuation – a 'casevac'.

The helicopter, with the Immediate Response Team of medics aboard, was ordered to go to Sangin first. One of the wounded, Lance Corporal Luke McCulloch, had been hit in the head and looked close to death. The casevac chopper was flown by Major Mark Hammond of the Royal Marines. The flight took twenty minutes. As Hammond began his final approach, the JOC fizzed with tension. This was when the helicopters were most vulnerable to the Taliban RPGs and heavy machine guns. The loss of a chopper would not only be a human disaster. It would be a huge victory for the Taliban, and could lay the ground for a British tactical defeat. There was already talk in London of pulling out of the farthest-flung platoon houses to minimise the risk of a helicopter being shot down.

As the Chinook swooped towards the landing site, Hammond saw green tracer fire flowing towards him from the fields, thickly planted with tall crops that lay south of the base. Reluctantly, he swung the Chinook away and headed back to Bastion.

He and his crew had been on the ground only a few minutes when they were ordered off again, this time to try to retrieve the two casualties at Musa Qaleh. The base doctor there had warned Tootal that he could keep one of his patients alive only for another six or seven hours. Musa Qaleh was the helicopter crews' most hated destination. The landing site was in the middle of a built-up area full of insurgent firing points. When they reached the town at 8.15 p.m., the Taliban were waiting. One of the escorting Apaches saw two RPGs swish past the Chinook, missing it by 10 yards. To attempt a landing would be suicidal. Again Hammond was forced to return to base. When they arrived at Bastion they found their chopper spattered with strike marks. One round had hit the root of a rotor blade, inflicting potentially lethal damage.

Tootal decided to risk another attempt before the night was over. A replacement was found for the damaged Chinook. Artillery batteries and aircraft were put on alert to batter Taliban positions around the two bases as the helicopter darted in. Hammond, along with his three crewmates and the four members of the medical team, took off for Sangin once more. He brought the Chinook into the landing site low and fast. As it settled in a whirlwind of dust, a Spartan armoured vehicle raced up to the back ramp, where the crew snatched the casualties aboard. The helicopter had barely touched the ground before it was climbing again, chased by streams of green tracer spouting from the Taliban positions. The sound of the engine was drowned out by the ear-battering din as the crew returned the fire from the door guns.

The ambulances were waiting at Bastion to hurry the casualties away to the base hospital. It was too late for Luke McCulloch. The twenty-one-year-old, one of the contingent of Royal Irish Regiment soldiers fighting alongside the Paras, was pronounced dead before he got there.

In the course of the day Mark Hammond had experienced

enough danger to last most pilots a lifetime, but he volunteered for a last, risk-laden task. For the second time that night he went back to Musa Qaleh. Tootal had racked up every aircraft available, amassing an escort of Apache attack helicopters, A-10 'Tankbusters' and a Spectre gunship to shepherd the Chinook in. As the chopper arrived, just before 1.30 a.m., the aircraft strafed the Taliban firing points around the base. Despite the barrage, the insurgents managed to launch an attack and bullets cracked around the Chinook as it touched down, picked up the wounded and climbed into the night.

The Chinook finally arrived back safely at 2 a.m. Before he collapsed into bed, Stuart Tootal found time to write up his diary. It had been an extraordinary day, one that those involved in its dramas would never forget. He had spent the previous fourteen hours 'endeavouring to get our wounded out from three different locations. Two died on the way and three have had legs amputated. Some will return to combat and some will not.'

There had been many times since the Paras had deployed when he had turned to RSM Hardy before heading to his cot and said, 'That was a day of days.' But there had not been a day like this one. There had been tragedy, he wrote, but also 'much courage, both by the wounded and those who went to get them. There has been sorrow, sadness, fortitude and even humour. A difficult day, no doubt, but one to be proud of, having seen the way people have behaved.'

His last thought before he dropped into an exhausted sleep was, 'I really don't want tomorrow to be like today but it just might be. It might actually be worse.'

2

Green On – Go

3 Para had a saying: 'Be careful what you wish for.' When word got around that they might be on their way to Afghanistan, everyone welcomed the news. There was a feeling that a major operational deployment for the Parachute Regiment was long overdue. It had been twenty-four years since they were involved in heavy fighting. That had been in the Falkands, a campaign that loomed large in the Para legend.

The Paras had returned from the South Atlantic wreathed in glory. There were two VCs to add to their hoard of medals. They won famous victories at Goose Green and Mount Longdon. But in the interval between the Falkands and Helmand they had done little war fighting. They were not sent to the first Gulf War and were given only a subsidiary role in the second. The Kosovo deployment in 1999 was uneventful. There had been the odd exciting excursion, like the mission to Sierra Leone in 2000 when 1 Para helped rescue eleven Royal Irish Rangers held hostage by the rebel West Side Boys militia. But 3 Para's duties in recent years had mostly involved gruelling but increasingly routine tours of Northern Ireland and Iraq.

By the summer of 2005, when the rumours of a deployment to Afghanistan began to gain substance, everyone was ready for a demanding task that would allow them to measure themselves against the soldiers who had gone before them.

The Parachute Regiment was one of the youngest in the British Army. But in its short life it had developed a strong identity and a powerful sense of its own capabilities and worth. The formation of a permanent airborne force was Churchill's idea. The new regiment was intended to bring together the fittest, most motivated and resourceful men available. Its purpose was to cause the maximum damage to the enemy with minimal or no support. It was expected to operate behind enemy lines undaunted by overwhelming superior enemy forces. Its spirit was summed up in its motto, *Utrinque Paratus* – Ready for Anything.

The first British airborne assault took place in February 1941 when a small band of daredevils jumped into southern Italy and blew up an aqueduct. In the remaining four years of the war the Paras built a tradition as illustrious as that of many of the ancient regiments they fought alongside. They were in North Africa and took part in the invasions of Sicily and Italy. They played a key role in the Normandy landings, notably at Merville, where they knocked out a gun battery protected from air attack by 12-foot-thick concrete, which threatened the invasion fleet.

They were at the heart of the most famous airborne operation in history, Market Garden. The Paras, alongside two airborne divisions of Americans and one of Poles, were dropped 100 miles behind the German front lines to clear a corridor across the Netherlands for the advancing Allied armies. The 10,000-strong British 1st Airborne Division was all but wiped out and the key bridge at Arnhem it was tasked to capture remained in German hands. But the episode established an imperishable reputation for courage, resolution and coolness that was celebrated in the film *A Bridge Too Far*. During the Suez crisis in 1956, 660 paratroopers dropped into El Gamil airport in darkness, securing it in the face of heavy opposition.

Memories of Merville, Arnhem and Suez still colour the Para ethos. New recruits might not know the name of the last prime minister but one, but by the time they finish their training they will be fluent in the history of the regiment. This pride in the past provides a reservoir of spiritual strength to draw on in hard times. 'We are here to uphold something that has gone before,' said John Hardy, the 3 Para RSM. In nasty moments in Helmand, when fortitude was flagging, he would remind his men that their performance was under scrutiny, asking them,'The blokes who went through the war, through Arnhem – what would they think?'

The path to the Parachute Regiment is long and hard and strewn with obstacles. After an initial three-day selection, would-be para-troopers begin six months' basic training at the army training centre at Catterick, a sprawl of brick blocks, plonked down in the rolling farmland of North Yorkshire. Inside its gates someone, somewhere always seems to be barking a command. No one walks and everyone marches. A surprising number are hobbling, poling themselves along on crutches. The chances are they are Para candidates whose limbs have failed to withstand the rigours of the course.

The training washes out the unfit and the unsuited. The final selection, for officers and men, is made at Pegasus Company – known as 'P' Company. It is designed to sort out whether or not you have the Para DNA. It is a rite of passage that those who have endured still talk about with pained awe years afterwards. It is above all a test of determination. 'The thing about P Company, which is difficult to explain to anyone who hasn't done it, is that it's not really a physical test, it's a mental test,' said Captain Hugo Farmer, who won a Conspicuous Gallantry Cross in Helmand. 'If you want it and you are determined enough, you will pass it. You have to have a reasonable degree of fitness, obviously, or you will fail early on. But it is people who are mentally tough that are wanted. That's the most imporant thing.'

P Company lasts three weeks. The first two are taken up with daily battle marches with kit, squad runs and intensive circuit train-ing sessions designed to physically exhaust candidates before the final 'Test Week' begins. This starts with a stint on the Trainasium – an aerial assault course over high, narrow walkways and a tower built out of scaffolding and wood. Candidates are ordered to do an 'illusion jump', which means running along a plank suspended 30 feet up and launching themselves at a cargo net 15 feet away. In this way, the instructors test whether the candidate can handle heights. It also tells them whether he will throw himself from a height with-out question. 'It takes quite a lot to run up to the end of the plank and launch yourself off not knowing whether you will make that net or, if you do, if you will bounce off,' remembered one survivor.

This is followed by a 10-mile battle march carrying full kit and weapon. The next day starts with a 2-mile steeplechase and three circuits of an assault course. Then comes the log race in which teams compete to carry a telegraph-pole-sized piece of timber over a difficult cross-country course. Anyone who fails to keep up can expect to flunk the course. Day Three begins with a 2-mile best-effort run with kit. The afternoon is given over to 'milling'. This involves two candidates standing toe to toe, slugging it out for sixty seconds. The fighters are not allowed to defend themselves, only punch. They wear heavy, 16oz gloves and protective headgear, but many still finish the bout spattered in blood.

The candidates get the weekend off to recover. When they return, they are sent off on a 20-mile endurance march with full kit, weapon and helmet. The course ends with another cross-country race. This time the teams carry a 'casualty' on a stretcher. About half of those who try fail P Company. Many drop out through injury. Women have attempted it, but none has yet passed.

The successful candidates go next to RAF Brize Norton, where they undertake eight increasingly difficult parachute jumps, the last made in full kit at night-time.

Parts of the selection process seem at first glance to be anachronistic and out of tune with what is required of a modern professional army. 'Milling' is a term that dates back to the days of bare-knuckle prizefighting, and the Paras is the only regiment in the British Army to practise it. Arriving on the battlefield by parachute is almost as bizarre nowadays as turning up on a horse. The Paras, however, have an almost mystical belief in the value of jumping. They tried to get permission for a classic parachute drop operation in Helmand. The idea was rejected by higher authority as charming, but impractical.

Their loyalty to these habits is based on the belief that they have an intangible worth far greater than their apparent practicality. 'When you are on the log race and and you have got 200 metres to go and you are absolutely knackered you do not give up,' said Lieutenant Andy Mallet, an accountancy executive in his former life. 'If anything you go faster. When you are in the ring and you are milling someone and they are bigger than you, you don't give up, you keep milling. It's that ethos that nobody else has.'

The final test of courage and commitment is the jump. At the end of training 'your initial reaction is to do whatever you are asked, so when you are standing in the door of the aircraft and you see the green light go on and you are given "green on – go", you go. It's that principle that we take forward in everything we do.'

Jumping in the Parachute Regiment is not the same as sports parachuting. It involves, according to Stuart Tootal, throwing yourself 'out of a perfectly serviceable aircraft at night with a heavy container of equipment often weighing upwards of a hundred pounds strapped to your legs, with another eighty or so people trying to leave the same aircraft ... the hazards of doing that are quite significant'.

Whatever its tactical limitations in southern Afghanistan, Tootal felt that the psychological bolstering parachuting provided was a great preparation for what the Paras would face there. The nerves experienced waiting at Bastion to lift off to what might well be a 'hot' landing zone struck him as very similar to the low hum of dread that preceded a difficult jump. 'Parachuting doesn't allow you to conquer fear, but the experience of doing difficult parachute descents does give you a familiarity with managing it. Lots of people said that and I felt it myself. Regardless of what happened, I was fairly convinced, based on my experiences of parachuting, that I would do the right thing.'

Climbing out of the back of a Chinook into a Taliban ambush, 'you might be thinking of the implications of being killed or wounded, but I think the biggest concern is how you're going to perform. Are you going to freeze?'

The 'green on – go' reflex was the cure for that. 'It doesn't matter if we haven't parachuted for years in an operational environment ... it's what that training experience gives you – the type of soldier it breeds.'

The toughness of the training and the ruthlessness of the selection create some marked characteristics. One is an intense feeling of camaraderie that blows down social barriers. Class and background seem unimportant. There is a feeling of communal concern and mutuality that is hard to find in life beyond the barrack walls.

Surviving the process, making the cut, also encourages feelings of superiority. Paras love being Paras. 'They are the best at what they do,' said Andy Mallet. 'It doesn't matter what anybody else says. I know, having served with the Third Battalion, The Parachute Regiment, we are the best regiment in the army without a shadow of a doubt.'

'You have got the Guards regiments which are hundreds of years old, which can hark back to Waterloo, but that doesn't matter,' said Captain Nick French, the Mortar Platoon commander. 'It doesn't mean anything to you. We can hark back to victories in the Second World War, Suez, Northern Ireland, the Falkands. Instead of talking about history, the blokes make history. That is why we are so proud. We have proved ourselves time and time again as opposed to relying on some mystique that was created at Waterloo. That's why the blokes are so fiercely proud of who they are.'

Private Peter McKinley, who won a Military Cross in Helmand, says simply, 'We are airborne gods. The whole army hates us because we are fucking mega. They hate us for the way we act, the way we walk and hold our heads high.'

To be an elite requires someone else to be crap. In the eyes of the ultras of the Parachute Regiment, such as McKinley, that designation applies to everyone else in uniform. The phrase 'crap hat' is used for all who do not belong to the Parachute Regiment. No one knows where it comes from. It is usually abbreviated to just 'Hat'. Nick French's mobile phone tone is a recording of an old-fashioned voice declaring, 'Paras believe in themselves and each other – everyone else is a crap hat,' lifted from a 1980s documentary.

Para pride was on full display one wintry night at Colchester Barracks in 2007 when the 3 Para boxing team was taking on 2 Battalion, The Yorkshire Regiment – the Green Howards – in the semi-finals of an army boxing contest. On one side of the ring sat the 'Toms', as the foot soldiers of the Parachute Regiment call themselves. On the other were the Green Howard 'Hats'. The officers of the two battalions, poured into scarlet bum-freezer mess jackets and tight black trousers, sat facing each other across the canvas. It was a late Victorian scene with only a pall of cigar smoke hanging from the rafters missing from the picture. 'Drop the Hat! Drop the Hat!' yelled the Toms. 3 Para's fighters obliged, winning all but one of the bouts. In the seventh fight, a spectacular knockout within twenty seconds of the first round brought every Para in the hall leaping and cheering to his feet. At the end of the evening the Green Howards trudged out into the dank Essex night where coaches were waiting to trundle them off on a joyless three-hour journey home. The Paras streamed away to the messes for a night of drinking and revelry.

A sense of fun and outrage forms a structural part of the Paras' image. In this too they regard themselves as superior to the rest. Their attitude is illustrated in a series of cartoons stuck on the wall of a senior NCO's office in Catterick. The first shows the contrast between a Tom and a Hat in their off-duty down time.

The Tom has a shaven head ('deters pubic lice') and is wearing an old bomber jacket and jeans, the knees of which are heavy with grass stains from an illicit, al fresco bunk-up. He clutches a foaming beer bottle in one hand. The Hat is primly attired in a blazer with a bowls club-type crest on the breast pocket. He sports a gelled, tinted and highlighted 'Take That' haircut and is wearing 'gay' socks. He too is drinking – a bottle of low-alcohol gnat's piss.

The message is that the Paras are desperadoes, real men in an age of wimps and wusses. They care little about their appearance and detest bullshit. But when it comes to the battlefield the roles are reversed. In the cartoons that follow, the Tom is in immaculate battledress, his gleaming weapon lovingly maintained. Here, clearly, is a man who is overjoyed to be where he is. The Hat, on the other hand, is a shambles. His uniform is wrinkled, his rifle is dirty and his expression suggests he would rather be out clubbing.

The cartoons are, of course, a gross libel on non-Paras. But there is some truth in the picture of the Tom. It is certainly how some of them like to portray themselves to the outside world – that is, in the worst possible light. Some members of 3 Para were well known to the Colchester constabulary. The Toms' favourite boozer was the Fox and Fiddler, their favourite drink a Cheeky Vimto, an appalling concoction made up of one bottle of Blue WKD with two shots of port and plenty of ice. It could be a recipe for trouble when the pub closed.

'You will find there is very much a live today, die tomorrow attitude among the blokes,' said Nick French. 'They blow their wages, get up to all sorts of antics in town with people they shouldn't.' But the fun is rationed. The cartoons are accurate. To the Para mentality, it is the battlefield that matters and everything, ultimately, is subor-dinate to preparing for it.

Despite the shared beliefs and characteristics, the men who went to Helmand were a diverse bunch. Membership of an elite also implies tolerance towards fellow members of the club. Individualism, the courage to be yourself, was regarded as a Para virtue.

All military units are shaped to some degree by the personality of their commanders. In Stuart Tootal, 3 Para had a leader who was complex and reflective, but also assured and determined to succeed. He took over command in October 2005 from Lieutenant Colonel Matt Lowe, described by one of his officers as a 'good old-fashioned CO ... rather aloof'. Another regarded the two men as 'two different beasts. Matt Lowe was more considered in his outlook. Stuart is probably a bit more intuitive, instinctive, more aggressive.'

Tootal was forty-one at the time of the Helmand deployment. He arrived relatively late to the Parachute Regiment, and adopted its ways with all the zeal of the convert. He came from a strong military background. His grandfather was in Bomber Command and was killed over Germany. His father, Patrick, was a career RAF officer who ended his service as a group captain. Tootal went through a statutory rebel phase as a teenager. His father remembers him turning up to meet him at the Ministry of Defence building in Whitehall wearing a Greenpeace T-shirt. But he had taken to heart Samuel Johnson's maxim that every man thinks less of himself for not having been a soldier. He joined his school's Combined Cadet Force and after studying history and politics at London University went to Sandhurst. He was commissioned in 1988 and joined the Queen's Own Highlanders. He served in Northern Ireland and was in the desert for the first and second Gulf Wars. On the way to his command he studied for a master's degree in international relations at

St John's College, Cambridge, and an MA in war studies at King's College London, where he later spent six months on a visiting defence research fellowship. This made him a very well-educated officer, even in the modern British military, where academic achievement is admired. His main area of expertise was counter-insurgency. He had had a chance to study it first-hand when he went to southern Iraq in 2003 as second-in-command of 1 Para.

At the time of the Helmand deployment Tootal was a bachelor with no family distractions to blunt his appetite for work. He expected the same degree of dedication from his men and worked those under him hard. Yet no one doubted his commitment to his men. 'When Colonel Tootal came in it was quite clear that he had a human side,' said one of his platoon commanders. 'His heart was very much in the right place. He cares a lot about the blokes and their welfare and he wants to look after them. We instantly respected him because he had the right priorities. He didn't treat the blokes like assets.'

Tootal was supported by a second-in-command who was not afraid to challenge his boss's thinking. The phlegmatic approach of Major Huw Williams was much appreciated in the many moments of crisis. 'Huw was a great foil to Stuart,' said one officer. 'When he came up with a proposal he would say to him, "Yes, this is plausible, no, that is not."' They made a good team and won the confidence of those who had to execute their orders 'We were all happy with what was coming down from above,' said one platoon commander. 'I never heard anyone say, "This is fucking stupid, this is madness." [They] just came up with good sensible plans ... you can't ask for more than that.'

During the Helmand campaign Tootal would come to rely greatly on the support of his regimental sergeant majors. Nigel Bishop was his RSM for the first three months until he moved on to another posting. He was replaced by John Hardy, a twenty-year veteran known as 'the Razman' to the troops, who regarded him as a surrogate father. His relationship with Tootal was a vital element in the battalion's human chemistry. Tootal was the senior officer. Hardy was the senior soldier. As such, they had a bond that transcended the vertical hierarchy. 'I bark to one man and that is the CO,' Hardy said. 'I don't wag my tail for anyone else.' Hardy had many responsibilities. The most important, though, was to act as a conduit between the blokes and the boss – 'telling the CO how it was'.

3 Para, like all infantry battalions, is configured in tiers. At the top is the CO (commanding officer) and his headquarters staff, who manage and direct the battalion. The fighting soldiers are formed into companies. Each company is divided into two or three platoons and each platoon into sections. The number of men in a company varies, but it can be as many as a hundred or as few as sixty. In 3 Para 'A', 'B' and 'C' Companies were the rifle companies, the basic fighting unit. The were sustained and augmented by Support Company, which provided additional firepower in the shape of machine guns, mortars and anti-tank weapons. 'D' Company was the ISTAR company providing specialised Intelligence, Signals, Target Acquisition (snipers) and Reconnaissance expertise.

Each company was commanded by a major. At thirty-six, Will Pike, the OC (Officer Commanding) 'A' Company, was the most senior. He was the son of Hew Pike, who led 3 Para in their days of glory in the Falkands, and had his father's strong, square features and thick, blond hair. He had long ago given up worrying whether this connection was an advantage or a burden. 'In the end I don't think it makes a blind bit of difference,' he said. 'I don't think that anyone else thinks that either.' Those under him sometimes felt he was hard to please, but noted he was as tough on himself as he was on others.

'B' Company was commanded by Giles Timms, a blunt, cheerful fitness fanatic, who had been destined since adolescence for military life. He joined the Combined Cadet Force of his public school. After learning of the army sholarship scheme, 'everything I lived and breathed from then on was geared to getting into the army'. He joined 4 Para, the reserves, as a private soldier while at university. The artillery sponsored him through Sandhurst, 'but my allegiance was really to the Parachute Regiment'. It was only at the last minute that he told his sponsors that he would not be joining them. 'I got quite a hard time for that, for disloyalty. [But] you have got to be true to your own ambitions and I wouldn't have been happy in the Gunners.'

'C' Company's OC, Paul Blair, known as Paddy, was a soft-spoken, good-looking Ulsterman with a gentle, courteous manner. He did a four-year business course before deciding that office life was not for him and set off for Sandhurst in July 1995. Cadets are required to put down a first and second choice of regiment they want to join when they pass out. 'I was very much, it's the Parachute Regiment or nothing,' he remembered.

Adam Jowett, who commanded Support Company, joined the Paras from the Grenadier Guards and served with them in Kosovo and Sierra Leone. He was working in a staff job when the word came through that 3 Para were likely to be sent to Afghanistan but wangled his way out of it to go with them. Jowett was the most reserved of the company commanders, but a robust soldier when the time came.

For all their combined experience, in the spring of 2006 there were only three men in 3 Para who could claim to have had real experience of a proper war. These were the last remaining members of the battalion who had served in the Falkands campaign. The intervening years had been spent in worthy but uninspiring deployments that hardly matched the expectations of 3 Para's members when they joined up. As they prepared to leave their drab headquarters in Colchester for the burning plains, soaring mountains and lush river valleys of Helmand province, the atmosphere was charged with the premonition that things were changing. 3 Para were about to get what they wished for.

3

'The Lawless Province of Helmand'

On 26 January 2006 Defence Secretary John Reid announced to the House of Commons that British troops would be sent to Helmand province in the spring. The decision caused immediate controversy. Britain was already deeply committed in Iraq. Pessimists recalled the history of British military interventions in Afghanistan. They raised the grim precedents of the First and Second Afghan Wars and retold the story of the retreat from Kabul in January 1842. Of the 16,500 soldiers and camp followers who set off, only a handful stumbled into the safety of Jalalabad. The rest had been killed by the freezing weather and the relentless attacks of Ghilzai tribesmen.

It was not just the British who had come unstuck there. All the might and brutality of the Soviet military had been unable to crush the spirit of a people who, however incapable they might be of living together harmoniously, were united in their hatred of outsiders.

The Paras had known about the deployment for months. Rumours had been circulating since the previous summer and they had been officially 'warned off' to prepare to go in August 2005. They were used to false alarms. But this one sounded genuine. For many in the battalion this was the news they had been waiting for all their military careers.

Sergeant Craig Mountford was coming up for thirty-five when the buzz started gathering volume. He had started his working life as an apprentice welder in Stoke-on-Trent but had always liked the idea of army life. He had first heard about the Parachute Regiment through their exploits in the Falklands. He was attracted to them by an early reality TV show, *The Paras*, which followed a group of recruits from day one of basic training to acceptance or rejection. In 1989, aged nineteen, he joined up. So far, though, his operational experiences had been disappointing. 'It was really frustrating,' he said. 'We weren't getting a look-in. We were constantly being told – "Right, you are being stood by, you are going to go." And we never went. This isn't warmongering. You just want to do your job – go away on operations, to see what it is like, to experience it.'

In the spring of 2003 the second Gulf War seemed to offer great possibilities. In the end 'it was just a case of securing a couple of oilfields, patrolling in Basra and that was it. We didn't do any war fighting as such'.

With the news of the Afghanistan deployment, Mountford began to think again that he might finally see some serious action. 'It was in all the papers. Mad Max country. The lawless Helmand province.' But by now he was inclined to be sceptical of media prophecies. 'They said the same about Iraq. Fighting through to Baghdad. Millions were going to be killed. Initially everyone thought it was going to be good, but then it began to die away. We started thinking, "It probably won't come to anything. It probably won't happen."'

Iraq had been an anticlimax for most of those who had been there. Hugo Farmer went to Basra on his first deployment with the Paras in December 2005. He was unlikely to be satisfied with the sort of duties that awaited him. Farmer was twenty-six. He had had a stellar university career, graduating from Bristol with a double first in Chemistry and Law. His first ambition had been 'to make as much money as possible'. The City snapped him up. It did not take long for him to decide that a career in corporate finance was not for him.

My life was pretty rubbish. There was very little satisfaction and lots of work that seemingly went nowhere, lots of people above me justfying their existence by creating heat and light but not actually doing anything substantial or proper. I would be in the office by eight a.m. Initially it wasn't too bad. I would be gone by seven p.m. But then I switched teams and it was eleven p.m. You go home, shower, go to bed and you get up and it all happens all over again. You couldn't guarantee you weren't going to be in the office at the weekend.

Farmer felt he was 'becoming a grey man'. He was haunted by the example of one of his colleagues, only a few years older, who had a wife and child and was saddled with the huge mortgage needed to buy the sort of house his status demanded. 'He was a beaten man,' he said. 'He was resigned to the facts.' There were lots like him, 'treading the same old boardwalk, just getting richer and fatter and older. I thought to myself, "I need to change tack here. I need to do something interesting."'

Farmer had no soldiers in his immediate family but knew some from university and thought they were 'fun-loving, always doing interesting things'. There was a friend of the family who had joined the SAS. He thought to himself, 'If he can do it then I can.' A little research told him that 50 per cent of the SAS had started off in the Paras (the figure now is 58 per cent). He left his job even before he had been accepted at Sandhurst. He went there in January 2004, sponsored by the Paras, and arrived at 'A' Company under Will Pike in the early autumn of 2005.

Most of the time in Iraq, Farmer led 1 Platoon on patrols along the border with Iran. He found it 'actually quite interesting'. The only real threat was from IEDs – improvised explosive devices made from artillery shells which the insurgents planted by the roadside and detonated remotely when a patrol passed by. There was an easy way of countering it. The patrols, operated in armoured modified Land Rovers, simply kept off the roads, an easy thing to do in the flat country bordering the Shatt al-Arab waterway which marked the Iraq–Iran frontier.

Their task was to stop Iranians sneaking in bombs, weapons, drugs or any other contraband. The border was long and porous and smuggling was part of the local economy. Farmer thought it 'a very good introduction as to how to run a platoon on operations … It wasn't high tempo by any stretch of the imagination but it was a nice way to learn.' The Paras were also supposed to mentor the Iraqi border security forces. That meant visiting border posts strung along the frontier, 'making sure they had the right equipment, making sure that they were trained and knew how to run it, and also to give them a warm fuzzy feeling that they were being looked after and that what they were doing was important'.

Iraq did not prove an uplifting experience for many in 3 Para. The Iraqis themselves seemed feckless and ungrateful. Martin Taylor had, like Farmer, turned his back on a conventional, modern career. After a media studies degree at Sussex University he spent two and a half years working for a recruiting consultancy and commuting to London from Kent every day. His family and friends were surprised when, restless with his life, he started talking about the army. 'But the more I looked into it the more I heard people saying, "I can see you doing that sort of thing."' He initially applied for the Royal Artillery but after his second term decided he wanted to join the Parachute Regiment.

He too spent his first operation patrolling the border. Taylor was cheerful, good natured and inclined to think the best of people, but he found it 'an enormously frustrating chore. For some reason the Iraqis just did not want to help themselves. It was frustrating just watching these guys living in squalor.'

If there was a lesson to be learned from Iraq, it was how not to do things. Stuart Tootal had watched the aftermath of the triumph of America's 'shock and awe' strategy with an expert eye and increasing dismay. He believed that 'our approach was fundamentally wrong. We rather assumed that once we'd finished the fighting it was merely a case of putting a new government in place, and we underestimated the difficulty of winning over the consent of the people for that regime. What we failed to achieve from the outset was proper security, and [we] stood by allowing a lot of looting to go ahead. And then we didn't improve the lot of the people.'

Tootal's background in counter-insurgency studies convinced him that there was much in Britain's imperial past that could be applied to the present. He was impressed with the example of General Sir Gerald Templer, the high commissioner appointed by Churchill in 1952 to find a solution to the communist uprising known as the Malayan Emergency. It was something he shared with another British officer, Lieutenant General David Richards, who had been appointed commander of ISAF (the International Security Assistance Force in Afghanistan), which was due to take over the whole NATO (North Atlantic Treaty Organisation) operation in Afghanistan from the Americans. Templer had wielded complete control of every aspect of military and civilian life in Malaya and had devised an intricate committee system that integrated counter-insurgency operations with the reconstruction effort. He once declared: 'the answer lies not in pouring more troops into the jungle, but in the hearts and minds of the people', thereby coining a phrase that would echo through counter-insurgency operations ever after.

The political situation in Afghanistan, which had a democrat-ically elected government under President Karzai, would not allow such overt control. But there was one aspect of Templer's approach in Malaya which could be applied without offending political sensi-tivities. This was the application of the 'ink spot' theory. It held that the best way of tackling an insurgency was to concentrate on securing specific towns and improving local services, including schools, hospitals, sewerage, water, roads and electricity. Life would then be so good that no one would want to support the rebels and the uprising would wither away.

John Reid had presented the situation in Afghanistan as another emergency. He told the Commons: 'Whatever the difficulties and risks of this deployment – and I do not hide them from the House or the country – those risks are nothing compared to the dangers to our country and our people of allowing Afghanistan to fall back into the hands of the Taliban and the terrorists. We will not allow that. And the Afghan people will not allow that.'

It was a reassertion of the claim that Afghanistan was the front line in a war whose effects, if it went wrong, would be felt painfully in the cities of Britain. That had been the argument for invading Afghanistan in the immediate aftermath of the attacks of 11 September 2001. Since then, Britain had been under pressure from America to supply troops to continue the ongoing NATO mission of stabilisation in Afghanistan. The plan was now moving into its third stage. The 'easy' parts had been done. The area around Kabul and the northern and western regions were relatively peaceful. Now it was time to concentrate on the south. Tony Blair answered the call willingly. Since 9/11, he had committed Britain to playing a major role in Afghanistan. His government had proved that it honoured its NATO responsibilities and would do so again, even though the deployment would place a further strain on the country's stretched military resources.

The south of Afghanistan had been neglected after the fall of the Taliban. In 2002 the Americans and their allies had put most of their effort into squeezing the life out of what remained of the Taliban and al-Qaeda in the mountainous east of the country. Since 2003, their military effort had been diverted into fighting the war, and then the insurgency, in Iraq. The American troops based in Afghanistan concentrated on targeted operations against Taliban and al-Qaeda leaders.

The material help that was promised after the Taliban were driven out of the main cities was slow in coming to the south. There had been little reconstruction and no large-scale deployment of troops to secure the region. In the absence of any Afghan or foreign soldiers to stop them, the Taliban, many of whom had fled to Pakistan after their defeat, began drifting back to Helmand and Kandahar provinces. It was their historic home. Kandahar was the birthplace of the movement. Most Taliban were Pashtun and the provinces were Pashtun territory, part of an ethnic belt that stretched across the border to Pakistan. At the beginning of 2006 they were trying to re-establish themselves through violence and intimidation, murdering and terrorising anyone associated with the government and its NATO coalition allies.

ISAF was led by NATO. It was set up by the United Nations Security Council to secure the country and allow the authority of the central government to take hold. Its operations had begun in the capital, Kabul, and slowly expanded throughout the country in planned stages. Now it had reached stage three – the establishment of Regional Command South.

The British would be part of a multinational force of about nine thousand soldiers. The contributing nations included Canada, Holland and Denmark. The command rotated among the lead nations. The Canadians would be the first to hold it. The battle group's area of operations would be Helmand, which was in dire need of development but was also the scene of increasingly vigorous insurgent activity.

Defence Secretary Reid made it clear that combating the Taliban resurgence would be one of the battle group's main tasks. The troops were being sent to 'deny terrorists an ungoverned space in which they can foment and export terror'. The underlying, long-term aim was to 'help the people of Afghanistan build a democratic state with strong security forces and an economy that will support a civil society'. In the British area of operations this would be done through the Helmand Provincial Reconstruction Team (PRT), which would work with the military, the British Foreign Office and the Department for International Development (DfID) to deliver a 'tailored package of political, developmental and military assistance'. The specific mission was to 'help train the Afghan security forces, to facilitate reconstruction and to provide security, thereby supporting the extension of the Afghan Government's authority across the province'. This last phrase would come to have a powerful significance when the battle group began their work.

As if this was not enough, there was a further aspect to the mission. Helmand was opium poppy country. Poor farmers relied on the poppy to make a living, selling their crop to local drug lords. The troops, said Reid, would be expected to 'support international efforts to counter the narcotics trade which poisons the economy in Afghanistan and poisons so many young people in this country'. Nine-tenths of all the heroin on British streets originated in Afghanistan, he claimed. Once again, decisive action in a far-flung place could benefit British society.

It would be claimed later that Reid had presented the mission as a risk-free exercise in nation-building. This was based on an interview he gave to the BBC's *Today* programme in April, just as the deployment was beginning. On a crackly line from Kandahar, NATO's main base in the south, he said that 'if we came for three years here to accomplish our mission and had not fired one shot at the end of it we would be very happy indeed'.

In the months that followed, as the British mission grew more and more hazardous and shots were fired by the hundreds of thousands, these words would be repeated by critics as evidence of his naivety. In fact the phrase was ripped out of context. Reid had been frank about the risks from the start. In the same interview he declared that 'although our mission ... is primarily reconstruction it is a complex and dangerous mission because the terrorist will want to destroy the economy and legitimate trade, and the government that we are helping to build up'.

The way the task force was structured made it clear that trouble was expected. The Helmand Task Force was drawn primarily from 16 Air Assault Brigade based in Colchester. At its heart was 3 Para, who, as its commander was proud to boast, 'fight on their feet'. Without air support, however, they could not function. That was to be provided by seven CH-47 helicopters provided by the Royal Air Force. The twin-rotored Chinooks, with their huge lift capacity, were the main workhorses of the task force. They were armed only with three machine guns and needed protection. This was the job of eight Apache attack helicopters from 9 Regiment of the Army Air Corps, which were being deployed for the first time with the British Army. They also played a crucial role in supporting ground troops when they were under attack. Four Hercules C-130 transports would be supplied by the RAF.

The fighting core of the force was 3 Para. They were reinforced by a company from the Royal Gurkha Rifles and a detachment from the Royal Irish Regiment. The Household Cavalry Regiment (HCR) with their Scimitars and Spartans would supply an armoured element. The Royal Horse Artillery's 7th Parachute Regiment (7 RHA) would contribute a battery of 105 light guns. The operation was supported by a parachute-trained squadron of engineers from 23 Engineer Regiment, units from the Royal Logistics Corps and the Royal Electrical and Mechanical Engineers and medics from 16 Close Support Medical Regiment.

An advance force of engineers were set to go to Helmand ahead of the main deployment to build camps, protected by a company from the Royal Marines' 42 Commando. By July, about 3,300 troops were expected to be in place in Helmand, excluding the engineers building the camps. The task force could also call on the assistance of American bombers, support and attack helicopters, and other NATO countries were considering offering fighter cover and transport aircraft.

The size of the 'force package', as it was called, had been the subject of long debate in London. Men and materiel were in short supply owing to commitments in Iraq. Reid described the deployment as 'substantial', and said that it was sufficient to 'maximise their chances of success and minimise the risks'. The battle group's senior officers were reasonably content with what they were given, though like all commanders they would always have preferred to have more. But that view would alter as the original mission changed and the force's responsibilities spread far beyond their original intended area of operations, stretching manpower and resources to the limits. 'The fact is', said a senior ISAF commander after the Paras had returned home, 'that the 3 Para battle group ... was woefully insufficient for the tasks that were being laid on it.'

The operational boundaries of the deployment were vague and elastic from the start. Reid said the British were not going 'because we want to wage war', and that the military assets were intended 'to deter and defend ourselves'. But the political and military landscape they were entering made war fighting inevitable. There were several powerful interests seeking to direct their actions, voices that could not be ignored. They were fitting into a multinational force whose members had different agendas. The most important were the Americans, who had little interest in the reconstruction effort and would expect the British to contribute to their campaign to decapitate the Taliban leadership. They would be leant on by Britain's ally, President Karzai and his representative in Helmand, to expand the government's authority into the badlands.

It seemed to the Paras themselves, as they made their preparations, that the fact of their presence in Helmand was bound, sooner or later, to provoke a fight with the Taliban. Will Pike emphasised to his company that 'we were there to enable development, to enable reconstruction and that the military arm was not the decisive thing, but winning the hearts and minds of the people'. When the Paras talked among themselves, however, Pike said, 'we all knew that it was easier said than done and we were very aware that this operation was probably going to be the most significant thing we had done as a battalion since the Falklands and it was going to involve fighting on a scale we hadn't seen since then'.

Pike knew Afghanistan from a previous tour – he had served in Kabul with 2 Para in the aftermath of the attacks of 9/11. As he understood it, Helmand was something of a sanctuary for the Taliban. The international military presence was sparse – some Americans engaged in targeted counter-terrorism operations – and the central government weak. The place was essentially run by the same people who ran the narcotics trade. 'We knew that people were going to oppose the strands of development that we wanted to try and secure,' he said. 'So whilst the ferocity of the fighting came as something of a surprise ... I don't think we were under any illusions.'

In their pre-deployment training 3 Para hoped for the best and prepared for the worst. Study days were organised and visiting experts gave lectures on the people, history and customs of Afghanistan. Several soldiers were sent off on crash language courses and everyone was taught a few Pashto phrases for basic interaction with the locals. There were bouts of intensive tactical training but it was hard to recreate the conditions they would be operating in amidst the cold and wet of a British winter.

Early in 2006, however, 3 Para were sent for a month's training to a much more useful environment – the stony hills and wadis of Oman. 'Much of the training involved going to mocked-up villages, establishing relations with the locals and displaying a culturally aware attitude to the people they would be dealing with,' Martin Taylor remembered. 'Much of it had already been learned in Iraq. We were rehearsing the less aggressive "hearts and minds" side of things.' But at the same time they were 'always, always rehearsing what would happen if we came under attack. We trained with helicopter gunship and air support. Among the exercises was a live firing exercise in which the scenario is that you are out patrolling and come under attack from the Taliban who are firing from a strongpoint and you have to go and attack that. The blokes trained really hard and were very fit when they came back.'

While they were in Oman, news trickled down to them of what was going on in Afghanistan. It seemed to confirm their instincts that there was trouble ahead. The reports mainly concerned the Canadians who were in charge of the Kandahar area of operations, the sector next to the Paras'. 'I was responsible to brief the blokes up,' said Craig Mountford,

> so every night in Oman I would sit down with the company commanders then pass it down to the lads. There were regular reports that someone had been killed in Afghanistan. But it wasn't the fact that people were being killed. It was how they were killed. I heard one particular story about a Canadian officer who went to one of these "meet and greets" with the locals. He went in, took his helmet off and sat down on the floor to take tea with them. He had a bodyguard with him. But someone came in and stuck an axe in his head. That brought it home to quite a lot of people, I think. People began to step back and think, 'Bloody hell, this might be something of a fight.'

The question of how to distinguish friend from foe, gunman from civilian, played a large part in preparations. The Paras were taught some likely indicators that would alert them to an approaching suicide bomber: heavy sweating, an absence of body hair, the mumbling of prayers and a refusal to respond to warning shouts were all signs to set alarm bells ringing. In the towns and villages they would be working in there would be many opportunities for making catastrophic errors that could deal fatal damage to the effort to win consent and trust.

Everyone dreaded shooting the wrong person. But they were also extremely uneasy about what would happen to them even if they had made an honest mistake. The spate of judicial actions against soldiers who had got into similar trouble in Iraq had created cynicism and a belief that justice was being bent by political considerations. Tootal gave reassurance that no one would be hung out to dry. 'The CO was very, very clear about what his approach would be if someone was deemed genuinely to pose a threat,' said Martin Taylor. As long as a soldier 'was acting in all honesty and was not misusing his power in any way he would be supported'.

On the other hand, Tootal also left no room for doubt that anyone who abused the local population could expect harsh punishment. He spelled out the difference in a talk to the troops, asking them to imagine that they were patrolling into a village at dusk. Unseen assailants had been shooting at them and they were tense and nervous. Suddenly a boy walks out of an alleyway, holding a shepherd's crook. In the failing light it looks just like an AK-47 rifle. Someone makes a split-second decision and shoots him dead. Tragic though it is, it is a consequence of the friction of war. In the circumstances there would be an investigation. But if it was shown that the soldier was acting with honest intent he could count on his CO's support.

If, however, the soldier had seen the boy and was about to shoot him, subsequently recognised his mistake but took him into the alleyway 'then kicked the shit out of him because he'd been given a good scare, then I'll have that soldier court-martialled,' Tootal said.

By the beginning of April 2006 the theorising was over and the practice was about to begin. After years on the sidelines, 3 Para was ready to take to the field. The thought was both alarming and exciting. 'There is one test that a parachutist wants to take,' said Nick French, 'and that is how do you react under fire. Are you going to flinch, are you going to hide or are you going to pass that test? If you do you will leave the army happy.' In the months ahead they would have many opportunities to try their courage.

4

Afghanistan's Plains

Rudyard Kipling's *Barrack-Room Ballads*, published in 1892, contained a poem, 'The Young British Soldier', which was much quoted by those predicting the dire consequences of getting mixed up with Afghanistan. One verse ran: 'When you're wounded and left on Afghanistan's plains/And the women come out to cut up what remains/Just roll to your rifle and blow out your brains/And go to your Gawd like a soldier.'

To the Paras arriving at Camp Bastion, in the arid flatlands north of the Helmand provincial capital of Lashkar Gah, it was heat and dust rather than the bloodthirsty attentions of fierce local women which seemed the main hazard. 'A' Company were the first to deploy, arriving on 15 April with the battle group's tactical headquarters and the Patrols Platoon. They had also been the last to leave Iraq and had less time at home than the other company battalions. There was some whingeing among the soldiers, but the logic of the decision was accepted. It was, in its way, a compliment. 'A' Company had the most recent operational experience and the longest-established command structure. Going in first confirmed its members' belief that they were the best.

First impressions of Bastion, though, did not raise spirits. To Corporal Chris Prosser, a machine-gunner from Support Company who was attached to 'A' Company, it came as 'a complete shock'. The Paras were used to roughing it in the field but expected a few basic comforts back at camp. Instead, 'there was nothing there. Inititally we were living in twelve-foot by twelve-foot tents with no aircon and nothing on the floor. We were living on ration packs for the first two weeks. Sandstorms came in every afternoon and swept through the tents so your kit was always covered in dust.'

'Bastion when we arrived was just a dustbowl,' said Hugo Farmer. 'There were no hard roads and we were about fourteen to eighteen to a tent.' The ablutions blocks were not completed and grey pools of waste water seeped into the gritty sand.

Other units at the base seemed to fare better than the new arrivals. Farmer speculated that there was an ingrained army belief that 'the Paras liked that sort of stuff'. In the end they just got on with it, living out of their bergen rucksacks.

Stuart Tootal, who reached Bastion on 18 April, was more concerned with how the base would be resupplied. As it stood, it was reliant on a fragile air bridge provided by the Chinooks and Hercules. The lack of comfort did not worry him too much. His overriding preoccupation was getting his battle group into place as quickly as possible. The camp conditions, however, were a major concern to the Permanent Joint Headquarters staff who oversaw the operation from thousands of miles away in Northolt, Middlesex. They preferred to hold the remaining troops of the battle group back until Bastion was in a fit state to receive them. Tootal was frustrated at their caution. Dribbling his men into theatre risked losing the initiative. His view was that

[we] were an expeditionary army and we should be able to go out into the field and set up. I was quite prepared to say we'll just live in the desert. We'll live off rations and draw water because there's plenty of water we can access. We'll shit in holes and we'll burn it off. We're going to be dusty and we're going to be uncomfortable. But actually, I've got all my fighting power with me.

In the end it was more than four weeks before all his infantry elements arrived. There was a further wait before key assets such as the artillery were in place. The Household Cavalry light armoured squadron did not reach the battle group until 10 July.

Fortunately for 3 Para, the Taliban were not yet ready to declare the fighting season open. The poppy harvest was about to begin. Once it got under way, the fields along the great river valleys that plough north to south through Helmand would be full of toiling men, women and children. The process was simple. First, the harvesters made four light incisions with a multi-bladed razor in the head of the poppy. They left it for a few days for the sticky, milky sap to collect. Then they returned to scrape it off with a wooden spatula. Each head had to be scraped up to seven times to collect all the 'milk'. The sap was shaped into slabs which were sold at established markets. They were then passed on for processing and transporting, increasing in value at every stage until the refined product reached the streets of Europe's towns and cities as cellophane 'wraps' of dirty, brownish powder.

The poppy farmers sold their crops to local drug lords, who sold it on to the processors. Helmand province was reputed to supply 20 per cent of the world's opium. The growers were expecting 2006 to produce a bumper crop – 50 per cent up on the previous year. When the Taliban were in power they had opposed the trade, coming close to eradicating production. But now they were trying to wrest back the power they had lost and were anxious not to antagonise either the peasants or the landowners who exploited them. Poppy was a vital part of the economy. Even a poor tenant farmer could expect to make £1,000 from a plot of land less than 100 yards square, a sum that went a long way in Helmand.

In their new, collaborative mood, the Taliban promised to suspend fighting so as not to disrupt the harvest. In return they could call on local chieftains to supply them with reinforcements from their private militias. They also imposed an opium tax which raised tens of millions of dollars to fund their supply and armaments needs. Until the opium had been sold, it seemed the Taliban were content to watch and wait.

Support for the eradication of the opium trade had been one of the stated aims of the British deployment. It was never explicitly said, though, that the military would be used to destroy crops. None of the senior commanders involved in the operation had any intention of doing so. Creating stability for reconstruction to take place depended on winning the consent, or at least the tolerance, of the local population. Burning poppy fields was a sure way of turning potentially friendly farmers and their dependants against the latest

batch of foreigners in uniform to descend on the province. Tootal
believed it was completely unrealistic to tackle the opium problem
without providing an alternative livelihood that came close to
matching the income local farmers made from the poppies. The
problem had been around for decades. No one had yet come up
with a viable solution. However desirable it may have appeared to
politicians in London and Washington, the folly of busting up the
local economy was fully appreciated by every soldier in Afghanistan,
from the Toms all the way up to the incoming ISAF commander,
General Richards.

3 Para's area of operations was the 'Triangle'. This was the district
bounded by Camp Bastion, the provincial capital of Lashkar Gah
and the market town of Gereshk, the second largest place in
Helmand, which lay about 20 miles to the north-east of the base.
This was considered a relatively benign environment. It was the
most developed region of the province, where there was sufficient
existing infrastructure for the reconstruction programme to build
on. Both towns lay on the Helmand river. Most of the province
was barren. The area around Bastion was called Dasht-e-Margo, the
Desert of Death. But the waters of the river were channelled into a
web of ditches and canals, creating a broad band of fertile land that
sustained life along the valley.

The central Afghan government controlled the two towns but had
little authority in the villages. There was a belief that the Taliban
regarded the area as something of a sanctuary and chose not to
draw attention to themselves. 'The level of enemy activity was low
because actually there wasn't a lot for them to fight and they were
really being allowed to do their own thing,' said one officer.

The original plan was for the Paras to begin patrolling in the
towns and the surrounding areas, advertising their presence and creating an atmosphere of stability. It was classic 'ink spot' strategy.
According to Martin Taylor the intention was 'to go into small
villages and say "Are the Taliban operating here? We can offer you
this, we can offer you that." If they tell us what their problem is –
say that they don't have running water – then we would get the guys
in who could bring them running water. If there were no schools

then we would get engineers in to build them schools.' 'A' Company saw its job as identifying what needed to be done. It was then the task of the civil servants of the DfID to come in and make it happen. This, as it was to turn out, was a very optimistic expectation.

The Paras approached the task with genuine enthusiasm. In its short life, the regiment had become a much more flexible and subtle organism than in its early years. Its suitability for any task less than full-scale war fighting had been called into question by the events of 30 January 1972 in Londonderry, Northern Ireland, forever known as Bloody Sunday. The Troubles were at their height and 1 Para had been brought into the city to support the Royal Ulster Constabulary, who were policing a protest march. The demonstration was organised by the Northern Ireland Civil Rights Association. By now, though, it was the gunmen and bombers of the Provisional IRA who controlled the direction of the Catholics' struggle for equality.

The march was illegal and the Paras had been given the job of arresting the leading 'hooligans'. As expected, the gathering quickly turned into a riot. In the confusion the Paras opened fire. When the chaos subsided it was revealed that they had killed thirteen males. Six of them were seventeen years old.

The deaths gave the IRA a propaganda coup and cast a long shadow over the reputation of the Paras. The charge against them was that they had indiscriminately killed unarmed innocents. These accusations were taken seriously by audiences in Britain, America and Europe. An inquiry under Lord Justice Widgery found that none of the dead or wounded had been shot while handling a firearm or bomb. It also judged that there was 'no reason to suppose that the soldiers would have opened fire if they had not been fired upon first'. Their training had, however, made them 'aggressive and quick in decision and some showed more restraint in opening fire than others'.

The charge of mindless violence was to hang around for years. Despite the controversy, the Paras continued to serve in Northern Ireland throughout the period. They were sent in as peacekeepers to Kosovo after the NATO deployment in 1999. By the time they arrived in Afghanistan they had millions of man-hours of experience handling the complexities of operating among civilian populations against a hidden enemy and a fine-tuned understanding of when to shift emphasis. 'Yes, we have a reputation for being very aggressive,' said Stuart Tootal. 'That's absolutely right. Sometimes we need to be. But we also have soldiers who are very self-reliant. They're bright, they think things through and they respond well to challenging circumstances, which includes having to decide when it's appropiate to adopt a non-aggressive posture. They're very good at it.'

But even after thirty-four years the events in Londonderry were still remembered. As he set off at the head of Patrols Platoon, the battalion's reconnaissance unit, Captain Mark Swann was aware of the need to make decisions that 'not only benefit your soldiers but will also reflect on you in the best way possible. People will say, "This bad thing happened in this village. Typical Parachute Regiment soldiers," regardless of how we behaved before then. One incident would very quickly give us a bad reputation'.

'A' Company were fully committed to the mission. 'We went there believing that this was a winnable situation,' said Martin Taylor. 'Yes, be prepared for very significant contact with the enemy. But we thought the vast majority of people would be on our side and we could win their trust and they would think perhaps the Taliban can't help us and the British can.'

It was in Gereshk that the first attempts were made to reach out to the local population, and it was 'A' Company which was given the task. Gereshk was relatively prosperous by Afghan standards. In the calm that followed the overthrow of the Taliban, the UN had installed pumps that provided clean, fresh drinking water. There was also a hydroelectric plant that supplied energy to about five thousand legal subscribers and an unknown number who simply hooked up a line to the main cable. There was a thriving market and shops on the main street. In its time, it had seen foreign armies come and go. The dominant building was a crumbling fort where the British had held out for sixty days during the First Afghan War. The Paras would be operating from a Coalition base on the outskirts. When 'A' Company got there they found that the camp was still being built and they would, initially at least, have to function without an ops room. They were also unimpressed by the state of the sangars – the base's defensive fire positions. 'We set to work for the next month tearing things down and building things up,' said one of the new arrivals. 'The message was, the Parachute Regiment is here and we are going to start establishing our authority.'

The compound was on the north-west outskirts of Gereshk and was known as Forward Operating Base (FOB) Price. To get into the town meant crossing a major road, Highway One, which loops through southern Afghanistan from Kabul. 'A' Company started patrolling immediately. Troops were taken to the edge of town by vehicle and then continued on foot. Walking was considered safer than driving. You were mobile and presented a smaller target. The streets were narrow and if you were stuck in a Land Rover you were vulnerable to the suicide bombers who, it was thought, could be preparing to descend on the town. It also reduced the risk from IEDs, which had already been discovered on surrounding roads.

Stuart Tootal joined the first patrol on 29 April. The Paras' arrival attracted great interest. The local people seemed reasonably friendly, especially the children. One child came out and offered a jug of cold water. Teenage boys and older men responded well to the soldiers' carefully rehearsed few words of Pashto. Tootal visited the local hospital and police station and asked what could be done to help their security and provide for their needs.

Even though it was not yet summer, the temperature was 40 degrees Centigrade. Patrolling on foot, wearing body armour and carrying a weapon, ammunition and radios was very hot and heavy work. After two hours on the ground, Tootal noticed how the troops' concentration and awareness of their surroundings faded as they coped with the effects of heat and fatigue. After nearly five hours, everyone on the patrol was thoroughly 'licked out'.

The first encounter with the citizens of Gereshk had gone off well enough. But 'A' Company's commander, Will Pike, was not convinced that the mood of the town was welcoming. 'There was a volatility to the situation,' he said. 'I described it as "West Belfast with an Asian tinge". The patrolling we did there was not dissimilar to what I had done in Belfast. It might seem benign. But there was an edge there.'

Moving slowly through the narrow streets, smiling and radiating good intent, the Paras began to notice that their progress was being marked by the sound of whistling. As they passed, they saw men whispering furtively into mobile phones. They soon suspected that they were being 'dicked'. 'Dicking' was a term from Northern Ireland. It was the name given to the warning system operated by IRA sympathisers to let the gunmen know British troops were approaching. The Taliban were invisible. But the Paras now had little doubt that they were there.

Mark Swann was walking along with his interpreter at his side when a truck drove by

absolutely full of men in black turbans, brown trousers and dishdashas [the cotton nightshirt-like garments worn by Afghan males]. They had black beards and were wearing eyeliner – why I don't know. The interpreter grabbed me and said, 'Taliban, they are Taliban!' I asked which ones and he said, 'All of them.' They drove through the middle of the patrol then shot off. As we turned the corner, we saw them sitting on top of the hill watching us. As we dog-legged left they also peeled off in the same direction.

It was not the Paras' intention to initiate a confrontation with the Taliban. The rules of engagement stated they could shoot only when their lives were clearly threatened. Swann decided to get his men away as quickly as he could. He recalled later: 'That's when I thought, this is actually quite sticky.'

An incident on 1 May seemed to reinforce this impression. Stuart Tootal made another visit to the town for his first *shura* – council – with Gereshk officials and elders. The meeting was friendly. The district administrator, Abdul Nabi Khan, spelled out his main concerns: worries about security and the lack of decent schools and health facilities. Tootal had arrived at the administrator's compound in an armoured 'Snatch' Land Rover. Soldiers from the patrols and sniper platoons had moved in the night before to secure the complex. As they left the meeting at midday, a warning came over the radio that a suicide bomber driving a car packed with explosives was on his way to try to catch the party as it left. This, Tootal recorded, 'added a degree of ... urgency to the extraction'. As they hurried away from the compound, the lead Snatch got stuck in an alleyway.

For a moment, chaos threatened. There were six vehicles in the convoy, trying to turn around on a sloping dirt path, now surrounded by a small crowd of curious children, while a Taliban car bomber was possibly bearing down on them. Tom Fehley, the officer commanding 2 Platoon of 'A' Company, was in charge. Very soon he had imposed some 'grip' on the situation and the vehicles turned round and moved off to the northern suburbs of Gereshk, where they formed a defensive ring and waited for Mark Swann and his men, who had been patrolling in the town, to catch up. They were making slow progress. The backstreets of Gereshk which they had to pass through to reach the rendezvous were 'rat-runs, dead-ends, alleyways, things like that'.

Eventually, they linked up with the convoy. As they climbed aboard the vehicles to head back to base, 'all of a sudden there was a burst of automatic fire', said Swann. 'I'm sure it was only from an AK rifle, but a burst of automatic fire in our general direction.' Four or five bullets kicked up puffs of dust from some nearby walls. No one saw where they came from.

It was a classic 'shoot and scoot'. No one was hurt and the decision was taken to extract immediately. By the standards of what was to come, the incident was barely worth recording. But the contact, in retrospect, took on a symbolic importance. It was a sign that no matter how positive the Paras' relations with the local population and authorities might seem, there were men among them who wanted to kill them.

The news of the contact, minor though it was, galvanised the battle group. When Swann got back to FOB Price he was called up immediately by his friend Matt Taylor, the Battalion Ops Officer.

They had been commissioned into the Paras at the same time and there was a friendly rivalry between them. 'He was saying, "Right, don't tell me, you've had a contact before me!"' In the other companies there was some mild annoyance at the fact that it was 'A' Company which had been the first to come under fire. This, it was feared, would only boost its members' already considerable opinion of themselves.

The flurry of excitement in Gereshk proved to be exceptional. The town remained relatively quiet throughout the rest of the deployment. This did not mean, however, that the process of reconstruction was able to take hold there.

The effort was meant to be coordinated through the 'Triumvirate' made up of the Ministry of Defence, the Foreign and Commonwealth Office (FCO) and DfID. DfID had a presence in Lashkar Gah, where the PRT was supposed to have its headquarters. Until there was stability and security in Helmand, however, there was little for the department to do. The functioning of the Triumvirate was hampered by personnel problems. The head of the MoD's Civil–Military Cooperation (CIMIC) team was unhappy in his post, and on 21 April it was agreed that he should return home.

At the same time, DfID's attitude was causing the Paras bafflement and dismay. The department's officials seemed anxious not to be associated too closely with the military presence for fear that they would come to be regarded as the enemy by the people who they were there to help.

Their approach was exemplified by the story of the Gereshk hospital washing machine. Captain Harvey Pynn, 3 Para's regimental Medical Officer, had taken up the cause of providing a functioning laundry for the hospital. It was just the sort of 'quick impact project' the soldiers were supposed to identify and pursue.

Pynn came from a military background. His father was in the RAF and his grandfather had been an RSM in the Parachute Regiment in the 1950s and 1960s. He was attracted to an army career but he also felt a vocational pull towards medicine. He combined the two by joining the Royal Army Medical Corps after studying at Guy's and St Thomas's. Following a stint with the Royal Greenjackets he joined 3

Para in the summer of 2005.

In normal times the MO's job was to look after the general health of the battalion. In war, there was the crucial duty of keeping the wounded alive until they could receive proper treatment. Pynn believed in being where the fighting was going on. He got his wish. The battle group overturned the normal procedure and posted their doctors forward with individual companies rather than keeping them back at base. He and other battle group MOs were to find themselves doing most of their work in the platoon houses, rather than at the high-tech hospital that had been set up at Bastion.

Pynn had a strong idealistic streak. He took the development side of the mission very seriously. When 'A' Company deployed in Gereshk he set to work surveying the health provisions in town. He was welcomed at the hospital and shown round. The conditions were grim. There was a resident surgeon and anaesthetist but very little equipment. Above all, the place was dirty, and bloodstained sheets littered the trauma room.

What they did have was a washing machine, which had been given to the hospital by USAID, the American international development agency, some time before. It sat there, still wrapped in factory plastic, useless without a water supply to plumb it in to. Pynn thought it would be a simple job for the battle group engineers to sink a well. It was cheap, easy and a palpable demonstration of the soldiers' goodwill.

The DfID office in Lashkar Gah was told of the plan. Word came back that there was no question of military engineers being allowed to do the work. The hospital was part of the Afghan healthcare system and an Afghan non-governmental organisation had already been given the contract. As far as the soldiers were aware, no NGO had been near the hospital. But the issue was a political one and they were forced to let it drop.

The failure to implement such a trivial piece of assistance did nothing for DfID's reputation with the soldiers. Their inability to carry out quick-impact projects (QIPs) was a continuing source of frustration for 'A' Company. Tootal shared their feelings. He made regular, forceful appeals to his superiors in the PRT, stressing the need for action. At a meeting at the Kandahar airbase, the NATO headquarters in southern Afghanistan, on 13 May he argued that DfID were wasting an opportunity. His men were unable to deliver small, goodwill-building measures not because of a lack of resources, but because of a bureaucratic doctrine. The Paras thought DfID's reluctance to associate with the military was naive. Most people in Afghanistan lumped all foreigners together. The first troops in Gereshk spent much of their time explaining that they were British. The locals assumed that any foreigner in uniform was American. The soldiers believed DfID would do better to work around perceived problems rather than surrender to them. After the meeting, Tootal went off to have dinner with the DfID reps. The potential for further disagreement was cut short when the meal had to be abandoned owing to one of the regular, but largely ineffective, Taliban rocket attacks on the base.

The Triumvirate structure did not render decision-making easy. But the complexities of the military chain of command complicated matters yet further.

It was Tootal's misfortune throughout 3 Para's tour to have to answer to several bosses. The multiplicity of nations and organisations involved in Afghanistan meant that direction came from a number of sources. The result was a lack of clarity about aims and coherence in achieving them that fogged the mission throughout.

When the Para battle group arrived in Afghanistan the Americans were in overall charge. They operated under the banner of Operation Enduring Freedom (OEF), which had been launched in the wake of 9/11. They were due to hand over command to the NATO-led ISAF, headed by the British general David Richards, at the end of July.

ISAF operations in the south were controlled by a Canadian brigade, led by Brigadier General David Fraser. 16 Air Assault Brigade operated under the Canadians. Its boss, Brigadier Ed Butler, did not have a formal tactical role in the Canadian chain of command. A joint command had been ruled out, and it was deemed improper for Butler to be subordinate to Fraser on grounds of military protocol – a brigadier should not take orders from another brigadier. Instead, he occupied a place outside the architecture of command. He took his orders directly from the UK's Permanent Joint Headquarters in Northwood and had political oversight of the operation. Butler had a rich array of talents and accomplishments which marked him for high command. He glowed with the special confidence that an Eton education seems to bestow. He was clever and looked beyond the obvious. In his opinion, the instability in Helmand was not a simple matter of the Taliban and al-Qaeda stirring up trouble. It had deeper causes, rooted in tribal dynamics and the struggle for resources.

Butler was unhappy with the command arrangements. In an attempt to overcome the difficulties of the set-up, a subordinate layer of command was inserted into the hierarchy. Colonel Charlie Knaggs, who had recently commanded the Irish Guards, was put in charge of the Helmand Task Force, and was therefore in nominal tactical command of every British soldier in the province. This appointment only added to the confusion. Finally, the Americans engaged in the counter-terrorism campaign in Afghanistan also had a formal interest in British operations. They were commanded by Major General Ben Freakley, a God-fearing, fighting soldier who rejected any idea of compromise with the Taliban and came to distrust the British approach.

Thus, for the first four months of the tour, Tootal had to answer to the Canadians, the Americans and also to Charlie Knaggs. Ed Butler was on hand to advise and listen to his concerns, but he operated at a tangent to the decision-making process. One of David Richards's first acts on taking over full command of ISAF in August was to place Butler below Fraser and give him tactical responsibility for British forces under Canadian command. It seemed obvious to many that this was what should have been done at the outset. The structure was extraordinarily cumbersome and guaranteed to generate fuzziness and ambiguity. This was before account was taken of Afghanistan's swirling political complexities. These difficulties would play an important part in the Para battle group's destiny in Helmand.

Despite the limitations on their hearts-and-minds activities, the Paras did what they could. On 1 June, to mark the United Nations' National Children's Day, 'C' Company, which had just taken over from 'A' Company in Gereshk, went to a local school and, with the approval of local elders, suggested a game of football. They handed out kit and, according to their OC, Major Paul Blair, were surprised when 'less than ten minutes later the local team ran out wearing the strip. A lot of them were playing in bare feet but we were royally thrashed.'

Even at this stage, Blair believed the outreach mission could work.

> Little things amazed me – the discipline of the children when we were playing football – one word from the teacher and they sat cross-legged around the pitch. Lots of the older students came out and said, 'This is amazing' because we had just dished out several hundred school packs with paper, pens, exercise books and so on. I thought, if we have got this amount of interest and as a lot of the elders involved with the school are on side, there is definitely hope.

Blair's first thought was that 'we must look after the kids. The kids are gagging for education and for extra supplies so I thought, we have delivered on that one.' But fear of the Taliban loomed over everything. The teachers told Blair how they received letters threatening them with death if they taught little girls. He nonetheless felt that 'if we can sort out security and some supplies we can at least nail the education bit. Gereshk, I thought, was a success waiting to happen.'

The arrival of a new CIMIC officer in the middle of May seemed an encouraging development. Captain Emma Couper had been on the point of leaving the army to go to a job in the UN when the abrupt return of her predecessor created a vacancy. 'As a female officer, to get an opportunity to go out to the headquarters of a Parachute Regiment battalion comes along once in a lifetime,' she said, 'and although all my friends thought I was nuts, when I said,

"Well, would you turn it down?" they all said, "No."'

Most of the women attached to the Paras were medics or administrators. Couper went into the army after studying English literature at Manchester University, where she joined the Officer Training Corps, mainly for the sport and outdoor adventure it offered – she played rugby and went climbing. Both her parents had been in the army, though they were out by the time she was born. For her first year at university, she had no intention of following them. Then in the second year, after doing some army attachments, 'all the pieces started to fit in. I really liked those I worked with. I didn't want a nine-to-five job. I wanted to travel and I wanted to work with people.' To her OTC buddies it seemed a natural progression. Most of them followed suit. Her other friends 'had different values. Maybe they were more materialistic. They wanted to have more control over their lives.' Her work in CIMIC had taken her to Bosnia in the nineties, Afghanistan in 2002 and most recently Iraq, where she liaised between the divisional headquarters and the local population.

She arrived in Bastion on 10 May and met Stuart Tootal, who thought she seemed 'enthusiastic, bright and experienced'. They agreed on the need for projects that not only delivered benefits but also put money in local pockets, such as digging new roadside drains.

Once in Gereshk she went out on patrols, 'establishing relationships with the key leaders, getting them in for meetings and starting to build a database of information that we could push up to Brigade and give them an idea of what was going on on the ground. The basics of water, electricity, power and all the things which potentially the larger agencies from the US and UN might in the long term get involved with'.

But all this depended on improving security, and it was clear to her that there was a very long way to go before real changes could be made. The police force were corrupt and malleable. Some of the twenty-two checkpoints set up at the entrances to the town were ostensibly run by the police but in fact subcontracted to gunmen. The police sat inside their posts while their hirelings extorted money from everyone passing through.

Attempts to instil some training and sense of duty had been discouraging. The course was four or five weeks long and was held in Kandahar, 80 miles away. The men were unhappy at being away from home and tended to run away after a few days.

Even with resources available, the Paras' experience so far told them that sorting out Gereshk would be a hard and tricky task. The time was coming, though, when all their manpower and assets would be needed for a tougher job.

5

The Road to Sangin

By the second week in May, all the elements of 3 Para had arrived in Bastion. Tootal felt he now had a battle group to command, although he was still waiting for some of his gunners and engineers and all of the HCR's D Squadron. The engineers in place were making constant improvements to the camp. Bastion was expanding all the time. No one could complain about the conditions now. There were rows of air-conditioned tents connected by duckboard runways. Soldiers could get their laundry done, eat decent food and call home on the welfare phones. Mobile phones had to be surrendered on arrival, for 'operational security' reasons. There was also a high risk that homesick Toms would run up crippling bills calling their loved ones in the UK.

At night you could sit outside a Western-style coffee shop, enjoying the relative coolness, drinking Cokes and smoking. Bastion was a cigarette-friendly zone, with men and women sparking up with abandon. Booze was another matter. The camp, like every other military facility in the area, was dry.

Tootal thought the time was now right to start delivering the 'Sangin effect'. This was his plan to expand the British presence northwards into the towns and villages that ran along Helmand's river valleys. It would deliver the British government's wish to 'deny terrorists an ungoverned space'. Discussions went on throughout April between the battle group and the Canadian forces in neighbouring Kandahar province as to how this could be done.

The intention was given impetus by the new governor of Helmand, Engineer Mohammed Daoud. The appointment of Daoud appeared to be proof of the central government's resolve to bring order to the province. He was a 'technocrat' from the east of

Afghanistan who had headed an NGO distributing wheat to the poor before the arrival of the Taliban. He was forced to flee over the Pakistan border to Quetta, where he met and became close to Hamid Karzai. His reputation contrasted favourably with that of his predecessor. Sher Mohammed Akhunzada had been forced out of office by pressure from NATO. Suspicions that he was a player in the drugs trade seemed confirmed, early in 2006, when counter-narcotics agents raided his offices and discovered nearly 9 tons of raw opium. His own men had seized the dope, he explained, and he was just on the point of handing it in. He was given the consolation prize of a seat in the upper house of the national assembly. To placate the powerful Akhunzada family, his brother, Amir, was put in as Daoud's deputy.

Daoud was considered to be as honest as it was possible to be in the treacherous and venal world of Afghan politics. He was a Pashtun, like most people in Helmand, but had no strong tribal affiliations. He was close to President Karzai and was identified with the forces of progress and modernity. 'He was the right man for the job,' said Ed Butler. 'He was a developer. He was a reconstructor. He could think long term.' He was also very insistent that the British were there to support him and that he had a right to call on their resources to shore up his authority wherever it was challenged.

Daoud had formed the unfortunate belief that the battle group was much more powerful than it in fact was. He assumed that the great majority of the 3,300 soldiers arriving in Helmand would be 'bayonets' and that, in the words of a senior British officer, 'there were going to be three thousand Paras running around all over the place'. The number of fighting soldiers in the battle group, including the Royal Irish, the Gurkhas and, later, the Fusiliers, was less than a third of the overall number. The others were there to support them. Try as they might, British commanders never succeeded in managing Daoud's extravagant expectations.

Daoud was also frustrated by the battle group's late arrival. The deployment had been delayed while the Dutch prevaricated over their contribution to the NATO effort in southern Afghanistan. As a result, said Daoud, there was a 'security gap' in Helmand, which the Taliban were now exploiting energetically. Encouraged by the security vacuum, they had been arriving in large numbers from exile in Pakistan and were urging local leaders to join them in a holy war. Four out of the twelve district police chiefs had been killed in the six months before the Paras arrived. In the spring of 2006, the outlying northern district of Baghran fell under insurgent control.

The British plan was to secure the Triangle, then gradually extend their presence northwards up the heavily populated Helmand river valley as conditions and resources allowed. The obvious place from which to begin delivering the 'Sangin effect' was a bleak desert camp, a few miles south of Sangin town, called FOB Robinson, which had been built by the Americans. It was easily defended and well placed to disrupt the insurgents' movements up and down the valley.

The possibility of putting a British company in there had been discussed. But Tootal was wary of placing his men in a fixed location where half their energies would go into defending themselves. His preference was to man the base with Afghan National Army troops who had passed through training courses that, in theory at least, had turned them into decent soldiers. They then received further instruction from British OMLTs (Operational Mentoring Liaison Teams) provided by soldiers from 7 RHA. The CO of 7 RHA, Lieutenant Colonel David Hammond, was happy to put an Afghan battalion, under the control of his OMLTs, into Robinson.

That would leave a Para company free to patrol the area, supporting the ANA and carrying out their own operations, engaging with the local people and generating a climate of security. They would spread the message about development and prepare the ground for the PRT, but also fight the Taliban where they found them.

This arrangement would be easier to sustain than a fixed presence. The force's movements would be unpredictable and, it was hoped, keep the enemy off balance. It required fewer men than the labour-intensive business of garrisoning a fixed base. Above all, the risk of getting bogged down was minimised.

Before the operation could be launched, however, the Taliban seized the initiative. On 18 May, gunmen launched a fierce attack on the district centre in Musa Qaleh, a small but symbolically and strategically important town in northern Helmand. About twenty members of the Afghan National Police (ANP) were killed. Musa Qaleh was 60 miles south of Baghran, which was already in insurgent hands. The attack suggested that the Taliban were now set on a campaign to seize the towns of the north, and use them as a springboard for the conquest of the whole area.

The operation was intended as more than just a challenge to the Afghan government. Mohammed Hanif, a spokesman for the elusive Taliban leader Mullah Omar, boasted to *The Times*: 'We are here to destroy the British. We will hunt and kill them. We will not let them go back to England and say that they have defeated the Afghans.' It was telling that he couched the fight in nationalist terms. For propaganda purposes, the Taliban presented themselves as patriots rather than Islamic warriors. Hanif's claim that 'the British don't have the capacity to fight us face to face' suggested a degree of confidence that the new arrivals lacked the resources to challenge the Taliban head-on.

Soon after he spoke, the Taliban had an indirect encounter with British troops. The Pathfinders, 16 Air Assault Brigade's elite reconnaissance unit, had been in the Musa Qaleh area at the time of the attack, scoping out possible landing sights. They were ordered to go and give what help they could to the beleaguered policemen. They arrived in darkness as the battle was dying out. It had lasted eight hours, but eventually the Taliban had pulled back. The next morning the ANP, bolstered by the deputy governor, Amir Akhunzada, and his personal militia, who had arrived from the south, piled into pick-up trucks and set off for Baghran, where the attackers had apparently retreated. The thirty-strong Pathfinder force followed in 2.5- ton Pinzgauer troop carriers and armoured Land Rovers. As they approached, they announced their arrival with a show of force. A coalition aircraft dropped a 2,000lb bomb on a hillside near the town. This prompted the Taliban to flee. The ANP then went into town for a *shura* with the elders.

The Taliban had not given up, however. Intelligence revealed that they had prepared five bombs along the convoy's return route. A suicide bomber was also standing by. The convoy avoided these traps but was still caught in an ambush that left two of the Afghan police dead and several wounded. The Pathfinders' sergeant major, Andy Newell, was impressed by the ANP's determination. 'They weren't shy of getting amongst it,' he said. 'One of them was shot through the calf and one through the shoulder and after they were patched up they wanted to get straight back to the fighting which I thought was quite hard of them.' He had also had a chance to see the Taliban close up. 'They put up a good fight,' he said. 'They obviously had some tactical awareness and knew how to use the country.' The clash ended when the Pathfinders called in an air strike by American A-10 Thunderbolts. After the Afghan casualties had been evacuated by helicopter the convoy carried on back to Musa Qaleh with no further trouble from the Taliban.

The poppy-harvest lull was definitely over. On 20 May, a four-vehicle convoy carrying Afghan soldiers, their American trainers and French troops was attacked on Route 611, which connected the important towns of Kajaki and Sangin. Initial reports indicated that up to fifteen ANA soldiers and two Frenchmen had been killed. The convoy eventually limped into FOB Robinson and a Chinook with a medical Immediate Response Team (IRT) on board was flown up to Bastion to bring back the casualties.

A number of Afghan soldiers were thought to be stranded somewhere along the route, at the mercy of the Taliban. Tootal was asked to send a force to secure the area and rescue the remaining men. It was a job for his 'Ops One' company, who were on permanent short notice to jump off on a mission. It was a rotating task and at the time 'A' Company were in the role. They set off in two Chinooks, protected by Apache attack helicopters, which were going into operational service with British troops for the first time. Finding the remnants of the convoy, if any, was going to be difficult. The French survivors, who were badly shaken by their ordeal, gave different grid locations for where the attack had taken place.

In fact there had been several attacks along a long stretch of road and there was no obvious place to put down. Looking down from the Chinook as it scudded at 60 feet over the valley floor, it seemed to Will Pike, the OC of 'A' Company, that the rescue plan was 'enormously difficult and the risk threshold was high'. The road ran along the Helmand river. On either side was a swath of irrigated land, about a mile wide, of orchards, small fields and enclosures, criss-crossed by irrigation ditches. 'It was all very flat, very, very difficult country to operate in,' he said. 'It's very good for them, but hard for us to get in there in any secure way, or be able to surprise them. It's a maze and you are facing a threat from three hundred and sixty degrees.' They carried on a fruitless search until low fuel forced them back to Bastion.

The following day, at first light, they set off again. This time they found three of the four trucks in the convoy. Two were burned out. An Apache fired a Hellfire missile into the last one to destroy any sensitive equipment that might remain.

There was no sign of bodies, but the following day local people handed over the corpses of the two dead Frenchmen and the nine missing Afghans to the troops at FOB Robinson.

Afterwards, the story of what had happened became clearer. A first attempt to drive south had been made on 19 May. Trucks carrying ANA troops, an American team who was mentoring them and the French forces had set off from Kajaki, near the hydroelectric dam that generated electricity for the province, for FOB Robinson and soon came under fire. Two vehicles were lost but no one was hurt. The convoy turned round and tried again the following day. The plan was to take the main highway for the first leg of the route then branch off east into the desert to avoid contact with the locals. Some vehicles appeared to have missed their turning, blinded by the clouds of dust thrown up by the trucks ahead of them. The Taliban had been warned of their approach and proceeded to shoot at them along a 6-mile stretch of road.

When the incident was analysed it revealed some disturbing realities. It underlined the fact that any vehicles moving along the roads of Helmand were liable to attack. The battle group was already aware of the risks from IEDs. But this was a full-on ambush. It made even clearer the value of helicopters over convoys when inserting large groups of men or carrying out resupplies. Local people appeared to have joined enthusiastically in the Taliban attack. According to Pike, the survivors reported that 'everyone was coming out of their houses and having a go – quite why, who knows – but the valley in that area kicked off'.

The search-and-recovery mission had used up precious helicopter hours. This meant a further delay in establishing the 'Sangin effect'. As preparations resumed, another emergency blew up, requiring another diversion from the programme. A panicky message from the governor claimed that the town of Now Zad, about 60 miles north of his seat in Lashkar Gah, was in imminent danger of falling to the Taliban. It seemed the Taliban had not been deterred by the setback at Musa Qaleh on 18 May. Daoud's office claimed that there had been several clashes and the police station in the centre of town had come under fire. 'B' Company was tasked to fly in and stiffen the meagre resistance that was all the contingent of ANP who were in the town were expected to be able to put up.

The laconic Giles Timms set off with about half his men. They were pleased to be doing something definite at last. The reports suggested that they would meet strong resistance from the Taliban on arrival. When they landed in Now Zad on 22 May, everything was calm. The smiling chief of police was there to escort them in. At the police station there was little evidence of an epic battle. 'There was a reasonable amount of brass and empty cartridge cases lying around,' said Timms. 'But there was no real evidence that Taliban had tried to make a concerted effort to take the place.'

Now Zad seemed to be dealing with the crisis admirably. It was 'a bustling little market town. Not every single shopfront was open for business but maybe two-thirds were.' They undertook an initial vehicle patrol through town. 'We got some funny looks, some scowls from people. But we didn't get taken on. It was just like a normal market town and still was when we left.'

'B' Company stayed for twelve days. They got to work building up the defences of the police station, which sat on the main street, refreshing themselves with Zam Zam, a sickly, strangely addictive soft orange drink. They were starting more or less from scratch. The existing fortifications amounted to no more than a few rice sacks filled with dirt. The police contingent had been in the habit of standing at their posts for only half an hour each evening before retiring to smoke dope. They were all from elsewhere in the province, Lashkar Gah and Gereshk. Their wages were poor and they often went unpaid. Many failed to return after going off on leave. 'They were pretty much a joke really,' said Timms. 'The moment we arrived they said, "We are glad you are here, we can sleep now," and took no further part in defending their district centre.'

Corporal Chris Prosser of Support Company, who went with Timms's men, felt some sympathy for them. They were, at least, 'trying to do something for their own country'. The Paras built six sangars. They put Afghan policemen alongside them on the front gate so the people of the town could see that this was a joint effort. Despite the apparent normality, there was an undercurrent of sinister activity in the town. Intelligence reports warned that the Taliban were watching the new arrivals. 'They were basically dicking us,' said Prosser. 'Trying to work out the layouts, how many people we had, what sort of weapons, basically the general set-up in Now Zad.'

One night there was a report that an attack was imminent and the garrison was ordered to stand to. But nothing developed, and on 2 June the Paras handed over to a small force from 'D' Company of the 2nd Battalion, The Royal Gurkha Rifles. Now Zad was to turn out to be a much hotter assignment than the Gurkhas' original task of protecting Camp Bastion. When 'B' Company returned later that summer, the place was unrecognisable. 'It was a complete war zone,' said Timms. 'Nobody was there any more. The shops were shut. A lot of the buildings had been demolished by air strikes.'

By answering the Afghan government's distress signal, the British were now committed to the defence of Now Zad. Tootal's intention was to support the Afghan forces rather than to do their job for them. The day after 'B' Company's deployment, despite the established risk of ambush, an enormous seventy-six-vehicle convoy was put together to deploy a fresh company of ANA soldiers to FOB Robinson near Sangin and take out those who were there. It was led by the CO of 7 RHA and boss of the OMLTs, David Hammond.

The job of screening the convoy along the 70-mile route from Bastion was given to Mark Swann and Patrols Platoon. 'It was quite a tricky task because the vehicles kept getting stuck and it took twenty-odd hours to get up there,' he said. When they finally arrived at FOB Robinson, Swann was handed another task. The Canadians ordered Colonel Hammond to press on the extra few miles to Sangin town itself. Once again, the Afghan government was claiming that disaster was imminent. The district centre, the administrative compound that was the symbol of its flimsy authority, was supposed to be under siege.

Hammond asked Swann to carry out an old-fashioned recce, probing forward to establish whether the Taliban were present, and if so, where exactly they were. Effectively, this meant driving around until they were shot at. After the long journey chaperoning the lumbering convoy, Patrols Platoon were exhausted. 'My boys were absolutely chinned at this point,' said Swann, 'but we had to do it.' The platoon was mounted in WMIKs, modified Land Rovers. The acronym stood for Weapons Mount Installation Kit, a reference to the rig that allowed a heavy Browning .50-calibre machine gun to be bolted on to the back. The man on the gun could swivel the weapon through 360 degrees and lay down a devastating stream of fire that could rip up anything short of a tank at a range of 1,300 yards. The firepower was further boosted by a 7.62mm GPMG (General Purpose Machine Gun), which was operated by the vehicle commander from the passenger seat. The Rover's 4.2-litre engine made it fast and powerful and its manoeuvrability was impressive if it was not too heavily laden. The WMIK looked like the descendant of the Vickers gun-toting jeeps driven by the Long Range Desert Group which operated in North Africa and was the precursor of the SAS. Swann and his men saw themselves as belonging to the same tradition.

It was the middle of the night when Patrols got their orders. The cover of darkness would be welcome. But it also increased the risk of running into one of the unmarked minefields left behind by the Soviet army. It was wiser to wait for first light, and the platoon took the very welcome opportunity to get their heads down for a few hours.

As they set off at dawn, intelligence warned that the Taliban were preparing an ambush. Swann altered course and set off on a dog-leg, diverting from the straight route to town. They arrived at Sangin District Centre unharmed and called Lieutenant Colonel Hammond and the Afghans, telling them to follow the route they had taken. Swann had been impressed by the incident. He said later: 'This was the point when I thought that this was not going to just be a few stray rounds being fired at me by some young lad trying to prove something. These people are organised.'

Hammond and the Afghans occupied the district centre and toured the police checkpoints. The local security forces denied that they were facing any serious threat from the insurgents. That did not mean that the Taliban were not there. The atmosphere seemed tense to Swann as he drove around Sangin. 'People ran away when we approached. Through our optics we could see people in the distance getting down into what could only be described as firing positions. We couldn't see the weapons so we didn't engage ... you saw people prowling.'

One of their Pinzgauer carriers broke down. The edgy atmosphere persuaded Swann to order his men to strip it and rig it with explosives. 'We thought if we are attacked now we are going to have to leave this vehicle and we can't leave it to them.' These were the sorts of procedures associated with war fighting. At dusk a Chinook flew in to lift the 'Pinz' out.

The Paras were beginning to get a practical understanding of the sort of enemy they were facing. The Taliban had shown that they were determined. They were also tactically cunning and used their knowledge of the terrain to mount well-thought-out ambushes. Furthermore, they could count on a degree of support from local people. Some of this was extracted through coercion. But some, as the shoot-out on Route 611 suggested, was given willingly. All this gave the insurgents a robust self-confidence. The realisation was growing that they meant it when they boasted of driving the British out.

Back in Bastion, Stuart Tootal was growing increasingly concerned at the direction the mission was taking. The Now Zad
diversion was unwelcome. It meant fixing troops that needed to be
mobile if they were to function properly in one location. The need
to resupply them would place a further strain on the helicopters.
The battle group could not function without support helicopters.
Helmand had few roads, which made land movement predictable
and vulnerable to roadside bombs and ambushes. The troops
would have to rely on the Chinooks to transport them around the
battlefield, supply them with food and ammunition and get them
back to the base hospital when they were wounded.

The Chinook was developed by Boeing as a heavy-lift aircraft and
came into service in 1962. It is still in military and civilian use all
over the world. The variant used by the RAF – the CH-47 – dated
back to 1966. It is a big, blunt beast, nearly 100 feet long with twin
engines and two 60-foot rotors throbbing in tandem. It can fly high,
with a ceiling of 18,500 feet, which made it especially useful in
mountainous Afghanistan. It can carry thirty to forty men depend-
ing on the weight of kit or 28,000 pounds of cargo. All in all it is a
fine machine. 'Chinooks are the ultimate battlefield helicopter,' said
Flying Officer Chris Hasler of 18 Squadron RAF, who won a
Distinguished Flying Cross piloting them. One of the squadron's
ships was over twenty-five years old and had seen service in the
Falklands. Age hardly made any difference. Fixed-wing aircraft have
a main spar running through the fuselage and wings that have a limited lifespan. Choppers go on and on. 'Helicopters are almost like
Lego sets,' said Hasler. 'You can bolt things on, take blades off, put
in a new engine, but you still have the same frame. You can make a
[Chinook] pretty new just by replacing some bits.'

The trouble was there were not enough of them. Seven were
assigned to the task force, of which only five were serviceable at any
one time, while the rest were in for maintenance. The heat and dust
of Helmand made it a tough environment for rotary aircraft and
regular checks were essential. The number of flying hours was
restricted for safety reasons. In order to get the most use out of the
helicopters, Tootal suggested that they be moved forward to Bastion

from Kandahar where they were based. From the beginning the pilots spent most of their time at Bastion, accompanied by a small engineering detachment who lived in a tent alongside the machines, permanently caked in the dust that was kicked up every time a chopper flew in or out.

The Paras were thankful for the Chinooks and grateful to the crews who flew them. They only wished there were more of them. None was available. The decision to carry on spending the bulk of the RAF's budget on fixed-wing fighter planes designed for a war with the Warsaw Pact countries which would never be fought had severely limited the air force's ability to do the tasks that now made up most of its duties.

Tootal knew it was inevitable that his soldiers would have to respond to unforeseen events. But if there were too many of them, the battle group could end up as a solely reactive force and lose sight of its original stabilising and reconstruction mission. Tootal felt that the force was paying too much attention to Daoud's demands and worried that local people would regard his soldiers simply as agents of the new governor. Daoud was unknown and untried. Bitter experience had taught the inhabitants to assume he was corrupt and self-seeking until he proved himself otherwise.

Even as Tootal was thinking this, another urgent request from Daoud was on its way. One of his key supporters, Haji Zainokhan, was in trouble. He was stranded in a village in the Baghran valley, about a hundred miles from Bastion in the north of the province, surrounded by Taliban who seemed intent on murdering him. On 24 May 'A' Company was sent to rescue him. They took off in two Chinooks with two Apaches hovering protectively alongside. Haji had got caught out while visiting some relatives. He had a bodyguard of twenty policemen, but felt they did not offer sufficient protection.

The helicopters flew low, following the contours of the river valleys. Given the reports of a Taliban presence it had been thought wise not to tell Haji when exactly they were coming, or how. Will Pike, leading 'A' Company, knew where the village was but not the precise location of their man. Just before they landed, they called him on his mobile satellite phone and told him to get his men to light a bonfire. The helicopters touched down into a scene of bucolic calm. 'It was perfectly peaceful,' said Hugo Farmer. 'It was actually a very nice place.' The chief and his entourage were loaded on and flown back to Bastion. He was, Pike remembered, 'pretty chipper, pretty chuffed'. One of his police bodyguards was little more than a boy and seemed terrified of flying in a helicopter. 'One would think that being left to the Taliban would be more frightening,' Chris Hasler, who was flying one of the Chinooks, noted in his diary. 'Each to his own, I suppose.'

The operation had gone off well but it was not what 'A' Company were supposed to be doing. Their energies were meant to be focused on delivering the Sangin effect, establishing the 'ink spots' that would bring stability to the province. 'A' Company was never to put the plan into practice. The ever-shifting dynamics of the Helmand mission were changing again. The Paras and the Taliban were about to collide.

6

Operation Mutay

On 4 June the Paras set off on what was billed as a 'cordon and search' operation. Their target was a mud-walled residential compound, 70 yards square, on the eastern outskirts of Now Zad. According to the sketchy information available, it was thought to be an ammunition and weapons dump, possibly a Taliban bomb factory and a safe house for insurgent commanders. The idea was to secure the compound, seize the materiel and grab any Taliban who might be there.

The job had been handed to them by the Americans. It was part of Operation Mountain Thrust, their ongoing hunt for 'high-value' Taliban and al-Qaeda targets. It seemed a relatively straightforward task. The intelligence brief warned that there might be some Taliban present, but not enough to pose a major threat. 'Cordon and searches' were a staple company-level activity in Northern Ireland. They had also been practised in exercises before the deployment. The terraced streets of Ulster and the empty desert of Oman, however, were very different propositions from the mud-brick mazes of Helmand. The operation was to turn into one of the epic clashes of the Paras' tour, a six-hour fight in which virtually everyone involved got their first, hard look at the face of battle.

Altogether there were about a hundred men taking part. The mission would be led, once again, by 'A' Company, the 'Ops One' company at Bastion. 10 Platoon of the Royal Gurkha Rifles, garrisoned in the Now Zad district centre together with some Afghan police, and Patrols Platoon, who were in the area, were tasked with setting up an outer perimeter to seal off the area. Then 'A' Company would arrive by air to capture the compound. The Gurkhas would take the local district chief along with them to give the operation an

'Afghan face'. Air power was on hand to come in and blast the enemy if needed, in the shape of A-10 jets and Apache helicopters. As it turned out they were to play a vital role.

This was a battle group operation and, as commander, Tootal went along with his headquarters team to oversee it himself. Even before he hit the ground, it was clear that the Taliban were waiting and eager for a fight. The Gurkhas had set off from the Now Zad district centre at 11 a.m. to establish their sector of the outer cordon around the target compound. They were expecting an uneventful day and thought they were unlikely to encounter anything more than a handful of fighters.

There were about thirty in the convoy, including eight or nine Afghan police. It passed through a village on the northern edge of a town called Aliz'ay, and along a wadi that led southwards. Rifleman Ananda Rai was driving the lead WMIK when they came across a small group of men who were apparently civilians. One of them broke away and ran into a house. Rai thought he had taken fright. But then he re-emerged carrying an RPG launcher. He 'screamed and dropped to one knee'. The RPG streaked across the bonnet of the vehicle.

Rifleman Kieran Yonzon was providing 'top cover', manning the .50-cal. He saw the man with the grenade launcher but he was only a few yards away and Yonzon could not bring the heavy machine gun's long barrel down to bear on him. Instead, he jumped down from his perch, snatched up his rifle and fired three shots, which killed the attacker. Another man popped up from behind a wall and fired fifteen or twenty rounds towards Yonzon.

Then unseen gunmen, crouching in the trees lining the far side of the wadi, opened up with more RPGs, a heavy machine gun and rifles. Lieutenant Paul Hollingshead, a twenty-four-year-old from Southport on Merseyside who had joined the Gurkhas after university, was three or four vehicles back in the convoy. He scrambled out of the lightly armoured Snatch Land Rover and started shooting back. Everyone was trying to get out of their vehicles to find cover and return fire. 'It was very, very quick,' he said. 'If we'd stayed in the vehicles we would have been cut to shreds.'

It was the first time Hollingshead had been on the receiving end of an RPG. 'They made the loudest bang I had ever heard,' he said. Rounds from the heavy machine gun were smashing chunks out of the wall behind him.

The Apaches were hovering over the target compound about a mile away, but there was no way of calling in an air strike. In the rush to dismount, the radios had been left on the vehicles. Hollingshead decided he could not ask his 'boys' to retrieve one so he ran forward as rounds zipped around him. He returned with an old Clansman-type transmitter, a notoriously poor piece of kit. This one had a label stuck on it reading 'Dodgy But Workable'. The Joint Tactical Air Controller (JTAC), Lieutentant Barry de Goede of the Household Cavalry, came to join him. But when they tried to get in contact with the aircraft in the area, the radio refused to work. 'We were beating it, hitting it, taking it apart,' said Hollingshead. Finally, de Goede managed to raise the Apaches and gave their coordinates. The Gurkhas signalled the air to identify their position and a few minutes afterwards the Taliban positions were raked from the air with 30mm cannnon fire.

The next step was to retrieve the vehicles and get out of the wadi. Hollingshead picked five of his men to come with him and lay down covering fire for the drivers. 'It was one of the proudest moment of my life,' he said. 'I said, "OK, you're coming with me." Then it was three, two, one, go.' The young Gurkhas, some of them only nineteen years old, ran forward unhesitatingly, with bullets cracking over their heads and ricocheting off the rocks around them.

Rifleman Rai was determined to get back to his WMIK, and rounded up two others to help him. But moving towards it, they came under heavy fire and had to stop. A little later there was a lull in the shooting and he ran forward on his own. He got behind the wheel and the bullet-shattered windscreen and tried to turn the vehicle round but his path out was blocked by a 'Pinz'. The temptation to panic was strong. 'I calmed myself down and told myself it didn't matter if I got shot,' he said later.

As they worked forward, firing and manoeuvring, Hollingshead realised that he was way ahead of his men. Before him was a low, flat-roofed building. Something that 'looked like a bundle of rags' was lying in front of it. It took him a few seconds to realise it was the body of the RPG gunner who had been shot dead at the start of the fight. As he was taking this in, 'this guy came skidding out of the building. He looked down at his mate on the ground. He hadn't seen me'. Hollingshead raised his rifle to shoot. The fighter was wearing a long green dishdasha kaftan and a sparkly skullcap and carrying a Kalashnikov. He had a bushy beard and appeared to be about thirty. He looked up as Hollingshead pulled the trigger of his SA-80. But nothing happened. An empty cartridge case had jammed on ejection, blocking the chamber. He tried frantically to clear it, as bullets from the continuing firefight kicked dust around his feet.

His opponent was only 15 yards away. Hollingshead yelled for help, steeling himself for the burst of fire. No shot came. The man was having his own problems. His rifle had also failed him, and after fiddling with it for a few seconds he ran back into the building. Hollingshead finally cleared the stoppage and laid down fire to keep the gunman occupied while the last vehicles jolted their way out of the wadi. He would later laugh at the 'Hollywoodesque' nature of the encounter.

Afterwards, safely back in Now Zad, the Gurkhas relaxed for the first time. 'Everyone was pretty elated,' Hollingshead said. 'We had all succeeded. No one had backed down, or done anything coward-ly.' They had taken only one casualty, an Afghan policeman who was shot in the stomach. It was all the more satisfying because the Gurkhas had not prepared for full-on war fighting of the sort they had just experienced. The company had been put together at short notice and had not practised more than basic infantry drills together. They were supposed to be guarding the camp. But they had been at the forefront of the first big fight of the deployment and they could feel proud of themselves.

While the fight was raging in the wadi, Patrols Platoon were also under fire. Sergeant Ray Davis and Lance Corporal Gav Attwell were in the first vehicles, leading the convoy to the cordon position, when they ran into a group of five fighters. This triggered a firefight that went on for forty-five minutes. The Apaches were called in again.

The helicopters were a British version of an American design and were awesomely destructive. They fired Hellfire missiles and 30mm cannon rounds with explosive tips. The systems were 'slaved' to a laser linked to the pilot's retina. Wherever he looked, the weapon pointed. Like everyone else, Mark Swann, the Patrols OC, had never seen an Apache in action before, and the harsh ripple of the cannon fire took him by surprise. 'It was cracking right over our heads and for a few moments I thought we were under heavy machine-gun fire,' he said.

These dramas were at the periphery of the operation. The main action was just beginning. Two helicopters carrying Will Pike and his company headquarters staff, the engineer search team and 'A' Company's 2 Platoon arrived just after noon, landing near a stand of palm trees to the north of the compound. One was flown by Chris Hasler, a twenty-six-year-old who had grown up in Nova Scotia. He joined the RAF after failing a medical for the Canadian air force. The Canadians had lost a good man. Hasler proved to be an outstandingly able and courageous pilot. They flew in fast and Hasler had to stand the ship on its tail, using the belly as a brake to slow it down. The Paras raced off the back and immediately saw fire coming towards them. Hasler did not notice at first until he heard a warning over the radio net. 'We couldn't see the tracer as it was too bright and we couldn't hear the sound over the din of the aircraft.' As soon as the last man jumped clear he lifted off and joined the other Chinooks, which went into a holding position to the south of the zone, waiting in case they were needed to evacuate casualties.

It was a huge relief to be airborne. Despite their size and a degree of armouring, Chinooks were vulnerable to the weapons that the Taliban could bring to bear. An American Chinook had been shot down in Afghanistan in June the previous year and sixteen soldiers killed. The pilots particularly feared RPGs, a staple of insurgents' armouries all over the world. Like the Kalashnikov they were invented in the Soviet Union and were cheap, robust, easily portable and simple to operate. They were fired from a 3-foot-long launcher, a steel pipe with grip, trigger, iron sight and a cone at one end to dissipate the blast from the gunpowder launch charge. The grenades were roughly the shape and size of a pointed bowling pin and weighed up to 10 pounds. Once in flight a rocket kicked in and fins flipped out to guide the grenade on its flight. It had a range of 1,000 yards. But RPGs were not the most accurate of projectiles and behaved erratically when they went beyond a third of that distance. They were designed to blow up tanks and could do severe damage, especially to an aircraft if the range was right. 'There's nothing you can do against an RPG,' Hasler said. 'If it explodes it either cuts you in half or takes off your blades and you go down.'

As the first helicopters departed, Stuart Tootal was still in the air. He had planned to use his helicopter as an airborne command-and-control platform, but it soon became obvious that this was impracticable. It was impossible to see clearly what was happening on the ground. He ordered his helicopter to land and made his way with his HQ team to link up with Will Pike, who by now had been on the ground for forty-five minutes. With the Gurkhas out of trouble Tootal's first concern was to move Patrols Platoon to a less vulnerable position. They were stuck in close country which severely limited their ability to manoeuvre. The walls and trees around made it difficult to see and make proper use of the .50-cals mounted on their vehicles. Tootal ordered them to shift to the south-west into more open country, but as they withdrew the Taliban launched two more attacks. Once again the Apaches came to the rescue, forcing them to break off and take cover. Patrols Platoon took advantage of the breathing space to launch a counter-attack. They broke into one compound and discovered bright splashes of blood drying in the dirt. There was no sign, though, of dead or wounded fighters. They were to learn that the Taliban, when they fell back, always tried to carry their casualties and their corpses with them.

As they moved on again to seek the open ground they came under fire once more. Private Bashir Ali felt something hot and heavy hit his chest. He looked down to see that his body armour was on fire. When the flames were doused he realised how lucky he had been. The thump had been caused by two AK-47 rifle bullets which ignited the tracer rounds in the magazines in the pouches of his chest rig.

Patrols Platoon's running fight was to last, with some lulls, for nearly four hours.

Will Pike and 2 Platoon had landed where they were supposed to, 50 yards to the north of the target. 1 Platoon, under Hugo Farmer, was meant to put down just to the south. Pike waited for the news that they were in postion. It was some time in coming.

Farmer and his men arrived to an alarming reception. As they piled off the tailgate and into an open field rounds flew into the back of the helicopter. The first man to hit the ground was Corporal Quentin 'Prig' Poll, whose skill and seniority made him the automatic choice as the lead man in the platoon's lead section – number 1. 'That meant being first off the chopper, first in, which gave me quite a bit of pride,' he said. Poll had been a butcher and run a vegetable stall in a market in Norfolk before hearing the call of the Paras. He had been in for eleven years and was highly experienced, having served in Northern Ireland, Kosovo and Iraq. But this, he knew, as he ordered his men forward in an extended line, was the real thing.

A hundred yards ahead he could see where the shots were coming from. There was a wall with a gap in it. Two gunmen were darting into the opening, firing, then dodging back into cover. The Paras returned fire but the small-calibre rounds of the SA-80 rifles made little impression on the baked mud wall. Poll decided to 'get on top of them' and bounded forward. He split his men into two groups for the real-life execution of the drill called 'fire and manoeuvre'.

'I got the blokes spread out into a single line and four of us moved forward while the other four fired,' he said. 'Then they would start firing and we would move forward so there was always fire going down and we were gaining ground on the enemy position.'

When they reached it, they saw the Taliban fighters retreating into an orchard. Through the sparse leaves they could see a compound with two entrances which the gunmen ducked into before emerging to start shooting again. Poll called on his section to 'go firm' – to stay where they were. It was impossible to know what was on the other side of the compound wall. He was also worried they might lose contact with the rest of the platoon. It was time to take stock.

He called up Farmer, told him what had happened and relayed his position. Farmer told him to carry on, and moved up to join him with another section. It had been Poll's engagement and Farmer left him to him work out how to proceed. Para doctrine was to allow commanders at every level to make their own decisions wherever possible and to encourage the Toms to exercise initiative. Poll decided 'I couldn't take all my section in because it was getting too tight.' He left four men behind and dashed forward with the rest. They fired into the doorway on the right and the gunman ducked away. Poll moved on to the left-hand doorway where another gunman was still shooting. He was on the point of throwing a grenade into the entrance when he saw movement inside the compound. He could just make out a group of people who were clearly not fighters trying to keep out of the path of the flying bullets. 'Straight away', said Poll, 'the idea of putting grenades in went out the window.'

He called up Farmer, who told him to stop his men firing. The gunman had disappeared now but shots were coming from inside the compound. Poll moved forward with Private Adam Randle and Private Damien Jackson. He ordered them to go through the doorway but not to open fire unless they could clearly identify whoever was doing the shooting. The gunman had dodged into one of the buildings inside the compound. It was full of women and children who had taken shelter there when the shooting began. As he continued to fire in the direction of the Paras, the civilians scrambled to escape through windows and doorways. Randle and Jackson took cover and held their fire. Poll darted in to join them. Some of the women were screaming, while other civilians seemed amazingly calm. Poll dredged up his smattering of Pashto to yell at the civilians to get down, and made wild hand signals. 'But the old ones and the young kids didn't understand and kept walking around.' The soldiers were to witness many examples of the incredible coolness shown by some civilians when bullets were flying about.

There was no sign of the gunman. It seemed to Poll that he had made his escape out of the back of the compound. 'We knew we had lost him and to carry on any farther would have separated me from

A Chinook is silhouetted above the Helmand desert. All the outstations relied on helicopters to fly food and ammunition in and casualties out.

Taliban fighters. They are wearing 'dishdashas' and carrying an AK-47 rifle and two rocket-propelled grenade launchers.

Now Zad from ANP Hill.

Private Damien Jackson during Operation Mutay. The mud walls, compounds and spindly trees are typical of the battlefield terrain. 'Jacko' was killed a month later, four days before his twentieth birthday.

ABOVE: Patrols Platoon during Mutay with smoke from fires started by tracer smudging the sky. The Paras' first major action 'poked a stick into a hornets' nest'.

RIGHT: Looking out over the wadi and bazaar from a Sangin sangar. The GPMG and pile of cartridge cases tell their own story.

Morning for the mortarmen at Kajaki dam. Even by the harsh standards of Helmand, Kajaki was tough duty.

Patrols Platoon Commander Captain Mark Swann (*front*) and Lance Corporal Andrew 'Chalkie' White breakfast by their WMIK in Gereshk.

A GPMG gunner in action on ANP Hill in Now Zad. The 'jimpy' was an essential piece of battle-winning equipment that was used in virtually every engagement.

'The thousand yard stare'. Private Martin Cork flying back from Mutay.

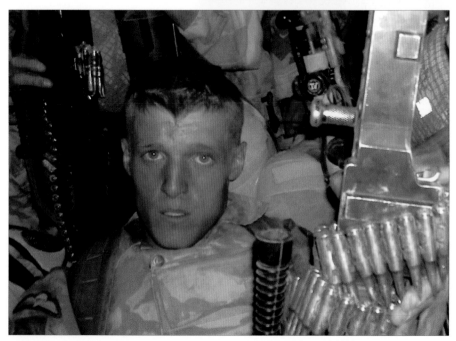

(*Left to right*) Captain Hugo Farmer and Corporals Quentin 'Prig' Poll, Stephen 'Hoss' Cartwright, James Shimmins and 'Chalkie' White sit in the shade cast by a stripped-down Pinzgauer as they wait for a helicopter to transport them from Gereshk back to Bastion.

Fighting Scot. Corporal Tam McDermott on the roof of the Sangin district centre. Note the makeshift sandbags made out of sacks. The weaponry includes a Soviet-designed Afghan RPK machine gun and an AT-4 light anti-tank weapon.

Hostile faces in Sangin. It was not always easy to tell friend from foe.

In the end, it all depended on the courage and tenacity of the 'Toms'. (*Left to right*) Private Neil Edwards, Lance Corporal Noel Brooksbank, and Privates Scott Boyle and Alistair Hartley in a Sangin sangar.

Sharp end medics. (*Left to right*) Lance Corporal Paul Roberts, Corporal Stuart Giles, Sergeant Brian Reidy and the Para's Medical Officer, Captain Harvey Pynn, in Sangin.

Sangin siesta. Dossing down on the floor for a few hours between 'stag' and patrolling.

orporal Mark Wright in the Sangin compound. He was to be awarded the George Cross for his selflessness and bravery.

Lieutenant Andy Mallet leads a patrol into Sangin town centre.

Loud and loveable. Sergeant Dan Jarvie was one of the most popular men in 3 Para.

Major Will Pike, OC 'A' Company. He was a tough boss. But no one doubted his devotion to his men.

Captain Martin Taylor showing the effects of three weeks in Sangin.

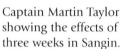

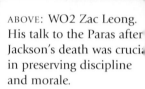

ABOVE: WO2 Zac Leong. His talk to the Paras after Jackson's death was crucial in preserving discipline and morale.

LEFT: Captain Matt Taylor in the field in Sangin. As Operations Officer, he played a crucial role in putting plans into action.

the rest of the platoon,' he said. They stayed put while Farmer came up to join them.

By now Farmer was feeling uneasy. The landscape and the buildings around them didn't seem to correspond with his map. Checking his Global Positioning System, he realised that the RAF had dropped them 350 yards to the west of where they were supposed to be. 'I can understand why they didn't drop us in the right place,' he said, magnanimously, later. 'For a start it's very confusing. Secondly it's a dangerous place for helicopters to hang around. So they saw a good place near where we had to be and they put us down.'

Farmer worked out a route to take them to their planned location, and having apologised as best he could to the civilians in the compound for the intrusion, set off. In their preparations the Paras had not formed a clear idea of the sort of terrain they would be operating in. They knew it was close country but did not expect it would pose too many problems. In reality it was a rural obstacle course. There were endless mud walls, thick and high, which made it difficult to see more than a few dozen yards ahead. Irrigation ditches cut a graph-paper pattern in the fields. All around were pomegranate orchards and fields of poppies, sunflowers and other high-standing crops. 'We hadn't expected it to be so lush,' said Will Pike. 'It was a bit like the South of France except flat. You couldn't see further than sixty yards.' The landscape looked pleasant and unthreatening. But it offered every advantage to a defending force and only hazards to those attacking.

The 400-yard journey to their correct position tested even the Paras' stamina. 'It was a nightmare,' said Farmer. Every 15 yards they ran into 8-foot-high mud walls that would have been impassable if not for the old-fashioned scaling ladders that someone had had the foresight to bring along. They had last been used to go over the back fences of suspects' houses on Northern Ireland council estates. They were to prove a vital bit of kit in these very different circumstances.

Even so, it was hard work clambering over them in full fighting order. That entailed webbing, body armour and a helmet, as well as the weight of your weapon and 'day sack' pack, crammed with extra ammunition. This was known as 'light scales', although it weighed from 70 to 80 pounds. Nonetheless, as Poll observed, when the bullets were flying, 'it's amazing how the weight just disappears. You feel it when you are coming down, when things go quiet. That's when it all starts niggling and pulling on you, tearing you apart. But during the contact you don't notice – it's out the window.'

After a quarter of an hour they met up with Tom Fehley and 2 Platoon. They could hear the snap of rounds coming from the Patrols Platoon's running engagement, and see smoke rising where the .50-cal tracer had set the vegetation ablaze. Farmer's men started to take up their positions to the south of the target compound. They were forced to take cover as shots started cracking overhead from unseen gunmen. But after ten minutes it went quiet and 2 Platoon moved in to clear the compound.

The search was a disappointment. They found a few hundred rounds of Kalashnikov bullets, a single grenade and a few bits and pieces of kit. There were also several bags of opium. The ammunition was removed. The opium was left where it was, in line with the battle group policy of disassociating themselves from any attempts to threaten the locals' livelihood. Either the intelligence was faulty, as it often was, or the Taliban had already removed the bulk of whatever guns, ammo and explosives had been stashed there. '2 Platoon felt a bit out of sorts,' remembered Corporal Scott MacLachlan. 'We just sat there saying, "What's happening?"'

For two hours the Paras waited where they were. It was hot in the afternoon sun. They sipped water continuously and tried to rest. Then, at about 3 p.m., Fehley called his section commanders together. A signal had come through from brigade headquarters in Kandahar saying that an important Taliban figure was hiding in the area. The new orders were to arrest him and Will Pike had given them the job.

From the outset, there was little hope of catching their quarry. The information could not have been more vague. They had no idea of what their target looked like or where precisely he was. The situation was in any event likely to have changed since the first intelligence was received. Fehley's orders were to move forward to a grid location 500 yards west of the target compound and deal with anything that he encountered on the way. If they found nothing, they were to return. At 3.30 p.m., 2 Platoon set off. 'We had only gone a hundred metres when we realised how difficult the terrain was and how vulnerable we had become,' said Corporal Tam McDermott, who was commanding 1 Section. 'There were high walls, high fences, little tunnels going through the walls. It just seemed to have been prepared for someone to have a go at us and withdraw. It was ideal ambush country.'

McDermott handed over point position to Corporal MacLachlan. They were both robustly Scottish, but Scottish in different ways. McDermott was assertive and outspoken; MacLachlan, who had once considered a career in marketing, was quiet and reflective.

Progress was slow. Every 30 yards there was another wall to climb. They thanked God for the scaling ladders. They were moving through a maze of 'long passageways, narrow channels, paths through orchards. You would think it would be good underfoot but in most cases it was marsh, quagmire', MacLachlan said. '[We] didn't know exactly who we were looking for – just Taliban types. We knew that what with everything else that had been going on, the chances were we would be hit. They knew all the rat-runs and escape routes. It was their battleground and we were the new kids on the block.'

After fifteen minutes they emerged at the edge of a large square of open ground. MacLachlan's orders were to push forward across it. Before he did, he paused to scope out the terrain. The field was about 150 yards across. There was an orchard on the far side. It was overlooked in one corner by a rocky mound, perhaps 250 feet high. He decided that from the Taliban's point of view, the field was 'a perfect killing area'.

Crouched behind the wall, he was understandably 'a bit apprehensive about taking that step forward, out from that cover, because if I did get hit there was no escape route for me with a brick wall behind me'. He consulted Fehley, who agreed that he should work his way to the left along a sandy pathway that ran round the field. As they approached the corner where the path turned away to the right, 'a sixth sense, a Para sense, was kicking in'. He told the rest of his section to stay put behind the wall while he and his lead scout, Private Dale Tyrer, came out of cover and rounded the bend. In front of them was a path that stretched for 100 yards before disappearing into the streets of Now Zad. 'As we started to advance I caught movement out of the corner of my eye, about seventy metres away in the shadows. Just at that point, three or four feet in front of me the sand kicked up.' The motion that MacLachlan had glimpsed was a machine-gunner dropping to the firing position on his belly. 'The next thing I knew', he said, 'there was machine-gun fire and rounds ricocheting off the walls, kicking up sand and dust.' MacLachlan guessed that the heavy fire was coming from a Russian-made PKM – the Taliban's equivalent to the British GPMG. It was a good weapon, capable of accurately blistering a position from 1,000 yards away. MacLachlan noted with some concern that at the range it was now firing at it was 'in a position to basically knock hell out of the street'.

Instead of retreating, MacLachlan and Tyrer stayed put, crouching in the lee of a wall skirting the path until they could identify precisely where the gun was firing from. Then, coolly, they began laying down accurate fire until the PKM stopped shooting. Taking it in turns to cover each other, they dropped back round the corner to join the rest, while marvelling that they were still both in one piece. 'How the hell we never got hit I have no idea because there were rounds all over the place,' MacLachlan said later.

The rest of the section were 'sat wide-eyed behind the wall. It was like, "lucky bastards!"' But it was not over yet. MacLachlan counted down, 'Three! two! one!', then he and Tyrer darted round the corner and 'put down a massive weight of fire'. Tyrer lobbed three 40mm grenades from the underslung grenade launcher on his rifle into the spot where the machine gun had been firing. With that, it all went quiet.

The pair fell back once more. There was a brief calm. Then across the field, from their positions among the trees on the far side of the big field, the Taliban opened up a scorching barrage of small-arms, RPG and machine-gun fire. The other sections of the platoon were strung out along the wall opposite the Taliban fighters. For the next one and a half hours Tam McDermott and his men traded fire with the Taliban across the field while the Fire Support Team pelted the insurgents with mortars.

Fehley was looking to take the battle forward somehow. He asked MacLachlan to move to the right to try to find a firing point from where they could look down on the Taliban positions. MacLachlan and his men plunged into the cover of an orchard, squelching through the waterlogged soil until they emerged by the side of the rocky hill overlooking the field. They moved cautiously and laboriously. After the adrenalin jolt of the ambush, MacLachlan's metabolism had calmed down. 'Time, instead of going at a hundred miles an hour, became treacle time.'

When they emerged from the trees, the Apaches were up, tilting and turning over the battlefield, trying to spot the Taliban. The risks of getting it wrong and unleashing a horrendous 'fratricide' incident were enormous. MacLachlan's men anxiously signalled the Apaches to warn them not to fire. They could see the hillock quite well now. There were a couple of men on top but MacLachlan could not make out whether they were carrying weapons. 'They were in typical Afghan wear with the old black turbans, beard and all the rest of it but I couldn't identify any AK-47s or anything.' In keeping with the rules of engagement, he told his men not to shoot unless they were sure the Afghans were fighters. Nonetheless, there was 'something dodgy' about one of them. 'He was a bit furtive. He kept looking up then ducking down as if he was looking out for us but couldn't see us.'

MacLachlan told his section to stay put while he pushed on to get better 'eyes on' the hillock. There was a wall to the left. He squatted down in the lee while he took stock. He could definitely see two figures on the top now. They were about a hundred yards away. He was reluctant to call his men forward and expose them to fire so he decided to deal with them himself. His plan was to 'sucker them into engaging with me'. He moved out of cover, deliberately exposing himself to attract the men's attention.

As soon as the men saw him they raised their rifles, which had been slung behind their backs, and began shooting, in wild 'spray and pray' bursts. MacLachlan 'drew a bead on one of them' and fired four or five single shots. His victim fell back against the tawny dirt of the hillside. MacLachlan turned to the second and fired again, and again the gunman toppled. There seemed to be no more of them. MacLachlan called his men forward and radioed Fehley to report their success. He told them to stay put and put the occasional burst into the hilltop to dissuade anyone from reoccupying it.

The Taliban were now under attack by land and air. Pike had sent his Forward Artillery Observer (FAO), Captain Matt Armstrong, and Forward Air Controller (FAC), Corporal Shaun Fry, forward with Fehley. They now put in a request for extra help from the Americans, who ordered A-10 jets and B-1 bombers to the area. The A-10 Thunderbolt was a terrifying prospect for anyone underneath it. It was known as the 'Warthog' in reference to its clunky profile and 'Tankbuster' owing to its ability to chew up armour with 30mm cannon shells at a distance of 4 miles. It had a range of 800 miles and could manoeuvre well at low speeds, which allowed it to loiter over the battlefield for protracted periods in support of ground troops. Not long after 2 Platoon's fight began, an A-10 made its first run. Hugo Farmer could hear it from where he and his men were hunkered down outside the target compound. 'I didn't see it come in,' he said. 'All I heard was the noise. It was absolutely incredible. It's very difficult to describe but it sounds like an angry dinosaur.' He was talking not about the engine note but the cannon shells. They fly out of the nose-mounted guns at a rate of 2,100 or 4,200 rounds a minute, splitting the air and ripping up everything in their way. It was said that pilots could fire bursts only for a maximum of four seconds before the counter-punch of the recoil caused the engines to stall and the Thunderbolt to fall out of the sky.

Farmer was eager to get his platoon into the fighting. He moved over to Will Pike's command post so that he was on hand to be tasked if reinforcements were called for. The fight had turned into a mosaic of separate encounters in which each side was trying to dominate the other. There was no front line, which suited the Paras, whose ethos and training were founded on the notion that they would have to fight on their feet an enemy that was all around them. It seemed to Pike that the Taliban were 'operating like packs of hyenas, and I think there were about seven packs, each about ten or fifteen strong'. Sometimes there seemed to be some order to what they were doing. At other times the Taliban 'were just floating about'.

Farmer was to get his wish as the action was now moving in the direction of his men. Taliban fighters were streaming eastwards to escape the battering they were getting from the Paras and the jets. Their line of flight took them straight towards the 1 Platoon positions. Farmer had pushed Prig Poll and the lead section up to a wall 30 yards to the west of the main platoon position. 3 Section under Corporal Chris Wright were a little to the north. Poll had split his men into two groups, placing one, led by Lance Corporal Johnathon 'Billy' Smart, a little to the north, on the far side of one of the ubiquitous walls. Private Randle was with him. As they hunkered down, Randle thought he heard Afghan voices coming from the undergrowth about twenty yards away and called out a warning to Smart, who was farther forward. According to Poll, Smart reported back to him, 'I'm afraid we've got fucking enemy coming straight towards us'. Poll told him to shoot if he was sure they were gunmen. By now two men were clearly in sight. One was carrying an RPG and the other a Kalashnikov. Smart still remembered to yell a warning – the Pashto phrase for 'Stop, I am a British soldier'. When the gunmen kept coming he and Randle opened fire, killing both. The necessity of shouting a warning had been drummed into everyone. 'The view is', said Pike, 'that you take life when there is a threat to life and if you don't have to kill an insurgent or anybody else then don't because an insurgent is better alive than dead and we are not here to kill people wantonly.'

Poll heard the shooting and spoke to Smart on the Personal Role Radio (PRR) net. Each soldier is electronically connected to his comrades by an individual microphone and transmitter which allows short-range communication on the battlefield. Smart described what had happened and warned that a third gunman was moving in his direction. Poll scaled a wall and looked over. Ahead, a man was coming towards him. 'He was walking backwards, looking at the two of his muckers that [the others] had just dropped and he looked confused and dazed at what had happened,' he said. 'Then he turned around and saw me.' Both men froze. They were

15 yards apart. The gunman was carrying an AK-47. Poll glanced through his SUSAT (Sight Unit, Small Arms, Trilux) telescopic sight and got to the trigger first. 'I dropped him,' he said. 'I put about four rounds into him, dropped him there.' For a second or two Poll looked down at the dead man, the first he had killed. He had black hair and a black beard. He was wearing a black dishdasha shift which he had tied between his legs to stop it dragging on the ground. As well as the Kalashnikov he had a small pack on his back full of RPG grenades. Poll had no time to think about what he had just done. More Taliban were coming towards him and the deaths of three of their comrades had made them angry.

'They were giving us everything they had,' said Poll. 'They were firing RPGs, PKMs ...' Poll decided to fall back with Privates Stephen Halton and Andrew Lanaghan who had joined him, 'because it was too naughty in there', but left Smart and his group in place.

From their position to the north, Chris Wright and 3 Section had heard the noise of the firefight. Private Peter McKinley had climbed a tree to get better 'eyes on'. About a hundred yards away, he saw a man in a dark dishdasha, wearing an assault vest and carrying a rifle, clambering over a wall. McKinley 'flapped' at first then 'finally got my safety catch off. By that time, I think he had seen me and tried to get back over the wall. I shot him'. McKinley got off nine rounds. The Paras fired only single shots. It saved ammunition and made their shooting far more effective than the extravagant approach of their enemies. The gunman dropped on to the wall then slipped back over the other side. His comrades responded with a volley of shots that chopped through the branches of McKinley's perch, showering him with twigs and leaves.

When Poll met up again with the OC, Will Pike, and his platoon commander, Hugo Farmer, there had been a shift in the battle. Some Taliban fighters had been seen falling back southwards from the area where 2 Platoon were fighting. Poll suspected they might be planning to take cover in a compound that 1 Platoon had passed earlier in the day when making its arduous way to meet up with the main group. He asked to take his section towards it and try to cut them off. Pike advised Farmer to give him his head. Poll was delighted. According to Dan Jarvie, the platoon sergeant, in his elation Poll 'called out the immortal words: "Married men with families stay here! Single men with me!" Then it was a case of "Hold on a minute, Prig. Take your section. Let's not start jumbling things up."' Prig saw sense and set off with Lanaghan and Halton. Farmer went with them, taking his radio operator, Private Philip Briggs. They entered the compound, checking the buildings inside as they went. One was empty except for a generator. Another was someone's living quarters. A gaggle of silent women and children were huddled inside. On the far side of the compound a small open doorway, about four feet high, was set in the wall, which led into a field. It seemed the obvious line of withdrawal for the retreating Taliban. The Paras moved towards it carefully. As they approached they were met with a flurry of badly aimed shots that whizzed harmlessly over their heads.

At this point the Paras might well have considered they had done enough and fallen back. Instead, Farmer ordered Poll and Halton forward to charge the doorway. 'No sooner had they passed through [than] they came under a huge, concentrated weight of fire that peppered all around the door,' Farmer remembered. 'Corporal Poll and Private Halton fell to their belt buckles and crawled back through the door.' Poll managed a joke as Farmer and Briggs helped drag them into cover. 'I think they know we're here,' he said. Farmer could not believe that they had not been hit.

They could hear radio chatter from the Taliban on the other side of the doorway. Through it they could see only a densely planted field, with head-high foliage. Despite their previous experience, Poll and Halton were adamant they wanted to go again. Private Lanaghan volunteered to go with them. Once more they dodged through the doorway. Once more they were met with a riot of fire. To add to their problems, a deep irrigation ditch lay just beyond the doorway. To cross it would mean getting cut off. It was impossible in any event to see anything clearly through the thick crops. They turned round and crawled back through the doorway. Farmer decided that 'the enemy had gone firm and had the entrances to the location in their killing area'.

As they considered what to do next, they heard a thud and something bounced down in the middle of the group. Farmer screamed, 'Take cover' and everyone dived. They were within 5 yards of the grenade when it exploded. Miraculously the only casualty was Farmer, who got a bit of blast debris in his backside. He fell back 20 yards to the middle of the compound and covered the doorway, hoping that the Taliban might decide to emerge through it to counter-attack.

Poll, Halton and Lanaghan also moved out of grenade range. As they took up their new position they were surprised to see a group of Taliban suddenly appearing on their left. They seemed to know what they were doing, leapfrogging forward in a classic fire-and-manoeuvre. For the first time, Poll was impressed. His experience in Iraq had not taught him much respect for the fighters of the region. His attitude had been: 'What do they know, this bunch of flip-flop, dress-wearing bastards. This was the first time I looked round and went, "Fuck, they actually know what they are doing."'

He yelled at his men to pull back. As they withdrew, another four grenades exploded on the other side of their position. 'That shook us a little bit, knocked a couple of the blokes down, but again there were no injuries.' They dragged themselves back 20 yards, hid behind a mound of crops and hay and laid down fire which forced the Taliban back. But the respite was temporary. The Taliban moved forward again and it took another flurry of fire from the Paras to drive them back.

For a while it went quiet. As they lay there behind the flimsy cover, the indefatigable Poll decided to try once more to get through the door. As he advanced, 'the sixth grenade came over, which rocked me a bit. This time I knew I couldn't go forward.'

Hugo Farmer was now weighing the merits of launching a direct assault on a group of Taliban who had begun firing from behind a wall to the right of his position. They were protected by a dense orchard. 'There were only a couple of holes in the wall and there were dozens and dozens of rounds coming through,' he said. He moved round with 2 Section, led by Corporal Charlie Curnow. They lined up to go, and Farmer took a deep breath. 'I looked at the approach. I looked at the blokes in the line. I looked at the section commander [Curnow], who could see what I could see. I hummed and hawed for a minute. We were talking to each other. I was saying, "Right, this is the way to go," and he was saying, "Good, right, OK, fine." Then I looked down the line and I thought: "Stop."' Machine-gun bullets were spitting from the wall of vegetation ahead. It was impossible to see the firing point. Suddenly the whole thing seemed suicidal. He told himself, 'This is just not on. This next bit is not going to happen.' He turned to Curnow and said, 'I'm not going out there and if I'm not going, you're not.' Curnow accepted the decision philosphically. 'He said, "Yep, happy with that, boss."'

As Farmer explained in a post-operational report: 'It was clear that the … density of the vegetation … was such that an assault into it would have been totally blind and would certainly have resulted in casualty and most likely death.'

The clash had lasted an hour. There were only about forty-five minutes of daylight left. Unless they were to stay the night there it was time to get out. The shooting died away to the odd, distant crackle, and the sun slipped down the sky, gilding the leaves and lighting up the mud walls with a buttery, innocent glow. Farmer and his men trudged warily eastwards to the prearranged helicopter landing site on the far side of the wadi.

2 Platoon had found it harder to extract themselves from their battle to the north. Tam McDermott's section were strung out along the wall facing the Taliban positions inside the treeline at the far side of the open field. Extracting under fire would be a dangerous operation. Two of his men, Privates Paul 'Flash' Gordon and Anthony 'Zippy' Owen, had been tasked with protecting the platoon's left flank and were lying out in the open. Despite being given the choice of retreating they chose to stick it out and cover the withdrawal. The artillery and air control team of Matt Armstrong and Shaun Fry, who were ahead of the Para positions, decided to stay put and call in an air strike on the Taliban lines, giving everyone the chance to break clean. The target area was less than 70 yards away. There was a huge risk that the strike could result in 'fratricidal' casualties. Scott MacLachlan watched the A-10 roar in to 'chew up

the entire main orchard area that the Taliban had been occupying'. As it did so Fry and Armstrong jumped up and sprinted to safety.

The Paras fell back slowly, covering each other as they negotiated the obstacle course of walls and ditches. On the way back they came across a man pushing a friend along in a wheelbarrow. His legs were covered in blood. The pair had come looking for medical help and Harvey Pynn was called over. After the two men had been searched, he examined the wounded man. He had been hit by shrapnel and one of his legs was badly broken. Pynn 'patched him up, splinted his legs, gave him painkillers and antibiotics'. When they left they took him with them to Bastion for proper treatment. It was an ad hoc hearts-and-minds project, but not of the sort that had been originally envisaged.

The Chinooks lifted off into the gathering darkness at 6.15 p.m. It was hard to talk over the roar of the engines. Most men sat alone with their thoughts. For the first time, they each had the chance to look back over what had been a remarkable and important experience. Everyone was carrying away a feeling that the day had gone well. 'Throughout the section, from the newest, freshest faces who had only been in the battalion a couple of months, right the way through to the more senior Toms, everybody pulled their weight and did what they were told,' said Scott MacLachlan. 'The sense of achievement was something else. Everyone felt on a bit of a high after that.' Tam McDermott felt they had passed a test. 'We had not needed a wake-up call. We were not arrogant. We knew the Taliban had been fighting for years and years. But they were no match for us.'

The Paras had proved the value of their intense training. Their drills had worked smoothly and command-and-control was coherent and effective. But it had been a strange encounter. In terms of achieving the original objective the mission had to be counted as a disappointment, given the meagre haul carried away from the target compound. Nor had they managed to capture the second 'high-value' Taliban target. Many were to describe the incident later as 'poking a stick into a hornets' nest'. The Paras had stung the Taliban into coming out to fight. That had certainly not been the original intention. They had gone there intending to carry out a simple 'cordon and search'. They had expected some resistance, but nothing on the scale that developed. It was only when they returned to Bastion that they learned that the intelligence they had been given was incomplete. Information had come through that there were dozens of Taliban in the area. But it was not passed on to them before they set off.

The Paras had enough skill and resources to handle the unexpected. Tootal had decided in his pre-planning that deliberate operations such as Mutay should be undertaken only if there were enough men, guns and aircraft to ensure against unforeseen turns for the worse. They had not expected, however, to be shot at as soon as they arrived, nor to be under continuous attack once they had set up the cordon. The Taliban had shown impressive aggression and determination, as well as an ability to organise, fire and manoeuvre. The Paras had easily outfought the Taliban. But there was a feeling that they had also been touched by luck.

'Flying back in the Chinooks everybody was quite clearly jubilant, buoyant,' said Hugo Farmer.

But they were also thinking through their own thoughts as well. I can remember looking out of the window thinking, 'Christ almighty, that was a bit different, that was good fun.' I didn't think it at the time, but the miracle of Mutay was that everyone was on the Chinook, no one even got injured. Coming back, hitting the ground at Bastion, people were coming up and saying, 'What was it like, what was it like?' For the first time you felt legitimised. You felt that actually you had done it for real now and it was good, it was good. As time went on, the lustre came off that a little bit.

7

Rapid Reaction

Stuart Tootal noticed a 'definite buzz' in Bastion after Operation Mutay. 'A' Company were proud of their performance. The rest of the battle group units were anxious for their turn. Tootal, though, was not looking for another fight. His hope was that he could use the encounter to win the trust of the local population. The success of Mutay, he believed, might help persuade them that the British were a good thing. The conventional doctrine was that the majority of the civilians were 'floating voters'. Decades of chronic violence and instability had taught Afghans that it was best to watch and wait before committing to one side or the other. The Taliban had boasted that the British were no match for them. The action at Now Zad should have dealt a serious blow to their prestige.

What was needed now was a 'non-kinetic' operation that would demonstrate that the fighting had a point and that suppression of the insurgents would be followed by positive, peaceful action. Tootal's desire for a quick confidence-building effort was to be frustrated. Once again, the battle group's energies were diverted into other tasks.

The opportunity to show the positive side of the British presence was dwindling away. Tootal worried that his men were being used merely to react to events. He was also concerned that using them to reinforce the government's authority outside the Triangle would mean British soldiers doing the job of the Afghan army and police for them. As a result, the Paras would find themselves stuck in fixed positions, unable to manoeuvre and dangling on the end of a long and slender supply chain.

Intelligence estimates put the Taliban losses at Now Zad as a result of Operation Mutay at between twenty-one and thirty-six.

They had died in what they regarded as their own territory, a place of safety where they did not expect to be disturbed. The encounter had shown them that their new enemies were determined and professional. The Paras, in Will Pike's words, 'had sent a bit of a signal to the Taliban that we are happy to come into your backyard, do a task and extract, and there is not much you can do about it'. The insurgents also appreciated now the wide range of weapons ranged against them. The Taliban fought largely with rockets, rifles and machine guns. They were facing a force armed with the most efficient killing instruments Western technology could devise. In a conventional war it would have been clear who would win. But the Taliban were not conventional warriors. They were fighting for God, and death held fewer terrors for them than it did for their opponents. It was a contest of wills, and patience and resilience were among Taliban fighters' outstanding characteristics. Within a week of Operation Mutay they were busy again, this time around FOB Robinson near Sangin.

Robinson was a bleak spot. It was an enclosed patch of featureless, gritty desert, filled with vehicles, tents and containers. The Americans who set it up called it the Poor Bastards' Club. In the second week of June it was home to elements of 7 Parachute Regiment, Royal Horse Artillery. 7 RHA are airborne gunners. They played a vital part in the battle group. They provided a battery of seven 105mm light guns which were brought into play on many occasions to crush Taliban attacks on Sangin and, later, Musa Qaleh. They also coordinated and directed all artillery, mortar and aerial bombardments by helicopters and jets. Although they were gunners, the demands of Helmand meant they were often called on to fight as 'infanteers'. At the same time they were involved in one of the mission's vital tasks: they ran the OMLTs that trained units of the Afghan National Army. An ANA *kandak* (battalion) was currently deployed at the base under 7 RHA control.

On 11 June the men at Robinson were asked to retrieve a Desert Hawk UAV (Unmanned Air Vehicle) that had crashed in the desert. UAVs are a cheap and risk-free way of gathering intelligence from the air. They fly by remote control and are equipped with a camera which transmits images back to base for intellligence scrutiny. They are made out of light wood, have a 52-inch wingspan, weigh only 7 pounds and cost about £12,000. They look more like model aeroplanes than instruments of war. The UAV had gone down on the west bank of the Helmand river, not far from FOB Robinson. A mixed patrol made up of members of the OMLT, soldiers from 18 Battery, Royal Artillery, who were also in camp, some Gurkhas and an ANA contingent set out, late in the afternoon, to find it.

FOB Robinson was on the east bank of the Helmand and the patrol crossed over by commercial ferry to the search area. They drove around fruitlessly for a while before learning from some local people that the Taliban had already picked up the Desert Hawk. They set off back to camp. It was dark by the time they recrossed the river. When they reached the eastern bank, a sizeable Taliban force was waiting for them. In the fight that followed Bombardier Thomas Mason was hit by a bullet that passed through his arm, below his body armour, through his chest and out the other side. The patrollers managed to fight their way out of the ambush zone and called in a casevac helicopter to get the casualty out. They then stayed put to await the arrival of a quick reaction force from Robinson. It was led by Captain Jim Philippson, a twenty-nine-year-old who, at the end of his tour with 29 Commando Royal Artillery, had volunteered for service with 7 RHA in Afghanistan. The men in the reaction force parked their vehicles by a police station near the ambush site and moved forward on foot. Before they had got far they were hit by another ambush. Philippson was killed in the firefight. The speed of the attack led everyone to suspect that the Taliban had been tipped off by someone at the police station.

When the news reached Robinson another quick reaction force raced out from Robinson. They linked up with the original rescue team and managed to retrieve Philippson's body. They returned the few miles to the base then set out again to try to link up with the original patrol. On the way, the Taliban intercepted them once more. In the exchange of fire Troop Sergeant Major Andy Stockton from 32 Regiment, Royal Artillery – the unit responsible for UAVs – had his arm blown off by an RPG.

After the injured man had been casevacced back to Bastion, the men pressed on, eventually met up with the original patrol and settled down to wait for morning. There were now nearly thirty vehicles in the group. They made a large and visible target. Yet the Taliban held off, apparently waiting for first light. With dawn came reinforcements: 3 Para's 'B' Company, under Giles Timms, arrived by helicopter. 'We literally walked them back alongside, with their vehicles trundling along at walking pace the seven kilometres or so to FOB Robinson,' he said.

The incident caused some bad feeling among British soldiers. Why were men's lives being put at risk for the sake of a £12,000 toy plane? Why was the patrol sent out just as it was getting dark? Why had Philippson's group set off on foot from the police station? Jim Philippson, who came from St Albans in Hertfordshire, had been with 7 RHA only a few months but was already a popular figure. He possessed a 'unique combination of fierce professionalism, relaxed style of command and sense of fun', according to one of his colleagues. He was a key member of the mentoring team, where his patience, responsiveness and touch of charisma had made his Afghan charges warm to him.

These incidents again demonstrated the Taliban's energy and aggression and underlined the risks of using predictable routes. The lesson was learnt anew, only two days later, when an American convoy was attacked along the main road between Sangin and Musa Qaleh. One man was killed and three vehicles were shot up. The Paras were summoned to the rescue. Tootal sent off an 'A' Company force under Will Pike. No one had had any idea the Americans were in the area. By this stage it was obvious that any foreigner travelling along the route could expect to be attacked. 'It was an example,' said Pike, 'of people doing stupid things and other people having to come and dig them out of it.'

'A' Company flew off late in the afternoon. It was some time before they found the convoy. The Paras put down and scrambled out of the rear door. The Americans were about four hundred yards away. One group set off to secure a patch of high ground overlooking the highway. Another went to round up the Americans and help them out of the ambush site. The attack had taken place close to one of the settlements that straggle along the highway that runs by the Helmand river. To British eyes, it seemed an ideal place to launch an attack. It appeared the Americans thought they had missed a turning and had driven back and forth looking for it, giving the Taliban time to get into place.

As the Paras closed up on the Americans, the Taliban issued a reminder that they were still there, firing an RPG from the built-up area at one of the three Apaches that had escorted the Paras in.

It was already getting dark. The Chinooks had gone. They would not be back until dawn at the earliest. The Paras decided to spend the night on a slope that overlooked the ambush site. It was far from ideal but it seemed to offer the best cover in what was bare, exposed terrain. With night falling, the dangers of blundering on in the darkness seemed greater than the risks of staying where they were.

Pike had with him his HQ staff, two rifle platoons, the machine-gun platoon commanded by Captain Rob Mussetti and some mortars. They spread themselves out, setting up defensive arcs that would cover the approaches from the road, scratching shallow shell scrapes in the stony ground with entrenching tools, and then settled down for the night. The plan was to sit it out until dawn, then move off westwards into the open desert, where they would be picked up by helicopter.

Private Peter McKinley and his mates obtained what cover they could from a foot-high ridge running across the slope. They went through their drills, switching on their night vision optics and standing to in readiness for any attack. The Americans and their vehicles were behind them, in a fold in the ground that offered a little protection from the first buildings, which lay about fifty yards away. One of their Humvees was parked on the ridgeline, its .50-cal machine gun pointing down the slope. McKinley was not impressed by their behaviour. 'We were all stood to and the Americans were behind us, smoking and having a chat, fucking about,' he said. 'If you are in the middle of a dark field and you light up a fag, everyone is going to see it.'

McKinley was twenty-one years old and was one of 3 Para's

prominent personalities. He was lean, funny and aggressive, even by Para standards. One NCO described him as 'a social hand grenade'. He was born in Cornwall, where his father was in the navy. The family later moved to South Ayrshire. It was the *Braveheart* era, and he was the only boy in class with an English accent. He 'fucked up school – wasn't that good at it and I was always getting into trouble, fighting and whatever'. He left without taking his exams and got a job as a greenkeeper at the Royal Troon golf club.

Looking for something more fulfilling, he went to the local careers office. 'They brought up all the jobs on the screen, the jobs I could do,' he said. 'I had never heard of the Paras before and so I said, "What's a paratrooper?" The guy turned round and said, "You don't want to join them, they are full of thugs, ex-cons, people like that." I just laughed and said, "Can I at least find out about them?"' McKinley joined soon afterwards and served in Northern Ireland and Iraq. The Paras were now his home. He was, in a way, the personification of the cartoon Para. 'He is the sort of character who might be a pain in the arse in barracks but actually does the job when it comes to it and does it very well,' said one officer. McKinley was resoundingly to prove his worth that night.

At about 8.40 p.m. the 1 Platoon commander, Hugo Farmer, was 'sitting with my radio op, Private Briggs, chatting about the day, when he asked what the likelihood of being taken on by the Taliban that night was. Just as I said, "Briggs, they would have to be fucking mad," all hell broke loose. Tracer fire from AK-47s came snapping over our heads along with RPG rounds.' Rocket-propelled grenades are set to detonate after nine seconds if they have not hit something solid. These were bursting in the air, pumping molten shrapnel on to the earth below. Green tracer from a heavy machine gun a few hundred yards away flashed through the position.

Farmer and Briggs dived for a shallow scrape they had gouged in the stony soil as the platoon's front sections opened fire. McKinley had been sharing a similar conversation with his section commander, Chris Wright, a moment before. 'I said, "Chris, do you think anything will happen tonight?" He said, "Generally speaking, from the books I have read, the Taliban don't attack at night."' With that McKinley made himself as comfortable as he could in the un-forgiving dirt and stones, using his helmet as a pillow.

Now he was up and blazing away, pumping rounds and 40mm grenades from his underslung launcher into the blackness ahead of him wherever he saw a muzzle flash.

He was interrupted by a shout of 'Medic!' An RPG had struck one of the Humvees parked on the ridge. Everyone in 3 Para has basic first-aid training. McKinley had taken some further courses and had some added expertise. He answered the call, running up the hill across open ground over which grenades were exploding.

I got to the Humvee and there were two blokes at the back of it. One of them had a big gash at the back of his neck but he was talking. He was all right so I left him. The other guy was fucked up big time … I think the RPG that hit the Humvee had just shredded him. He was in rags. His eye was hanging out and his arm was in a shit state. He had some damage to his leg and he was finding it hard to breathe.

McKinley did what he could with the bandages, IV fluid bags and tourniquets in the team medic pack that he always carried with him. There was no light and he worked with a torch stuck in his mouth. There was no question of giving his patient morphine on account of the head injury and breathing difficulties. Mercifully, the man seemed to be in deep shock anyway and was drifting in and out of conscious-ness. McKinley was interrupted by an American medic arriving on the scene with a much more lavish aid kit. 'He took one look at him and said, "Sorry, I'm not trained for this."' The reaction confirmed McKinley's views about the US military. 'I thought, you fucking dick, this is one of your mates here and I am having to fix him.'

McKinley had been joined by the 'A' Company Combat Medical Technician, Lance Corporal Paul Roberts, who had been working on the other casualty. Reckoning he had done what he could, he set off back down the hill to his shell scrape. After about two and a half hours, when the tempo of fighting dropped, a Black Hawk arrived to take the wounded Americans out.

The fighting had died down but the Taliban were still there. Through their thermal sights the Paras could see ghostly white figures moving into a compound facing their position. McKinley and Private Jim Thwaite, next to him in the shell scrape farthest forward, had also spotted two men with weapons moving around on the ambush site less than a hundred yards away. They opened up. An Apache flying overhead confirmed that the Paras had killed both attackers.

Corporal Mark Wright, the mortar fire controller, had now moved up to the forward line, closest to the village. It was very dark, but through his night vision goggles he could now see the activity in the compound, where men seemed to be forming up. He began calling down fire, thirty-five rounds in all, which scattered the Taliban, killing six of them. The attack set off a chain of firefights. By now, an A-10 had arrived overhead. But the Taliban were shooting from among the houses strung along the road and the aircraft could not engage without risking civilian casualties. The Tankbuster flew away after a few passes. Eventually, the crack of gunfire slackened and silence settled on the hill again. It was broken by the arrival of a Chinook, which brought in more mortar rounds, a platoon from 'C' Company, commanded by Captain Ben Harrop, and a team equipped with Javelin guided missiles. Javelin missiles are aimed and fired usinga Command Launch Unit. This is a thermal imaging sight thatpicks up heat from human bodies to create a picture. With it, the Paras now had a clear view of Taliban movements on the ground around them. The new arrivals settled down to cover the western approaches to the position but there were to be no further contacts that night.

At dawn, the vehicles pulled away from the village, followed by the Paras, who 'tabbed' westwards through the empty desert to a high plateau. The convoy formed a circle and called the helicopters to come and collect them. It was to be a long wait.

As the sun climbed up the sky they sat in their shell scrapes and tried to preserve the dwindling water supplies. They had each taken about six litres of water, which was supposed to be enough to get them through twenty-four hours. Now it was running out. Hugo

Farmer began to appreciate 'how people in cartoons must be feeling, crawling along going, "Water, water." It was terrible. I was sipping a thimbleful at a time.'

There was no indication of how long they might be there. An American relief convoy was supposed to be on its way to escort their soldiers out, but no one seemed to know when it would arrive. Will Pike got on the radio and demanded a resupply chopper. It took several hours to arrive but 'morale just flew through the roof as soon as boxes of water and rations were being dropped'. The Paras could not leave until the American rescue convoy arrived, however, and after the load had been kicked off the back of the helicopter, the Chinook took off again.

Time dragged by. Then, out of the heat haze, they saw a column of about forty vehicles approaching. Pete McKinley, Chris Wright and Jim Thwaite watched as one of the Humvees from the convoy rolled by. An American wearing what McKinley judged to be 'fucking silly sunglasses' turned to them and said, 'This country sucks.'

The Americans brought cigarettes, which the Paras gratefully blagged. They also brought with them a contingent of ANA, who had a CD player with them that blasted out local pop. Private Peter Parker got into a dance competition with one of the Afghans. 'It was one of the funniest things I've ever seen, watching those two dancing,' said McKinley. 'All the Afghans were loving Peter because he is a young lad and they were all bender boys.'

The Paras had to wait fourteen hours in the desert heat before the choppers arrived to extract them to Bastion. The whole operation had taken thirty hours rather than the two hours they had been told to expect. Hugo Farmer thought back on what had been the second big contact of his tour. Operation Mutay now seemed almost too easy. 'The tone of this one was totally different. We were in very poor positions, literally hollows, because there wasn't time to make decent positions so we just dug in where we could. We were a sitting target. If the Taliban had disposed themselves better they could have covered us with fire.' As it was, 'some of it was bloody close'.

Scrabbling in the grit trying to offer as small a target as possible, he had felt that he was 'digging in with my chin strap and so was my radio operator, with rounds bouncing around us'. It had not been an encouraging experience. Back in camp, everyone was keen to know what had happened. Farmer told them, 'it was pretty grim, that one'. It had taught him 'that it is not good to be out there and be vulnerable. It is much better to take the advantage rather than trying to be reactive'.

Once again the Paras had been lucky. 'A' Company had come through unscathed. But the battle group's responsibilities were about to be extended once more, and with it their level of risk. The dam at Kajaki was the most strategically important site in their area of operations. It stems the Helmand river, creating a 32-mile-long reservoir. The water powers turbines that provide electricity for much of southern Afghanistan. It also feeds the irrigation system that sustains life along the river valley below. Work on the dam had started in the early 1950s when USAID began pouring money into the project. It had been completed in 1975 and somehow kept running throughout the Russian occupation and the fighting that accompanied it. It had been damaged by allied bombing late in 2001 but had been patched up since. Now it was under American control once more. The dam complex was protected by Afghan guards under the command of a US special forces veteran who now worked for an American security company.

The Taliban found it an irresistible target. Why they did so was unclear. If they succeeded in capturing it, it was unlikely they would be able to hold it for long. The best they could hope for was a short-lived propaganda victory. Blowing it up would require an enormous amount of explosive. If they succeeded, the result would be to cut the power supply to the region, wreck the delicately balanced irrigation system and destroy the agriculture of southern Helmand. It was hardly a recipe for winning the backing of the people on whose behalf they claimed to be fighting. These considerations did not seem to occur to them or, if they did, to trouble them, however. For the rest of the summer they hurled themselves at the dam, apparently unconcerned by the cost in blood.

The first British troops to be deployed there arrived early in June. An eight-strong OMLT team with twenty ANA took over a compound and an observation post overlooking the dam that had been abandoned some sixteen years before by the Soviet army. They had fought many battles defending the dam against the mujahedin.

After all these years, bits and pieces of the junk the Soviets had abandoned were still lying around. The new arrivals drew no melancholy lessons about the transience of invading armies in Afghanistan. No one expected the Taliban to be able to match the firepower that the British and their allies could bring to bear.

Nonetheless, they were capable of making life inside the dam complex unpleasant. The American running the show was known as Kajaki John. He headed a team of about eight to ten Afghans and Americans, all in their forties and fifties, all ex-military. They controlled a shifting garrison of army, police and local militiamen whose numbers dwindled as the Taliban activity increased. Together, they were supposed to provide protection for a doughty force of technicians who kept the turbines turning. It was said that if a recently trained hydroelectrical engineer were to turn up to service the power plant he would not have a clue where to start. Years of makeshift repairs had made it a mechanical mystery whose secrets were known only to adepts like 'Joe', a local technician who had been making do and mending the works since the dam was completed.

In the early part of June the Taliban grew bolder. In one week they managed to land forty mortar bombs in the dam complex. Kajaki John and his men had no heavy weapons with which to defend the place. He could appeal for helicopters to come to his aid but the Taliban had worked out that they took twenty minutes to arrive. This gave them time to drive in from bases about ten miles from the dam, set up their mortar barrels, fire a few rounds into the compound, then leave. The main effect was to demoralise the Afghans inside. If the attacks were not dealt with firmly, the chances were that they would all clear off.

The OMLTs and their Afghan pupils were not strong enough to counter the threat. The Americans running Operation Enduring Freedom were applying strong pressure on Britain to send a company up to Kajaki to restore the situation and persuade the

American contractors not to withdraw. Tootal was reluctant to fix another of his scarce companies in a static location and thought the threat could be dealt with differently. The attacks on the dam complex had become almost routine. It was decided to insert a temporary force into the dam area secretly and, when the Taliban appeared again, ambush them with mortars and machine guns.

The job went to Nick French, the OC of Support Company's Mortar Platoon. The idea was to take on the Taliban at their own game by hitting them with their own weapon of choice. Along with the mortars French had with him half of 'B' Company's 5 Platoon and some machine-gunners, snipers, signallers and medics – about forty-five men in all, 'a little marauder force', as French put it.

French was twenty-nine years old, cheerful, confident and seemingly bred for action. His father had been in the navy but French preferred the air force and spent six years in the air cadets. In the end, though, he decided he 'didn't find flying that exciting' and switched his allegiance to the army. After studying politics at Liverpool University, where he joined the Territorial Army, he went to Sandhurst, and applied for the Parachute Regiment. He had served in Northern Ireland and Iraq. He was proud of the Paras' tradition of controlled aggression. Now he was flying up to Kajaki to put it into practice.

The insertion was done with a minimum of fuss to fool the watching Taliban into thinking that it was a routine resupply. 'I wanted to keep pretty covert,' French said. 'I didn't want to scare these guys away. I wanted to sort this Taliban team out. I wanted to kill them.' Once in, French and his men quietly occupied an area to the south of the dam complex along a ridge. French placed his mortars in concealed positions in a line along the slope, together with the machine guns and some Javelin anti-tank missiles they had also brought along. He placed the others into three observation posts (OPs) 50 metres in front of them. One of them was already occupied by the ANP. Their presence was, at the very least, a nuisance.

Local politics were extraordinarily complex and confusing. The police were meant to be on the opposite side to the Taliban yet they kept in touch with each other by walkie-talkie. The contact ensured that both sides could make an informed calculation as to where their best interests lay. The arrival of the Paras got the ANP 'very excited', said French. The reinforcements boosted the belief that they were now on the winning side. They could not resist calling up the Taliban and boasting about the array of weapons they now had supporting them.

The element of surprise seemed to have been lost, but for a while it looked as if the Taliban had been discouraged. There was no attack on the night the Paras deployed. The following evening, though, they appeared as usual, perhaps suspecting the ANP had bluffed them.

The Taliban liked to attack at dusk. Now, without bothering to hide their intentions, they were gathering under the eyes of the Paras. Even though French was convinced that the police had already given away their position, he and his men strained to remain invisible, lying still and showing no lights. 'I got a call back from one of the OPs,' French remembered, 'saying, "Boss, there are two truckloads of Taliban with a mortar on the back and about twenty guys, about fifteen hundred metres away."' The Russian 82mm mortars that the Taliban used had a range of about two miles. The quality of the bombs was poor, though, and to be accurate they needed to be closer in. The Taliban performance was remarkably casual, 'like some military demonstration', said French. The trucks stopped and the men dismounted. Some began setting up the mortar barrel while the others fanned out to protect the firing point.

French instructed his men to hold their fire until the first Taliban round went off. The rules of engagement that the battle group was operating under made it permissible to fire if there was a clear per-ceived mortal threat. That already appeared to be the case here, but if the Taliban fired first, then there could be no doubt about it.

The mortar teams lined up the target and waited. The first Taliban round fizzed out of the barrel and landed just behind one of the OPs. The Paras' answering salvo was well off target and landed 100 yards short. The Taliban now knew that their enemies had mortars of their own, but the discovery did not seem to bother them. To

French's surprise they popped off six rounds in rapid succession, which cascaded down around the OPs.

The Paras responded immediately and the second salvo hit the Taliban full on. 'We could see through our binoculars blokes flying apart,' said French. 'Mass panic ensued ... we saw six or seven guys trying to sneak up the hill so we engaged them with heavy machine guns.' In the half-hour fight that followed, ten Taliban were killed and two wounded. French thought that 'the initial shock and the fact that we could react within two or three minutes of them firing really put them on the back foot. They had been doing this for a week completely untouched and then within two minutes of them firing we had ten of their mates spread across the desert sand.' The racket alerted Taliban gunmen arrayed along the edge of Kajaki town, about 900 yards from the ridge. They could see the British positions and opened up. French calculated that there were 'maybe ten or twelve guys with light and heavy machine guns'. He called for help from the Apaches but was told there was none available and he would have to crack on with what he had. Luckily, it seemed the Taliban had had enough and the firing died away.

French was highly satisfied with his men's performance. 'It was like a case of duelling mortars, like you [imagine] gunslingers in the Wild West,' he said. 'You stand at either end of the street and you go for your guns and the first one who hits the other guy wins.'

Up at the dam complex, Kajaki John and the local police chief were equally pleased. The Taliban seemed taken aback – intelligence was that they had been badly shaken by the mortar barrage as well as by the experience of being on the receiving end of a Javelin, which had also been fired in the fight. The weight of fire convinced them there were 1,000 men on the ridge, rather than the forty-five there were in reality. French and his men stayed on for another two days. A continuous Para presence was established shortly afterwards, placing a further burden on the battle group's resources.

Even by Helmand standards Kajaki was exceptionally tough duty. Corporal Andy Key was attached to the first deployment as a sniper. Much of his work was spent in visual intelligence gathering, observing the lie of the land and movements across it. He occupied an OP in one of the old Russian positions with four others. It was a tight fit. 'We each had a space about two feet wide,' he said, 'and that was with all our kit on.' They stretched a camouflage net overhead but it did nothing to alleviate the pounding heat. They settled down into a routine of one hour on watch, followed by three hours off for sleeping and eating. No one wanted to eat much. Water was something else. It might be warm but it still tasted good. Crouching in their positions, stifled by the heat, they could not afford to relax their vigilance. Their experience with the British mortars was not enough to deter the Taliban from continuing mortar attacks throughout July and the first half of August.

Despite the increasingly 'kinetic' nature of the battle group's activities, attempts were still being made to pursue its goodwill mission. In the middle of June 'C' Company expanded its patrolling out of Gereshk with the aim of establishing friendly links with some nearby villages.

Mid-afternoon on 27 June, a convoy set off from FOB Price and headed eastwards into a parched landscape of rolling sand. It was made up of ten Snatches, four WMIKs and a Pinzgauer troop carrier. Leading the patrol was Paul Blair, the OC of 'C' Company. Alongside his own men he had with him a detachment from 9 Platoon, The Royal Irish Regiment, and a Fire Support Group. The FSG were there to provide firepower from the .50-cal machine guns mounted on their WMIKs. There was also a mortar team, who travelled in the 'Pinz'. Unusually, some journalists came too – Christina Lamb from the *Sunday Times* and photographer Justin Sutcliffe. Lamb had been covering Afghanistan since the days of the Soviet occupation. The Paras had called on her expertise before deploying, inviting her to come and talk to them about Afghan history, politics and culture. She was notably brave and unflappable. The day's events were to test her to the limit.

They were heading for Zumbelay, a village to the east of Gereshk. It was the first time the Paras had been in that area. Blair's intention was to meet some villagers, listen to their concerns and establish some 'ground truth'. The journey took about ninety minutes. Zumbelay was a pleasant contrast to the terrain they passed through. It was a lush place of poppy fields, tall grass and plantations, watered by irrigation ditches that fed off a broad canal.

They stopped about a mile from the village. The FSG drove their WMIKs up to a ridge overlooking Zumbelay from the north on the far side of the village. The rest of the vehicles, together with the mortar team, followed, and parked up to the west of them.

The patrol set off towards the mud walls of the village. The working day was over and men were herding their goats back to their pens, churning up clouds of dust that hung in the late afternoon sunlight. It was very hot. The soldiers took off their helmets. All seemed quiet and peaceful. It was only afterwards that Lamb realised there was something missing from the scene. Where were the flocks of inquisitive children who invariably run out clamouring for sweets and pens whenever a foreigner approaches?

They came across a few men sitting on a bank under a mulberry tree. Blair announced through his interpreter that they were British, not Americans. They were there at the invitation of the Afghan government and they came as friends and brothers who wanted to help.

One, who seemed to have some authority, explained that there was no one around at present. They were all at prayer. If the soldiers came back two days later at ten in the morning they could hold a proper *shura*. They spent about twenty minutes sitting down and chatting, before the leader of the group suggested they leave the village at the opposite end to that by which they had come. There was a bridge there which would get them across the waterway. They shook hands and headed out of the village towards where the vehicles were waiting.

Blair was encouraged by the reasonably friendly attitude of the villagers. Lamb was less sure. Afghans had a reputation for hospitality. Why had they not been offered tea? Her question was answered almost immediately by the crack and rattle of gunfire coming from the ridge where the FSG was parked. Over the radio came the superfluous news that they were in contact.

The incident had begun when a satellite patrol pushed out from the main group noticed a group of about a dozen men moving towards the high ground and radioed the FSG. The group was commanded by Captain Alex Mackenzie, a witty, confident Scot who had gone to Sandhurst after studying law at Edinburgh University. Mackenzie decided to take a look, ordering the convoy vehicles grouped near by to provide cover while he and his WMIKs investigated. As they were about to set off, an RPG crashed into their position followed by a spray of small-arms fire. The air was swamped with the deafening racket of the .50-cals as two of the WMIKs commanded by Sergeant Paul McMellon opened up on the Taliban firing point inside a derelict building on the far side of the cluster of convoy vehicles.

Mackenzie left them to it and raced over to the convoy. Some of the drivers had dismounted and taken cover behind the Snatches. He ordered them to get back in and head for the cover of some dead ground to the south-east, where they would be out of the line of fire. It seemed to Mackenzie that the Taliban's aim had been to destroy the vehicles first before turning their full attention to the dismounted patrol that had gone into the village. 'If we lose the vehicles then we can't pick up the patrol, and that is why we were attacked,' he said. 'They are not stupid, so they hit us first.' The Snatches hurried into cover, protected by the WMIKs. All four .50-cals were pounding away, yet the Taliban kept up an impressive rate of fire, with RPGs, small-arms fire and the occasional mortar.

Down in Zumbelay, Blair and his men were watching the firefight. They had just left the village and were walking through a field in search of the bridge that had been recommended to them by the village elder.

Suddenly Kalashnikov rounds buzzed over their heads. There was a yell of 'Helmets on!' and the Paras and their media companions ran blindly forward. The field was ploughed and sun-baked into hard, ankle-twisting ridges. They stumbled forward with bullets singing in their ears. Justin Sutcliffe tripped and fell, landing on his back. He looked up to see an RPG scorching over his head. He struggled to his feet and lumbered on, weighed down by body armour and camera gear. A few seconds later a mortar landed just where he had been lying.

By now, the fire was coming from several different directions. The soldiers scrambled for the cover of the deep irrigation ditches that cross-hatched the fields at the edge of the village, slithering gratefully down the slimy mud walls. The patrol was scattered and the men were out of each other's line of sight. The gunfire mingled with shouts and yells as they tried to restore communications with each other. Red and green smoke rose across the field as marker canisters were set off – even though they gave away the soldiers' positions to the Taliban.

There was no question of staying put. The Taliban mortar men had them at their mercy. The only thing was to keep moving forward, towards the ridge and the vehicles. It was terrifying lying in the clammy ditches, with rounds snapping overhead, waiting for the mortar bombs to arrive. The fire was coming from all sides now. Fear drove everyone on. They hauled themselves and their kit up one slippery bank and down another, splashing into the muddy water.

Blair had been beseeching Bastion for close air support since soon after the start of the contact, and was initially told that two A-10s were in the area and would be overhead in twenty minutes. The relief that this message brought turned to anger when it was announced that the Thunderbolts had been diverted to the Sangin area to help out British forces who were stuck in a heavy firefight with insurgents.

Lamb found herself in a ditch with Private Kyle Deerans, a twenty-three-year-old South African who was one of the snipers. Alongside them was Colour Sergeant Mick Whordley, thirty-nine, who had only a few months left in the army after twenty-two years' service. He had begged Blair to let him off his normal duties at base to go out on the patrol. Whordley noticed some movement behind a mound of earth and shouted out to Deerans, who swung his sniper rifle towards a man in a blue dishdasha. As the man popped up out of cover, Deerans shot him through the chest.

Dusk was falling. A haze of smoke floated over the fields from burning poppy stalks which had been set on fire by the tracer. In the middle of the battle zone, a tethered donkey serenely contemplated the madness going on around him. There was no sight or sound of aircraft. The Paras and the journalists were going to have to get out of this on their own.

It was the FSG which eventually turned the battle. Mackenzie and his men had left the convoy vehicles to the south, where they were out of harm's way and could provide flank and rear protection. Mackenzie then returned with Sergeant McMellon and the WMIKs to try to help the patrol. It was almost impossible to see what was going on amid the tall grass and the deep ditches. The only indication of their comrades' whereabouts was the drifting smoke from the phosphorus grenades they had set off in order to obscure their attackers' visibility. Radio messages did not help. 'They kept saying, "We are two hundred metres or three hundred metres from the edge of town," but they had been saying that for a long time so I was starting to think, "Do they actually know where they are?" because there was nothing visible to me,' said Mackenzie. Two or three times he and his men ventured into the battlefield, drawing harassing fire from hidden Taliban, but were forced out again because they could not identify targets and were in danger of getting shot up by their own side. They pulled back to the south.

Night was about to envelop the battlefield. Mackenzie thought: 'If we keep fighting for much longer … we are going to be fighting at night or we are going to run out of ammunition. We were looking for an opportunity to change things.' About half an hour before last light, Corporal Scott Mitchell spotted a group of about a dozen armed men moving westwards. Mackenzie led the WMIKs off up on to a low rise and as they reached the crest, there below them, only 100 yards away, were a group of about a dozen Taliban. They were bunched up together, 'just as if they were queuing up at Sainsbury's', said Mackenzie. They were standing in a lane 'like a little path in an English country garden' that ran along a line of trees into town.

They saw the Paras just as the Paras saw them. 'They all opened up and they all missed,' said Mackenzie. They were firing RPGs, small arms and a 'Dushka', the Soviet version of the .50-cal. The only damage was a wheel cover that was whipped off a WMIK by shrapnel from a grenade.

The Paras did not miss. All four WMIKs opened up. The four

.50-cals and the four front-mounted GPMGs poured a cone of fire into the hapless Taliban. 'It was pretty brutal,' said Mackenzie. 'There were body parts flying everywhere and you could see people just like ... exploding.'

The bass throb of the .50-cals put heart into the men in the ditches. 'C' Company's sergeant major told Mackenzie afterwards that 'when they heard us firing, they felt their whole morale lift – it was like something out of *Star Wars*'.

They could now see salvation in the shape of the WMIKs, which laid down a sheet of covering fire to keep the Taliban's heads down while the exhausted patrol struggled out of the fields and into the open ground towards them. 'When they came out they were moving very, very slowly,' said Mackenzie. The WMIKs shepherded them towards the vehicles.

At last they heard the desperately welcome sound of aircraft engines overhead. The Apaches had arrived. But the danger was not yet over. The direct route back to FOB Price involved crossing a bridge across the Helmand. In view of what had happened it was a sure bet that the Taliban had set up an ambush there or planted an IED.

Blair decided to head out into the relative safety of the desert, keeping in constant radio contact with the Apaches to scope out the way ahead. They drove at a snail's pace for several hours, stopping only when they were sure there was no one in the vicinity. When at last they paused, the vehicles drew into a defensive circle. Everyone dismounted and went over the events of the day. Even the old and bold like 'C' Company's veteran sergeant major Mick Bolton were impressed. 'It was quite scary,' he said later. 'I have never been in a firefight like that ever and hopefully I will never get into another like it. Zumbelay was a tight spot.'

There were obvious lessons to be learned. Whether through coercion or sympathy, the villagers had played their part in the ambush. They had explained the absence of people by saying everyone was in the mosque – but the time the Paras arrived was not the hour for prayer. The Taliban had shown that they could organise themselves quickly if a patrol turned up out of the blue and could mount a competent ambush. The blessing was that their marksmanship was very poor. It was decided that from now on any *shura*s would be conducted in open country with the elders coming out of the villages to meet the soldiers on ground of their choosing.

They had to wait several hours before there were aircraft available to watch over their journey back to base. Air assets had been tied up overnight helping out an operation near Sangin, which had run into trouble.

Just before they reached the dangerous bridge over the Helmand, two American A-10s swooped low to scare off any lurking insurgents and the convoy trundled safely across and back to FOB Price. It was first light. Mackenzie remembered that for a few minutes, as they arrived, it rained, 'which was weird. It was the only time it rained in the entire tour.'

News of the episode had reached the camp. Everyone was anxious to hear the story. It was a dramatic one, as readers of the *Sunday Times* would learn when they read Christina Lamb's epic account and saw Justin Sutcliffe's front-line pictures. It was the first real glimpse the public had been given of how the Helmand campaign was shaping up. It did not match the rosy official picture painted before the deployment. Henceforth the campaign was to be fought mostly out of sight of the media.

8

Platoon House

On 21 June, the Paras were sent to Sangin for an operation that was supposed to last a few hours, or at the most a few days. As it turned out, the 3 Para battle group would be stuck there for the remainder of its time in Helmand. The town would come to symbolise the unexpected war they were fighting, surrounded by fanatical enemies, under constant attack, and totally dependent on outside help to keep going. The sketchy details filtering back to Britain suggested it was the War on Terror's version of the Alamo or Rorke's Drift. The comparisons were inaccurate. The Taliban were never to get close to overrunning the base. But Sangin was a grim, bloody, frightening and exhausting place to be in the summer of 2006.

Once again, the Paras were acting at the behest of Governor Daoud. His supporters in the town were in trouble. Two days before, the Taliban had ambushed a convoy carrying Jama Gul, a former district chief in Helmand, near the town, killing him and his four bodyguards. A large group of Gul's relatives set out to retrieve the bodies. They too were attacked and twenty-five were killed.

Among the wounded was the son of the district chief, who was said to be in a critical state. Daoud asked Charlie Knaggs if he could send a force to evacuate him for treatment. As commander of the Helmand Task Force, Knaggs had a close relationship with the governor. According to the commander of British Forces, Ed Butler, Knaggs 'invested hugely in [the relationship], a lot of time drinking tea and reassuring, persuading, cajoling, correcting, advising and empathising'.

The Paras' orders were to find the injured man and take him back to Bastion for treatment. They were also initially tasked with extracting the local police chief. He was in danger of being lynched after being accused of raping a little girl.

Everyone was understandably uneasy about going to the rescue of an alleged sex offender. It was hardly likely to endear the British to the locals. According to Martin Taylor, 'there was definitely a feeling among the blokes of "why the hell are we going to support this guy? We should go and kill him, then we would get the locals on our side straight away."'

The police chief's alleged behaviour came as little surprise. The ANP had a reputation among much of the local population for abusing the people they were supposed to protect. They were notorious for stealing, extortion and the molestation of juveniles. From what the Paras could see, they contributed little to the security of the town and were suspected of collaborating with the Taliban when it suited their purposes. It was no wonder that the local population were said to hate them more than they did the insurgents.

There were other reasons to feel anxious about the operation. Intelligence reports said that there were swarms of Taliban in the area who would almost certainly react forcefully to the appearance of a large British force.

Tootal was concerned about the risks to his own men and also about the possible damage that would be done to Sangin and its inhabitants in the event of a major fight with the insurgents. He passed this up the military and political line to Kabul. The judgement was that it was essential to support the authority of President Karzai and Governor Daoud in Sangin. The district governor's position was precarious. His predecessor, Amir Jan, had been murdered while visiting Musa Qaleh on 3 March. The operation was more than a rescue mission. It would help preserve the Afghan government's position in the town.

The problem with the police chief was resolved when the elders of Sangin expelled him themselves. That still left many worries, notably the possibility of a major clash with the insurgents when the helicopters put down. The final decision was left with Tootal. Despite the risks, he recognised the political imperative.

Once again, he chose 'A' Company for the job. They had been first into theatre and the first to move on to the ground. They had also been the first of the battle group to get involved in a major fight, at Now Zad during Operation Mutay.

Preparations began on 18 June and the plan was trimmed and altered several times before it was finalised in the early hours of 21 June. The Paras were expecting the Taliban to be waiting for them, and the 105mm battery at FOB Robinson and air support were warned to stand by to strike if needed. Martin Taylor, who sat in on the deliberations, walked away from the last meeting glad that he would not have to listen to any more calculations of 'significant casualties' on the helicopter landing site.

Pre-operation nerves were not helped by a delay in the departure time, meaning that the Paras took off in daylight. Twenty-five minutes after leaving Bastion, four Chinook-loads of anxious men settled down in great clouds of dust in a wadi south-west of the Sangin district centre.

Jacked up with adrenalin, the Paras sprang off the back ramp and into a scene of bucolic tranquillity. The predicted mayhem had failed to materialise. 1 Platoon under Hugo Farmer led the way to the district centre, 400 yards from the landing site. When they got there they were welcomed by the beleaguered district governor and his entourage, 'who were all very happy to see us'. They warned Farmer that there were 'Taliban all over the area'. 1 Platoon pushed on and set up a cordon between the centre and the edge of the town, a few hundred yards away, while the rest of the men took up positions round the buildings.

The wounded district governor's son was examined by Harvey Pynn, the 3 Para MO. The final order to move had been given just twenty-five minutes before take-off, and it was only when Pynn heard movement outside his tent during the night that he realised the operation was definitely on. He grabbed the 'A' Company medic, Corporal Paul Roberts, and another medical specialist, Sergeant Brian Reidy, and reached the landing site just in time to catch a helicopter.

Now he was looking at the cause of all the fuss. The young man was accompanied by two young doctors from the local hospital.

Pynn noted that his stomach had been operated on efficiently, the internal wounds patched up and the debris removed. There was 'a bit of tummy discomfort' but he was 'actually very, very stable'. Pynn concluded that 'he didn't need any intervention from me other than another shot of antibiotics, a bit more fluid and some pain relief'.

The patient was put on a stretcher, strapped on to a trailer and towed by a quad bike the Paras had brought along out to the chopper, then whisked back to the gleaming medical facility at Camp Bastion.

It seemed a lot of effort for a minor drama but the job was now done. Instead of returning to Bastion, however, Pike was told that 'A' Company would have to stay on for another forty-eight hours.

The decision appeared to follow an intervention by President Karzai. Sangin was clearly vulnerable and its fall would mean a huge loss of prestige. It was the nearest population centre to the Triangle. The town lay on the banks of the Helmand river. It was the site of the main bazaar for the chain of villages and communities that ran along the river valley. Farmers flocked there each week to sell their crops and livestock. About fourteen thousand people lived there. In the past many of them had been Taliban sympathisers. According to Governor Daoud, however, the people of Helmand had turned against them. They knew from bitter experience what life was like under Taliban rule: 'No development, no education, no healthcare, no economic progress.' It certainly seemed a better place to allocate resources than distant outposts like Now Zad and Musa Qaleh. Pike had no problem being there. 'I always felt that Sangin was an important place that we needed to do something with,' he said. 'More so, perhaps, than other areas we were involved with.'

Nonetheless, there was a feeling among the men that the British were too compliant with the wishes of the Afghans and that their own mission was being twisted out of shape by local political considerations.

Daoud, however, was a difficult man to deny. He had the ear of Karzai and would appeal to him when the British tried to resist his requests for help, pleading lack of resources. He was also, in the opinion of some who had to deal with him, inclined to 'flap'.

According to one senior officer, 'he didn't do crisis. He would say, if you don't do this then there is absolutely no point in you being here because if the black flag of Mullah Omar flies in any of these places, then we've lost Helmand and we might as well all go home.'

The British were there, after all, to help the Afghan government. As the most senior British officer in the area, Ed Butler had to field Daoud's demands. 'You're placed in this predicament when you have a sovereign state, which has accepted democratic principles and has invited us in,' he said. 'It's a key battle in the war on terror. They've asked you to do something, what do you say? To do nothing, to prevaricate, is not an option.'

So the Paras were staying. The forty-eight hours stretched into an open-ended deployment that would last until the end of their tour.

The fact that 'A' Company had landed without a shot being fired did not mean that there would not be trouble. The important thing was to prepare for it, at the same time as trying to win the confidence of the locals and to persuade them that the newcomers were there in a constructive role. Pike got his men building up the district centre's flimsy defences. The compound stood on the western edge of the town with the Helmand river and its sandy flood plain a few hundred yards behind it. The wadi that ran through the town from east to west lay directly in front of it. It was there that the bazaar was held. The wadi led to a footbridge which was used by traders on the western bank of the river when they took their goods to market. A straggle of fields and mud-walled enclosures stretched to the north and the south. Sangin town lay to the east.

The compound was shoddily built out of roughly plastered breeze blocks and mud bricks. There was no running water or electricity. There were a few plastic garden chairs to sit on and no beds. It was dirty and dusty but no one joined the Paras to be comfortable. Pike placed his FSG on the flat roof of the main building on the northern edge of the compound. The FSG tower, as it became known, was two storeys high and commanded a sweeping view over the town. From there, the eastern and northern approaches to the base could be covered by GPMG and .50-cal machine guns, Javelin anti-tank missiles and sniper fire. It was also an excellent vantage point from which air and artillery controllers could call in fire.

Twenty yards to the south was a block that became the administrative hub of the base. One room was turned into the ops room, with an old table as a base for the radios and maps stuck on the wall. Next door, Harvey Pynn set up the Company Aid Post. Other rooms were used as dormitories.

The two buildings were separated by a garden area with a few trees providing some welcome shade. The mortar team chose this as their fire base. Behind, to the west, was a small, fast-flowing canal.

In the first days the Paras spent every spare hour shovelling dirt into any container they could find. Andy Mallet, who had taken over from Tom Fehley as OC 2 Platoon, went into town to search for materials to buy and came back with 750 two-foot-by-one-foot baked mud bricks. Pike tried to contract local builders to build a wall but fear of Taliban reprisals deterred them. Then sandbags arrived and the sangars on the FSG tower grew taller and stouter. Another five sangars were constructed to protect the approaches to the compound not covered by the tower. Two were placed on low buildings inside the compound perimeter. The other three were pushed out 30 yards beyond. Each one had a designated arc of fire, demarcated by two features in the ground ahead of it, interlocking with the sangar next to it.

The Paras were vulnerable to attack on three sides. To the northeast, about 400 yards away across the wadi, was a row of shops which provided cover from which to fire. To the east was a line of garages which marked the edge of the town. The south was full of trees and high-standing crops, watered by irrigation channels that fed off the canal. To the west, though, the ground stretching away to the Helmand river was bare and open for three or four miles. Even the most reckless Taliban would think twice about launching an attack from there.

The platoons split the duties, doing twenty-four hours on each. While one manned the sangars, the other would carry out patrols and stand by as a quick reaction force in the event of trouble. There were five men in each sangar. At any time, two were on 'stag', hunched over the guns, while the other three stood by or slept in a sandbagged pit behind.

The Paras had arrived in 'light scales' – basically what they needed to live and fight for one day. There was no room for luxuries among the supplies that were later flown in. Sangin district centre was not a place for the fastidious. The daily water ration was six or seven litres. That was for drinking, not washing or shaving. Everyone started to grow beards.

'As for loos,' one officer remembered, 'we dug some ditches and managed to get hold of some poles so that if you needed a shit you would just hold on to a pole and away you went.' Things were to improve on the ablutions front but it was remarkable that in the early days there was only one serious case of diarrhoea and vomiting.

While the district centre's defences were being strengthened, Will Pike got on with his plans to build a relationship with the locals. On the day after their arrival, together with the district chief, he called a *shura* with the town's notables. About sixty attended. 'I was quite impressed by how many of them rocked up,' Pike said. He started off telling them through his interpreter that 'we are here at the invitation of the Afghan government. We have come a long way from the UK to help the Afghan people'. He candidly admitted that he was sure they had heard these promises of help many times since the NATO invasion of Afghanistan in 2001, only to be disappointed. But he went on: 'our presence here today and [the fact we are] staying is the first sign that the government is coming to the Sangin valley'.

He emphasised that they alone could not bring security, telling them 'you need to help us with it. It's about you and us and the Afghan forces coming together to say, "We want this to be a flourishing place, a place free of risk."'

This was rousing stuff, but his audience seemed unmoved. 'They came back with, "Well, we've seen this and heard this before. Nothing has happened in four years. Why should we believe you?"'

They also pointed out that the Taliban were strong in the area and they were powerless to defy them. Pike formed the impression that the people he was addressing were not the elders but their delegates, who would report back after the meeting. He was also convinced that some of them were Taliban supporters. It struck Martin Taylor that there were a suspiciously large number of men of fighting age present.

The town was busy and the pattern of life seemed normal. Sangin was no more than an overgrown village but it was the main commercial centre for the Sangin valley and a major centre for the opium trade. At the twice-weekly bazaar in the open ground in front of the base goats were on sale at one end and tinny Japanese 125cc motorbikes at the other.

Pike got his men patrolling in an unthreatening manner. They wore floppy sun hats rather than helmets and called out friendly salaams to everyone who crossed their paths. 'We didn't put on ground-dominating patrols at this point because there was no obvious visible threat,' said Hugo Farmer. 'It was more information gathering, getting to grips with what Sangin was like, what made people tick.'

Harvey Pynn checked out the local healthcare. There were several clinics, 'private medical facilities so people had to pay, but they were happy'. There was no need to offer any services so he concentrated on finding out whether there were any quick-impact projects that could be performed to boost the local welfare system, in the spirit of the great Gereshk hospital washing-machine saga. Cleanliness was certainly an issue. The standard of hygiene was the worst he had ever seen.

On the second day after their arrival Governor Daoud flew up from Lashkar Gah to hold a *shura*. Stuart Tootal and Charlie Knaggs went with him. This time it seemed that the audience were the real representatives of local interests. There were about thirty of them. They wore long beards and carried themselves with authority. They gathered under a mulberry tree in the district centre and listened to what the visitors had to say. Daoud argued that the British presence was a good thing. He also tried to persuade the locals to accept the authority of the men he had appointed to govern them.

Tootal had yet to be given his own translator so the soldiers had to wait until the meeting was finished before Daoud gave them a précis of what had been said. Halfway through the translation, they were approached by a representative with a statement from the elders. He carried the message that everyone wanted stability and good governance. But the reality was that they could not do anything without the agreement of the gunmen. He asked for three days' grace while they consulted with the Taliban and the local drug lords to see whether they would allow the British soldiers to stay in town.

The Paras agreed to undertake only limited patrolling for three days. But this response was not encouraging. The dilemma of the citizens of Sangin was close to the plight of Wild West settlers threatened by marauding outlaws, as seen in many an old cowboy movie. Like the peace-loving townsfolk of the Wild West Sangin residents hated the intimidation and extortion imposed on them by the bad guys. The information he had picked up from the interpreters on the street left Pike in no doubt that the locals lived in fear of the Taliban, though this did not mean that some did not share their ideological goals. 'There was talk about them dragging guys through the streets behind pick-up trucks. They are spoilers. They would burn schools, deliver threatening letters. They didn't really have anything to offer. Some of the people supported them because they didn't like Westerners being in Afghanistan. But I think mostly they were coerced, directly or indirectly.'

Whatever their feelings about the Taliban, the people of Sangin had good reason to be wary of siding with the British. They looked powerful. But were they inwardly strong? Did they have the staying power to see their oppressors off? The locals feared, with great justification, that for all their promises their would-be saviours might eventually tire of their mission and leave the people they had come to liberate to the mercy of the bandits. In the meantime, Sangin's civilians could expect to be caught in the crossfire as the two sides slugged it out.

The war between the Taliban and the coalition forces was moving closer to the inhabitants of the town. In the early hours of 27 June, a few miles south of Sangin, a Coalition operation to capture an important Taliban commander went awry. First reports said one of the team was killed in the raid and another was missing. A quick reaction force of Gurkhas was launched from nearby FOB Robinson. About sixteen men from 12 Platoon set off in their vehicles. They were showing no lights and the night was dark. As they approached a bridge near the eastern edge of Sangin they came under heavy fire from the west. They immediately pulled back, dismounted and got into cover. One Snatch was hit by four RPGs. The firefight that ensued went on for three hours. 'There are no words to explain how it feels to be in a firefight,' said Sergeant Major Trilochan Gurung, the OC of 12 Platoon. 'At first all the boys were confused and shouting to each other, but soon we got a grip as our Gurkhali blood started to flow.' They called in fire from I Battery's guns at FOB Robinson. After jets and helicopters had attacked the Taliban positions the Gurkhas moved forward and eventually linked up with the men they had been sent to find, then fell back thankfully to their base.

The whereabouts of the dead and missing soldiers was still unknown. 3 Para was asked to go and find them. 'B' Company and the battalion's tactical headquarters group were flown up before dawn.

They landed on the eastern bank of the Helmand river near Sangin and headed off to the grid reference they had been given. They had brought along a quad bike but it soon became clear that it would never be able to negotiate the wide irrigation ditches that lay in their path. The water was chest high and they had to hold their weapons over their heads as they waded across. When, just as dawn was breaking, 5 Platoon of 'B' Company arrived at the site of the clash, they saw the bodies of two men in uniform. There would be no need to search for the missing soldiers. Near by were four dead Taliban. The sight of their own dead was a shock. 'It really hit home,' said Mark Willets, 'B' Company's sergeant major. 'For a young lad to walk past the dead body of a Taliban, to be honest they're not bothered. He's the enemy. They're not fussed. But seeing the body of one of your own – you think, fucking hell, it could have been me.'

As the senior man in the company, it was Willets's job to collect the dead. He went forward with the company medic, Corporal Bradshaw, and the body bags, telling the others to keep back. When he got close to the bodies he realised with a start that he recognised one of them. He had sat down for a brew with him some weeks before, along with Giles Timms, who had known the dead man well.

The body bags were carried back to the landing site. Willets and his men pressed on to hunt for the Gurkhas' abandoned Snatch. When they found it there were inquisitive boys swarming all over it. They scared them away and recovered some kit from the vehicle before an Apache fired a missile into it to deny it to the Taliban.

The firefight seemed to have a marked effect on the mood of the people in Sangin. An intense battle involving artillery and aerial bombardment had been fought on the edge of their town. There had been power and water cuts to parts of the town, though whether these were due to the fighting was unclear. Hugo Farmer regarded the incident as a catalyst. Carrying out a low-tempo patrol in town the next day, he encountered a crowd who were 'clearly pissed off. They were asking us questions, saying, "You say you are coming here to rebuild and do all these good things but actually you are just destroying the town."'

The Paras in Sangin had also been kept in the dark about the operation in their neighbourhood. It seemed politic to blame the trouble on the Americans. The crowd were not buying that. 'They said, "Well, you are here with the Americans. The Americans tell you what to do."' Farmer replied that they were there to help and had no intention of fighting unless the Taliban started it.

'A' Company had been there a week. Until now the only sign of trouble had been a few potshots aimed at the district centre. The day before, Corporal James Shimmins, a machine-gunner, had been sitting in his sangar on top of the FSG tower. He bent over to fiddle with his gun and heard a crack. Bits of grit stung his face. Two shots had been fired at him from long range. It caused some excitement at the time. A few days later it would barely be worth mentioning.

There were strong signs that trouble was on the way. The ANP

passed on reports from their spies in town that people were beginning to move out. Some trekked away to stay with relations. Others
shifted from the likely confrontation zones facing the district centre
into less exposed quarters of Sangin. As the civilians drifted away
the Taliban filtered in.

After the early morning battle, a group of elders came to the
district centre and told Pike they wanted the British to leave. Their
presence, they said, would guarantee a fight with the Taliban. That
night the first attacks began. Initially they were low-key affairs,
apparently designed to test the Paras' responses. 'It was mostly at
night and so you would get flurries of RPGs, mostly on the northern
side,' said Pike. 'It would stop for a bit and then kick off again and
it would run through sporadically from as soon as it got dark until
about three in the morning.'

The first experience of coming under fire was never to be forgotten. Andy Mallet had just gone to bed after inspecting the sangar
positions. 'I remember taking my belt off and lying on my sleeping
bag, and thinking it was all quiet,' he said. 'I could hear insects
chirping and the sound of the river floating through the district
centre.' He drifted off to sleep then jerked awake as 'the whole world
opened up'. The Taliban were firing from the north-east with light
machine guns, rifles and RPGs. 'It's a hell of a shock when rounds
are fizzing above the building, over your head, snapping into the
walls. You get sprayed with plaster, it's complete darkness and you
don't know what's going on.' He grabbed his helmet, body armour,
rifle and webbing and ran out to check on those of his men who
were hunkered down in the sangars in the front of the compound,
while his platoon sergeant, Huw Davies, checked on the rest.

'Rounds of tracer were zipping over, smacking into the building,'
said Mallet. 'As I was running I was doing up my chinstrap and my
body armour on the move.' It was about a hundred yards to the front
sangar, part of it over open ground. When he reached it Corporal
Tam McDermott was blazing away with the GPMG at the enemy,
who were identifiable only by the muzzle flash of their weapons.
Mallet began 'putting down rounds myself'. Before long such
dramas would become routine.

After the initial night attacks the Taliban tried to maintain the pressure into the hours of daylight. Pike was sitting under the trees in the shady space between the main building and his ops room, talking to some elders, when there was a sound 'like a swarm of hornets coming over', as Kalashnikov rounds zipped harmlessly overhead.

One day Hugo Farmer saw 'a number of Taliban fighters trying to manoeuvre towards the compound. Some of them were in the open by the [bazaar]'. They were coming down the 'pipe range', as the Paras called the road that led from the district centre eastwards into Sangin. Two pick-up trucks raced up and pulled off to the left and right and armed men jumped out. They were under the sights of Private Martin Cork, who was manning a GPMG in one of the two sangars in front of the compound. He opened fire, hitting at least two of them.

On 30 June intelligence reports passed on from Bastion said that a big insurgent operation was in the offing. The assault began late in the evening. About twenty fighters split into three groups had advanced towards the compound from the north, firing RPGs and rifles and hitting the FSG tower.

By now the district centre was as well set up as it could be without the assistance of the battle group's combat engineers. There were ninety men in Sangin. All their extra weapons had been flown in. Amongst them they had two .50-cal machine guns, six GPMGs, the same number of Minimi light machine guns, 81mm and 51mm mortars and Javelin anti-tank missiles. They had plenty of ammunition. Their firepower easily outmatched the RPGs, machine guns and rifles that the Taliban could muster. The Paras also had all the might of the air force at their disposal. From their perch on the FSG tower the fire support team controllers, Matt Armstrong and Shaun Fry, could call in strikes by jets and helicopter as well as bombardments by the artillery based at FOB Robinson.

As the insurgents advanced over the open ground to the north and east of the compound the darkness was torn by the flash of outgoing tracer, and the steam-hammer thump of the .50-cals shattered the night silence. Before they could recover from the first shock, 81mm mortar rounds and 105mm artillery shells from the FOB Robinson battery exploded around them. There seemed something mad about the assault. Harvey Pynn speculated that 'they must have been on some mind-bending drugs to believe that they could assault our position from that direction using such schoolboy tactics'.

When the shooting stopped, up to a dozen of the attackers were dead, including the commander. On the defenders' side one man had suffered minor cuts from flying masonry and another was singed by the back-blast from a Javelin rocket. Inside the district centre there was quiet satisfaction. 'I don't think they knew who the British or the Parachute Regiment were,' said Tam McDermott. 'If they'd looked at history they'd have known that all the troops were up for a fight – itching to do something.'

As they dragged away their dead and wounded the Taliban now knew what sort of enemy they were facing. But they would be coming back again, and the next time the fight would not be so one-sided.

9

The Testing

When Harvey Pynn woke up the following day in Sangin his immediate concern was for the pharmacy, which lay at one one end of the row of shops across the wadi that the Taliban had chosen as a launching point for their attacks.

The pharmacy doubled as a dispensary, and the doctor who operated from it had become an ally. Pynn 'didn't want to wake up and see his surgery a sieve of holes'. He went up to the obser-vation post on the roof and looked across through binoculars. The pharmacy was still intact but the compound next to it had been flattened. A couple of families sat in adjoining fields, waiting for 'jingly trucks', the lorries painted psychedelic colours and decorated with chains that ply the roads of Afghanistan. 'I really feel for these people,' Pynn wrote in his diary, 'but really hope that after a short period … we'll have more control of the town and be able to com-mence the reconstruction effort.'

During the afternoon, Pynn joined a patrol into town. There were more families packing up their stuff on trailers and moving out. He went to one of Sangin's medical facilities, the Farooq hospital. They knew him now and were friendly enough. One of the lab tech-nicians told him that an elderly man had been killed and five women wounded in the shooting the night before. 'It never ceases to amaze me how blasé these folk are to weapons and gunfights,' he wrote. 'In my eyes last night was a major battle but to these locals who have grown used to it all over the years it must have seemed like a pea shooting contest.'

Later he visited the pharmacy. There were some bullet marks in the façade but it seemed otherwise undamaged. It appeared that the Taliban had taken over the roof of the building to use it as a firing point. The owner was pathetically grateful that the British had not bombed it flat.

Throughout the day, intelligence reports filtered in about the Taliban's next moves. It appeared that the top commanders in Helmand had decided to move to Sangin so they could direct the battle themselves. There was reportedly talk of sending in suicide bombers.

At dusk on 1 July, the men on the roof of the FSG tower watched the sinking sun paint the hills beyond the Helmand river red and prepared for another night of shooting and being shot at.

By now a pattern was emerging. Once darkness fell the first RPGs would scorch out from the line of shops across the dried-up river bed and thump into the compound. The defences were improving all the time. The bricks Andy Mallet bought had proved very useful. Earlier that evening, yet more sandbags had been humped up the stairs on to the flat roof of the FSG tower. There were about twenty men in the six positions on the roof. There were four machine-gun teams, two sniper teams and a Javelin missile crew, fourteen soldiers in all. There was also a shifting group of mortar, artillery and air fire controllers. Finally, there was the three-man signals team. As they settled down for the night the defenders felt reasonably secure.

The evening started quietly. Everyone had been given their tasks for the night. 2 Platoon was on stag duty, manning the OPs and sangars. Some of 1 Platoon were resting, or what counted as resting in the special circumstances of Sangin. There was no real relaxation. Men dozed off, still in their webbing, with their body armour, helmets and rifles by their sides, ready to race to their firing positions when the contact began. It was a Saturday. Thousands of miles away in Germany, the World Cup was reaching a climax. England had reached the quarter-finals and that night were playing Portugal. There was no way of following the drama. Some of the Toms asked optimistically whether the game would be broadcast on the BBC World Service, the only radio station they could receive.

At 9 p.m. Will Pike was in his ops room, talking to his sergeant major, Zac Leong. Leong was thirty-five years old. He was brought

3 PARA • 123

up in Cornwall and had spent all his adult life in 3 Para, apart from a two-year stint instructing. He too had been seduced by the TV series *The Paras*. 'I fancied a bit of it, just to taste it,' he said. 'I joined up and stayed in.'

Pike and Leong had worked together for two years. They had shared the burden of the Iraq deployment and respected each other. 'He was great in every regard and brilliant for me because I would set my direction, make sure that everyone understood that, then he would see that it was tidied up and done,' said Pike. 'He was very human, very humorous, just a terrific guy.' Zac Leong's qualities would be displayed to the full that night.

It had been a trying day for Pike. Earlier he had gone to visit FOB Robinson. There had been a suggestion that it would make sense if it was brought under his command. On the way back the Chinook dropped him off near what appeared to be the district centre. He jumped down from the tailgate of the chopper and into a huge cloud of dust. When it eventually cleared he looked around for Hugo Farmer, who was meant to be marking the landing site. Instead, a few yards away, he saw a pick-up truck with men in the back who watched him closely for several minutes before driving off in the direction of some compounds. It seemed 'pretty clear that something was awry'. Pike had no idea where he was. Night had fallen. The Chinook was dwindling into the distance, the throb of its rotors getting ever fainter. And now more men were emerging from the compounds and advancing towards him. Pike retreated through the fields adjoining a barren area that he thought must be the flood plain of the Helmand river. He tried to raise the aircraft or the district centre on his radio, but it had a limited range. 'It was extremely unpleasant,' he said. 'All the time I was saying "fuck" a lot and trying to put some distance between myself and the compounds.' When he reached the river, he crouched behind the bank. 'That got me a bit of cover so I could repel anyone who came.' Then he heard the sound of salvation. A helicopter was coming in his direction. It was one of the Apaches that had escorted the Chinook in. At the controls was Lieutenant Colonel Andy Cash of the Army Air Corps, who had flown to the correct landing site at the district centre, just over a mile from where Pike had been mistakenly dropped off. He had noticed the dust cloud when the Chinook put down and flown over to investigate. Pike began signalling to the helicopter, praying that the pilot would see him. Peering into the gloom below, Cash spotted Pike, called the Chinook back and hovered protectively overhead until it touched down about twenty minutes later.

Pike said later that 'in my judgement he saved my life'. Intelligence reports said that the area he was in, south of the district centre, was full of Taliban. 'Who knows what would have happened? It could have been horrific.'

Now, an hour later, Pike was hoping for a quiet night. At about 9.30, as he and Leong stood chatting, the compound was rocked with what Pike described as a 'God Almighty explosion, much larger than anything else we had had … we exchanged this look. It was like, "What the fuck was that?"' The blast was followed by a brief, sinister silence. Martin Taylor immediately radioed Bastion on the satellite link to report a 'significant contact', then called Matt Armstrong, the fire support team commander, to get him to request any jets in the vicinity to come to their aid. An old-fashioned land-line ran from the ops room up to the roof. Taylor rang the OP and one of the snipers answered. 'I said: "What the fuck was that?" He said, "Boss, we've been hit. I don't really know, but I've got blood coming out of my ears. There's a lot of blokes screaming."'

Now everyone's PRRs were buzzing. Taylor heard someone from the roof saying, 'I have got significant casualties up here, you have to come up here and sort things out.' As the message came through, the stretchers in the RAP were being broken out and Zac Leong, together with Paul Roberts and Brian Reidy, the company medics, was on his way out of the door.

Across the orchard, Leong could see smoke and flame pouring from the top of the main building. 'The shrapnel was glowing red hot,' he said, 'a massive shower of sparks.' He grabbed a stretcher and rounded up Prig Poll and some others to give him a hand, then ran over to the open concrete staircase that led to the roof. Fire was still coming in. On the roof he found a scene of devastation and chaos.

Three men lay amid the debris of burst sandbags and shattered concrete. One was clearly dead, with a massive wound to his head. Another lay on his back, with a film of dust over his eyeballs. Leong crouched over the third, looking for signs of life, checking pulse and breathing. There seemed to be some hope. He tied a tourniquet to the man's terribly wounded shoulder and frantically pumped his chest.

Leong placed the wounded man as carefully as he could on a stretcher and then Roberts and Reidy carried him down three flights of stairs to the Company Aid Post (CAP) and Harvey Pynn. The CAP he had set up next to the ops room was cramped and basic. Supplies and equipment were limited to the man-portable kit that was all the Paras had been able to bring in. The main resource was a Piggott's Pouch. This was a sort of suitcase which unzipped and hung on the wall, containing 20 kilos of medical supplies – enough to look after several seriously injured men. They used the stretchers for beds.

When they arrived, Pynn was already dealing with the walking wounded who had reached him first. 'Two dusty bodies fell through the small door in the CAP and staggered to the ground at my feet,' he wrote. Corporal Stephen 'Hoss' Cartwright, one of the mortar fire controllers, had severe shrapnel wounds in his backside. Private Paul Brown had injuries to his thighs.

Pynn started with Cartwright, whose condition seemed the worst. As he was dressing the wound 'a party of soldiers appeared at the doorway carrying a limp, bloodstained body'.

Pynn left the other casualties to his colleagues and concentrated on the new arrival. He blew air into the man's lungs and vigorously pumped his chest, continuing until long after it was clear the casualty was dead. Something told Pynn that it was essential that each soldier should know that every effort would be made to save him, even though that effort might be in vain.

The dead man was Lance Corporal Jabron Hashmi, a member of the signals team which had its base on the roof of the main building. He and his colleague, Corporal Peter Thorpe, and their translator, Daoud, were engaged in an important surveillance task, together with the company intelligence officer, Sergeant Emlyn Hughes. Earlier that day, Will Pike had decided to shift them from the position they had been occupying to some-where he thought was more safe.

Their new post was against the wall where the explosion struck. The force of the impact made people think at first that they had been hit by a recoilless rifle – a long, old fashioned anti-tank gun. Later it became clear that the damage was done by a 107mm rocket. These were Chinese manufactured and had a reputation for extreme inaccuracy. But the aimer had only to get lucky once. And this had been the Taliban's lucky night.

Martin Taylor's call to Bastion provoked a flurry of immediate demands for more details. Given the adrenalin-soaked confusion, it was impossible to answer their questions. Manning the radios, Taylor felt 'totally impotent'. There was nothing for him to do. Zac Leong was on the roof; Pike had gone out to oversee the firefight that had broken out after the initial impact; Pynn and his team were dealing with the casualties.

On one side Bastion was demanding information. On the other, Pike was reluctant to give an assessment until he knew exactly what the situation was. But the OC was adamant about one thing: they needed helicopters urgently to get the casualties out.

How many were there? Bastion wanted to know. Leong had just appeared, 'absolutely covered in blood', yelling that there was one definitely dead and two 'really bad'. Taylor tried to get information from Pynn. He ducked into the CAP.

'There was a really weird light in there. It was a gas lamp that he had procured from town somehow. He had his hand on [Corporal Hashmi's] chest and he was covered in blood. He was frantically pumping his chest. I said to Harvey, "What's going on?" He said, "Fuck off, just get me some helicopters."'

As far as Taylor could work out there were four or five casualties. He 'got on the radio and said there are three P1 casualties and five P2s'. Injuries are categorised in descending order of seriousness, with P1 the most acute. Taylor 'would much rather say someone is worse than they were and have someone come back later and say,

"Oh, he wasn't as bad as you said." It means that he is then in hospital and not with us.'

Taylor was told that Bastion understood the need for casevac helicopters, but at the moment it was too dangerous for them to fly. He 'went to Will and told him we had got bad news ... he was getting very worked up because he wanted to know when the helicopters were coming. He was getting equally annoyed with me because I wasn't giving him the answer he wanted.'

Taylor told Pike he would go and request a casevac again. Before he did so he looked into the CAP. Word had come down from the roof that Thorpe and Daoud, the translator, were also dead. There were by now another three P2 casualties who should be evacuated that night, making five in all.

Taylor got on the radio and reported 'five P2s and three P4s' (P4 means 'dead'). He was answered by Major Huw Williams, the second-in-command of the battalion. He was 'speaking in a very calm voice and that was very welcome because there was someone there who was cool and collected'. Williams could not quite believe what he was hearing and wanted to make sure. 'Do you mean P4 as in slightly wounded or P4 as in dead?' he asked. Dead, Taylor told him.

There was nothing that could be done for those killed. The living would survive until the helicopters could get in at first light. The firing had stopped now. The adrenalin seeped away, to be replaced by weariness and depression. There was work to be done, carting away the dead and clearing up the mess. About forty minutes after the explosion Taylor saw Zac Leong ask a young signaller to give him a hand getting Corporal Thorpe down from the roof. 'He said, "What, me, sir?" and [Leong] said, "Yes, you. Come on, son, let's go and get it done." And so they went up and put him in a bag and brought him down.' When he got back the young soldier was 'shaking, shaking uncontrollably, and he had this bit of tissue and he was trying to wipe the blood off his hands'.

The men took Thorpe into the CAP. 'He was motionless, grey and unresponsive,' Harvey Pynn wrote in his diary a few hours afterwards. 'The body count was rising. The only saving grace was that neither soldier would have felt a great deal.'

Elsewhere, others were trying to salvage some comfort from the situation. Martin Taylor clung on to the thought that it could have been a lot worse. If the rocket had struck half an hour earlier the roof and staircase 'would have been absolutely packed with guys who were ferrying sandbags up to the roof and very few of them were wearing body armour because of the heat. If that had hit then, we would probably have been looking at more like fifteen or twenty killed.'

The men began sifting their memories for what they knew of the dead men. They belonged to 14 Signals Regiment, which helped provide communications support for 16 Air Assault Brigade. They were outside the tightly bound fraternity of the Paras. They had got along well with them, though, in the eleven days they had worked together. Jabron Hashmi was twenty-four. He was born in Pakistan, close to the Afghan border. His family came to Britain when he was twelve and he was brought up in Birmingham. He joined the army in the summer of 2004 and was posted to the Intelligence Corps. His brother, Zeeshan, said he was 'fiercely proud of his Islamic background and he was equally proud of being British'. Hashmi had gone to Afghanistan to 'build bridges between East and West'. He was regarded by his comrades as exceptionally determined and keen to learn. His language skills made him especially valuable as he could give a soldier's estimate of what was being said rather than the local perspective provided by the interpreters. He was quiet and thoughtful and seemed to Martin Taylor to be 'a bit of an intellectual trapped in a soldier's uniform'.

Corporal Thorpe struck Taylor as 'a nice bloke, very clever. He was very proactive, always enthusiastic and helpful'. Peter Thorpe was twenty-seven and came from Barrow-in-Furness. He had already done one stint in Afghanistan. The two signallers had made an enormous contribution to the security of the base, providing warning of Taliban movements and impending attacks. So too had Daoud, the translator. 'The interpreters have become our lifeline here and are very much part of the team so the death of one of them is as much of a shock,' Pynn wrote later.

Zac Leong laid the bodies out in the orchard, where the mortars were set up, under the big tree where the *shuras* were held. It was a melancholy business. 'A' Company had brought only two body bags with them when they came in. Leong covered the third with a poncho. 'The blokes were having to walk past them,' he said. 'There was nothing we could do with them.' In the morning they loaded them on to the quad bike trailer and when the helicopter finally arrived drove them out to the landing site, where they departed with the injured.

Taylor was relieved that the survivors were heading off for treatment. 'But it didn't fill the guys with enormous amounts of joy to know that if they did get hit, they might not get picked up until the following morning ... There were understandable reasons. But it didn't do a great deal for morale and people started thinking, "Well, if I do get hit, I'd better not get hit too bad otherwise I am going to have to be here all night."' Even the ebullient Zac Leong felt down. 'My morale, I wouldn't say it was blown but I was gutted. I was gutted for the men who had died. But there's a job to be done and you just have to crack on.'

'Cracking on' was the Paras' answer to all setbacks. They tried to forget what was happening and carry on with a mission that now seemed starker and more daunting. Things had started to go wrong.

Harvey Pynn woke up to 'the most welcome dawn I've ever witnessed. The birds sang as usual but there was a grim atmosphere around the blokes.' It had been a traumatic night for him, sweating inside his body armour and helmet in the cramped, blood-soaked Aid Post, trying to blank out the background din of the mortars and machine guns and the incoming rounds as he tended to his patients.

Unable to see what was going on, he felt at times that they might be overrun. He had a contingency plan prepared – run out the back and into the river, which would carry him down to Gereshk and FOB Price.

After forcing down some breakfast Pynn went up to the roof to inspect the damage. The rocket appeared to have struck a concrete pillbox at the top of the stairwell. The need to wear body armour and helmets was constantly emphasised. Zac Leong had been drumming it into the men on the evening of the attack. But the two British dead had been under hard cover when the missile struck and had not been wearing theirs.

Pike took the death of the men under his command particularly hard. It was he who had moved them the day before to the position they had died in. 'They had been on another roof which was much more exposed,' he said. 'There was no cover, just a couple of sandbags, but that was it. I had moved them up to this place because it was more protected and that's what took the hit and that's quite difficult. I don't feel responsible for their deaths, but had I not moved them then they would probably still be alive today.'

Pike was regarded by his officers as a tough man. He was a 'very, very hard person to work for', said one. 'He was a super-perfectionist, very demanding. I think his natural default setting was he thought people would try and pull the wool if they could do. They weren't self-motivated enough and they needed constant direction.' But at the same time he was regarded as 'incredibly professional. He took his job very seriously.' His junior officers believed that, for all the rough edges, they learned a lot from him.

Pike's distress at the losses was obvious to those around him. Their view was that he had nothing to reproach himself for. 'He shouldn't [have felt] guilty in any sense whatsoever,' said Hugo Farmer. 'It was just one of those things, the luck of the draw.'

No one had ever doubted Pike's devotion to his men. The shrewdest and harshest critic of any company commander is his sergeant major. And Zac Leong was in no doubt about Will Pike's qualities. 'He dug out blind for the blokes,' he said. He had shown it in small ways, as when he wrung a Sky TV subscription for his Toms back at barracks in Colchester out of the bean-counters and got Internet access in the accommodation blocks. He showed it in big ways with the safety drills he rigorously imposed in Iraq, keeping patrols off the roads and minimising the chances of encountering IEDs. 'We must have covered more miles than any other unit in four and a half months in Iraq,' Leong said, 'and we had no casualties. That was down to him because of his determination and his planning and the way he dealt with himself and his company.' 'A' Company's preparations in Oman before the deployment had been exceptionally thorough. 'We were practising *shuras*, practising speaking to the locals and stuff like that. That set the benchmark.' All in all, Leong regarded Pike as 'a fucking good bloke'.

For all the work that had been done on building defences and for all the firepower at their disposal, the Sangin district centre on the morning of 2 July felt to those inside it like a very dangerous place. That was how Will Pike saw it. Stuart Tootal arrived with his headquarters team on the helicopter that took the casualties out. He had spoken to Pike before he set out and asked him whether he thought that the presence in Sangin was tenable. Pike believed that Sangin was important and that the battle group needed to be there. But in its current state it was too vulnerable. There was no bridge across the Helmand by which it could be resupplied on land. It was therefore entirely dependent on helicopters – which the previous night's events had shown could not be relied upon. Combat engineers were needed urgently to build proper defences and a position on the high ground across the river that would dominate the centre. Without these things, the Paras would 'pay an ever-trickling blood price'.

On arrival at Sangin Tootal was struck by the fatigue etched on the faces there. He listened to Pike and sympathised with most of what he had to say. 'A' Company were starting to question the point of being in Sangin. They were doing little more than holding the ground. By doing so they were boxing themselves in, losing the ability to manoeuvre, which was essential for the Paras to do their job. Tootal had similar concerns – not just about Sangin, but also the other outstations that had sprung up in the previous few weeks. The platoon houses depended for their existence on helicopters. And the risks of helicopters being shot down were increasing all the time as the Taliban got to know their likely landing sites.

There was another major worry. All this effort and the loss of life that now went with it was for the benefit of the Afghan government. At the *shura* the previous week Governor Daoud had promised to provide fifty extra policemen. They had never appeared. His representatives in Sangin inspired little or no confidence. The district governor, whose authority the arrival of the Paras was meant to reinforce, had left the district centre, where he had been staying, the night before the attack, saying he was going to visit relatives in Gereshk.

Ill feeling towards the twenty or so Afghan police living across the canal behind the compound was growing. There had been much talk among the intervening powers of the vital necessity of training the Afghans to take responsibility for their own security. On the evidence of the Sangin ANP there was a long way to go. To the Paras they seemed slovenly, undisciplined and often off their heads on dope. 'They were clearly high on something' much of the time, said Hugo Farmer. They had 'blurry eyes and were constantly laughing as if they were on some massive marijuana trip'.

There were serious reasons for doubting the good faith of the ANP. The Paras had begun to notice that when a patrol set off into town it would be followed in and out by one of the policemen. Farmer, like everyone else, was sure information was being passed by the ANP to the Taliban. In the charged atmosphere following the attack there were suspicions that the police had been in on it, perhaps even supplying the weapon. At this stage it was still thought that it was a recoilless rifle which had done the damage. When the Paras had arrived they had seen one on the district centre roof. It had since disappeared. Before Tootal's arrival, Pike had demanded that the chief of police produce it by last light and provide ten of his men to mount patrols that night.

Harvey Pynn sat in on Tootal's discussions with Pike. He 'could see the emotion in Will's eyes as he vehemently made the point that soldiers would die here on a nightly basis if we stayed any longer' in the same conditions. Pynn was 'impressed with the CO's listening skills' and thought he 'took little convincing'. But whether they would see it that way farther up the chain of command was another matter. 'It'll be a hard sell to higher command to withdraw now,' the

MO observed shrewdly. 'It would be seen as a victory for the Taliban – but let's face it, they control most of the town anyway.'

Pynn's feeling was that a good case could be made for abandoning Sangin on the basis that by defending themselves the British risked killing innocent civilians. Also, the governor had not stuck to his side of the bargain and had failed to provide the promised reinforcements.

Pynn's analysis turned out to be correct. The political and military interests which ultimately controlled 3 Para battle group decided that the loss of face involved in withdrawal was too great. As the day wore on reports came in that the Taliban were building up their forces around the compound. Tootal decided to spend the night in Sangin with RSM Bishop and other members of his HQ team. It was Pynn, thought, 'a good morale booster for the men', especially when the CO 'mucked in with filling sandbags'. Tootal toured the district centre's positions, chatting to his men and offering suggestions on how the defences could be improved.

He and his staff offered to build a sangar of their own on the main building roof which would cover the southern approaches to the compound. As they heaved the sandbags into place they attracted the attention of the Taliban, who started to spray them with small-arms fire. Tootal and his men had put in a GPMG gunner to protect them while they worked but had sited him in what, it was now clear, was the wrong place. They dived for cover then jumped up to shoot back, allowing the RSM, who had been caught in the open, to leopard-crawl his way to cover. 'I can't remember how many rounds I fired off,' said Tootal. 'But the feeling among us was one of euphoria. We were elated because we'd actually engaged with our weapons. You can go through your army career and never fire your weapon in anger and suddenly some quite senior people and the CO were up there trading fire.'

With nightfall the violence resumed again. Pike was taking no chances. He ordered his machine guns and mortars to fire on known Taliban forming-up areas and called in artillery barrages from FOB Robinson. The defenders were reassured by the drone of a C-130 overhead for much of the night. The Hercules was known to the servicemen and women of many nations as the workhorse of the skies, a homely aircraft that humped supplies and carried troops around the world. This version, though, had undergone a deadly modification. It was a C-130 Spectre gunship, which trundled over the battlefield pumping rounds from its 105mm light gun and 40mm cannon into the ground wherever the Taliban showed themselves.

The threat from the air and the guns at FOB Robinson were powerful deterrents. Intelligence reports revealed that the Taliban fighters were frustrated. The weight of fire from the air and from the base was devastating. The Taliban assault was doomed before it started. There was no rocket attack that night. Through their night sights the defenders saw the ground littered with the dead and dying. During the lulls in the shooting, foxes slunk out to feast on the fresh meat.

As light crept over the compound on 3 July, the only sound was the friendly racket of birdsong. Harvey Pynn noted the subdued mood. 'Stories were told but no one bragged or boasted about their actions,' he wrote. 'There was quiet contemplation. The eyes said it all. The thousand mile stare was out in force.'

'A' Company was reaching the end of its endurance. The Paras and their battle group comrades had spent seven consecutive nights under fire. They were dirty, exhausted and numb. It was obvious that fresh troops were needed. Tootal decided to bring in 'B' Company, and then send 'A' Company back to Bastion. 'B' Company began arriving just before last light. Pike and half of 'A' Company were ordered by second-in-command Huw Williams to go back to Bastion the following day. Pike wanted to stay until his men were out but was told he was needed for an upcoming special operation. Tootal was also returning. Before he set off, he called Ed Butler to report his concerns about the dangers facing the Sangin garrison. It was vital, he said, to get engineers in as quickly as possible to build up the defences. He also said more men were needed to hold the district centre – three platoons rather than two – and that the Afghans needed to live up to their promises to provide more policemen. Butler was sympathetic. It would take time to reinforce the base. But both men knew there could be no question of withdrawal. The Afghan government and its international supporters had staked their prestige on maintaining a presence in Sangin and the other outstations where the battle group was now scattered.

10

Jacko

Timms and the first elements of 'B' Company were subjected to the full Sangin experience immediately after their arrival. In the middle of the evening of 3 July, a shell from a recoilless rifle was aimed at the FSG tower. It missed, smashing into the compound wall, shaking the base but hurting no one. Looking across towards the town as night descended, Pynn noted that 'as the light dimmed, the town was eerily empty. Many of the private compounds had been vacated and the shops in the bazaar were boarded up. The Taliban had free rein to roam as they pleased and in turn we assumed anything that moved was enemy and was going to get a warning shot at least.' A Spectre gunship circled overhead. The snipers gazed into the darkness through night sights, occasionally calling in an artillery or a mortar strike. At one point a vehicle came into view with a recoilless rifle mounted on the back – presumably the one that had fired earlier. It was demolished, with a satisfying whoosh and thump, by a Javelin missile.

Will Pike and half of 'A' Company left the following morning. Timms was now in charge. The day passed relatively quietly. So did the night. The 3 Para Regimental MO Harvey Pynn, who had stayed on in Sangin with 'B' Company, thought the insurgents might be considering their tactics. 'Hopefully the Taliban have realised that we've got too much fighting power for them,' he wrote. 'As we get more ANA into this location we can spread our dominance throughout the town.' But on reflection it seemed as likely that they might 'just be licking their wounds and regrouping before they have another go'.

That night the rooms of the compound were full of snoring bodies, with the remaining 'A' Company soldiers getting the first uninterrupted sleep they had enjoyed for more than a week. The rest was therapeutic. On the morning of 5 July, everyone seemed in good spirits. Some more of 'A' Company were due to be extracted that day. 1 Platoon would have to hang on a little longer, however, and cover their departure.

The relief was due to take place in the afternoon. Timms ordered Hugo Farmer and his men to secure the area to the south of the compound where the helicopters would be coming in. It was one of several landing sites that had been used for resupply. 'We had been sent out to secure it on previous occasions and knew the score,' said Farmer. His platoon headed out at 2.30 p.m. Farmer took 2 Section over to the west, close to the landing zone. Prig Poll led 1 Section south and east through the densely vegetated plantations that fringed the eastern edge of the town.

'I had done that route no end of times by then,' Poll said. 'At least a dozen. I have a bad habit of putting myself at the front. It's not that I don't trust my blokes ... but it is nice to show them sometimes that I will go up front.' The fields were intersected by channels and ditches, linked together by sluices and small bridges. Shortly after leaving the compound Poll noticed a man crouching on a bridge with his back to the Paras, about two hundred yards away. He had often seen locals before at that spot, washing in the water-ways or using them as latrines, so it was 'nothing untoward really'. Nonetheless, Poll 'had a feeling, because of the way he got up and walked away. [He] wouldn't show his body to me. [He] walked away with his back to me, sidestepping off the bridge and disappeared into a doorway.'

Poll radioed Farmer and reported what he had seen. Farmer told him to 'go firm' while he brought 2 Section round to join them. When they arrived, they joined the end of the line and Poll pushed on again. He was still uneasy and after another 100 yards went firm again. He told Lance Corporal 'Billy' Smart, who was in charge of half the section, to move out to the right across a field and take cover in a ditch so that he could provide covering fire while the rest of the patrol pressed on.

When he drew close to the bridge where the suspicious-looking man had been loitering Poll stopped again. There was another small bridge to the right, which led in the direction the patrol was due to take. He ordered Lance Corporal Sharp and Privates Damien Jackson and Adam Randle to cross it. Poll dropped to his haunches, rifle at the ready, facing the scattered buildings on the southern outskirts of Sangin, where he judged any threat would come from. As he stood up to follow his men 'the explosion went off … I think I got lifted a few feet off the road and fell into a ditch'. He was knocked out by the blast – whether from an IED or an RPG was never established.

When he came to a few minutes later 'all hell was going off. The blokes that I had sent across were firing over the top of me, and the Taliban ambush I was caught up in were firing away at me'. The next thing he heard was the voice of the 1 Platoon sergeant, Dan Jarvie, coming over his radio asking, '"Prig, Prig, where are you? Are you there?" And I just said, "Look for my hand." And I stuck my hand up.'

By now Hugo Farmer and 2 Section had arrived and joined in the action. While Farmer laid down 'a massive rate of fire', Poll scrambled out of the ditch and scuttled over to his mates. He was met by the sight of his friend, Damien Jackson, being dragged by Randle into another ditch.

Hugo Farmer was just to the rear. He had seen the start of the ambush. The Taliban had opened fire with RPGs and machine guns from behind compound walls ahead and to the left of the patrol, forcing him and a young lieutenant, Simon Bedford, who was acting as his radio operator to gain experience, to duck behind the only cover available – a bale of straw. One of the grenades had hit just in front of Jackson. Farmer saw him fall. 'He was only six or seven metres in front of me and Randle pulled him into cover.'

Farmer's first reaction, instilled by his training, was to smother the Taliban attack so that Jackson could be evacuated. 'What you are thinking of is the security of the situation in order for you to allow your blokes to withdraw the casualty. So you are fighting the battle, securing the area so a sergeant can come forward or at least organise the evacuation of the casualty.'

That seemed a good plan. The problem was putting it into action. The front section was 'properly pinned down, people lying in shallow trenches, huge amounts of fire coming towards them. Some of the guys were able to return fire. Some weren't.'

This stasis had to be broken. The drills taught the Paras there was a way of doing it. 'When you have got seven or eight guys in cover and the enemy are firing at you there will always be someone who the enemy aren't concentrating on,' said Farmer. 'It is their responsibility to start locating the enemy and then returning fire. As soon as the enemy realise they are being fired on their heads come down, allowing someone else to join in – as long as the right target information has been given.'

It was all about delivering heavy, accurate fire. 'If you put down more than they do, then you will keep their heads down … that is called winning the firefight. That allows you to manoeuvre, which is the first step to winning the battle.'

This made it sound easy. That was not how it felt to Prig, hunkered down in the ditches with a severely wounded man struggling for breath beside him. Poll knew what he had to do. He got behind Jackson and, lying on his back, held the private's head between his knees so he could check his breathing. 'It was a small ditch,' he said. 'Rounds were coming in and the only way I could treat him was to lie flat on my back and pull him on top of me.' As he did so Private Randle crawled forward and tried to stop the bleeding from the wound in Jackson's stomach. In the meantime, Poll went through the first-aid drill: 'Jaw open, look in the mouth to see if the airway is clear, see if he has swallowed his tongue.' Jackson's airway was clear but it seemed to Poll that he had stopped breathing.

He looked up to see the platoon medic, Lance Corporal Stuart Giles, and Dan Jarvie approaching on their hands and knees. 'I just said, "Take over, he's stopped breathing." I thought he had gone at that point.' Poll's responsibility was to get on with 'winning the firefight'.

'My main effort was to get everyone out of this ambush now because people were getting cut up,' he said. 'I crawled back up and took charge of the remaining blokes and identified the firing positions of the Taliban.' He spotted two figures in the entrance to a building. Another man was shouldering an RPG launcher. On the roof of a nearby building he could see three machine-gun positions. He yelled out the locations to his men and they fired into them. The Taliban were well placed. They were also 'very determined, putting down good rates of fire on us'. Poll called Billy Smart to move in from his position to the right so he could join the fight.

As the others traded fire with the Taliban, Stu Giles and Private Sharp were frantically trying to resuscitate Damien Jackson. Dan Jarvie lay alongside them, alternately returning the Taliban fire and yelling requests for a casevac helicopter into the radio. He couldn't see his enemy but was blasting away in the hope of keeping their heads down. A few feet away, one of his men lay dying from a bullet wound to the lower abdomen.

'It was the worst thing I had seen in my life,' he said. 'He was lying back and I was shouting at him, "Jacko, look at me, look at me, don't fucking go, stay with me." We were trying to keep him stable, trying to keep him awake … but he was quiet, really quiet. He had gone white and he was looking up.'

Twenty minutes had now passed since the start of the shooting. Poll could hear an Apache overhead. He called Farmer, who, together with Charlie Curnow, was lighting mini-flares to let the pilot know their location. Prig passed on his position and the coordinates of the enemy and waited for the missiles to rain down. They never came. Instead, the Apache peeled away.

Angry and frustrated, Poll got on the net to Tam McDermott, who was back in the district centre, and asked for supporting fire from the mortars. Soon bombs thumped into the Taliban positions, forcing the fighters back and slowing their rate of fire.

By now Zac Leong had arrived from the district centre with reinforcements and a stretcher party. Tam McDermott, one of a small group from 2 Platoon who stayed behind when the rest left, was also there. He moved forward to join up with Prig Poll while Jacko was loaded on to a stretcher. Dan Jarvie watched him go. 'His kit was ripped off and he was looking at me. There was a feeling of helplessness when you see one of your men in such a bad way.'

It seemed to Stu Giles that Jackson was still breathing.

The Paras were now gaining the advantage. As they started to hit the Taliban positions with grenades from the underslung grenade launchers on their rifles, the incoming fire slackened. Farmer took his men to the right to seek better cover while the stretcher-bearers hurried away.

Farmer thought that Jackson might survive. 'It wasn't clear at that point that he was a goner,' he said. 'It was clear that he'd been hit hard but there wasn't much of an entry wound and there wasn't much of an exit wound. It had gone through soft tissue.'

Farmer was told to take his men to secure one of the established helicopter landing sites (HLS) in the wadi behind the district centre, about 900 yards from where they were. As they arrived, 'Martin Taylor got on to me on the net and said, "Come back." Not really thinking, I said, "What, don't you want me to secure the HLS any more? And he said, "No, no, no, come straight back."' Farmer was about to question the order when he realised, 'Oh, wait a minute, there is only one reason why they would be calling me back.' Jacko was dead.

Taylor had known it when he saw the stretcher party hurrying into the compound. Jackson's arm was hanging lifelessly down, jolting from the motion. Harvey Pynn had gone out to meet him. He had known him well as one of the team medics. 'Jacko was blue and unresponsive,' he wrote. For nearly half an hour they pumped his chest and filled his lungs with their breath. It was no good. A bullet had passed underneath his body armour, hitting him in the lower abdomen and exiting on the other side. It had struck a major artery, the abdominal aorta, causing catastrophic bleeding.

Pynn was devastated. He sat with his head in his hands while Paul Roberts and Brian Reidy zipped up the body bag. The MO then went in to tell Giles Timms the bad news. He found it harder to face Stu Giles when he arrived in the CAP drenched with sweat. Before Pynn could speak the expression on his face told Giles that his patient had died. 'He broke into floods of tears,' he recorded, 'followed by tears of blame.' Jacko had been breathing when the stretcher-bearers carried him away. Pynn believed that he had gone into cardiac arrest due to a catastrophic drop in blood pressure caused by fluid loss while he was being carried back to the compound. It would have been extremely difficult for the men on the ground to control the bleeding given that the bullet had passed neatly through the abdomen, and there was no open wound through which the injury could be accessed. They were also under heavy fire at the time. Pynn reassured Giles that 'even if I had been next to Jacko when he was shot it is unlikely I'd have managed to save him, such was his ill fortune that the round had struck a major artery'.

It was some time before the men were told that Jackson was dead. The danger was far from over. Dan Jarvie knew it, but 'wanted them to remain focused … it was "Right, lads, get your magazines rebombed up, GMPG gunners get your link, LMG gunners same detail, stand by ready to go again." It was a wee bit hard when you knew what had happened.'

The Paras were used to dealing with difficulties. The answer to every setback or 'drama' was to 'crack on', to deal with the difficulty and sort things out – 'screw the nut' in Para language. But the death of one of their own was more than a mere 'drama'.

It was Zac Leong who broke it to them. Jarvie called the men together under the shade of a tree, 'and then Zac gave the brief. He said, "Right, lads, Jacko has gone."' Leong went on to talk to them in a way that Hugo Farmer reckoned later was crucial in preserving the Paras' discipline and motivation.

[It was] not what I would call a rousing speech. But he made them buy into what they needed to buy into, which was that this wasn't going to change the way we were going to operate. It would only strengthen our resolve and make us want to succeed even more. Together, he got the platoon to give agreement that this was what we were going to do … that was a very, very important thing to do. Otherwise the blokes would start getting their own ideas about what we should be doing and it becomes fractious. The ethos and spirit starts breaking down … it was a very quick way to nip in the bud any possible negative reactions.

Farmer went round afterwards talking to each of his men in turn. 'They were shaken up, I was shaken up. It was a really shit experience. But it brought us together and that togetherness was reinforced by what Sergeant Major Leong had said.'

Dan Jarvie also stressed the need for cohesiveness and purpose. 'Paratroopers are paratroopers but they are still human,' he said. 'A lot of these boys were eighteen, nineteen. They were good friends of his. But without being callous I needed to make sure they were focused.'

Jarvie told them, 'this job is still the number one priority ... everything that you do, bear in mind that you are doing it now for Jacko. If we come across the Taliban we kill the Taliban. We take no chances with the rest of our lives.'

One by one, Jacko's section comrades filed into the CAP to pay their last respects. Billy Smart reverently laid his mate's maroon beret on his body. Jarvie, one of the hardest but also one of the warmest-hearted men in 3 Para, could not contain his grief.

Once they were outside, the intense emotion subsided, but Jarvie noticed that there was an added firmness to the men. 'There wasn't a feeling that they were going to go out and do anything for revenge. That's not what we were there for. We weren't going to hand out any punishment to anyone who wasn't Taliban. But we had a resolution ... we will go out there and fight harder, fight more aggressively because we know what we have lost.'

The deaths of Jabron Hashmi and Peter Thorpe had been a sobering reminder of mortality and a source of sadness for the Paras. But the death of one of their own created a special kind of grief. Damien Jackson was a much-loved member of the battalion. He was born in Sunderland and was a fanatical Black Cats devotee. Dan Jarvie had known him since he had arrived two and a half years before. 'Jacko came to me as a young Tom,' Jarvie said. 'When he first came he was always in dramas but he was a good soldier, a fit young soldier. He was intelligent and he had a good personality on him. He wasn't just one of my men. He was a mate of mine as well.'

Hugo Farmer thought he was 'a great bloke, really, really well liked. He was always happy, always smiling, very professional ... he

3 PARA • 145

had a great future.' Farmer had a picture of him taken during
Operation Mutay, posing with his gun and 'looking particularly
"ally"'. 'Ally' is a Para term of approval meaning 'cool'. His mates
called him 'Combi-teeth', reckoning his snaggle-toothed smile
looked like the all-purpose tool used for maintaining the SA-80
rifle. Jarvie relied on him as a link between the senior NCOs and the
young Toms who looked up to Jacko and came to him for advice.
Not that he was very much older than them. When he died he was
four days short of his twentieth birthday.

After discussions with his men, Hugo Farmer asked whether they
could go on guard duty that night. It seemed like the right thing to
do. The first attacks began at dusk, from across the wadi, the usual
RPG and small-arms fire. Just before midnight another big-calibre
round rammed into the compound.

On the night of 9 July, when all of 'A' Company were finally back
in Bastion, the men held a memorial service for Jacko. There was an
opening prayer, and then they sang some hymns. Will Pike and Zac
Leong read out tributes. The company was told that there were plans
to set up a new forward operating base across the river from the
district centre. It would be called FOB Jackson. 'The blokes liked
that,' said Hugo Farmer.

The plan came to nothing but Jacko would not be forgotten.

11

Musa Qaleh

Sangin was only one of five forward locations. By now there were troops in Now Zad, Musa Qaleh and Kajaki, as well as FOB Robinson. The parameters of the mission were gradually widening. Governor Daoud's philosophy was that if you didn't ask you didn't get, and he had proved very good at asking.

There were simply not enough men to do the job. It had been decided at the outset that everyone would be allowed a mid-mission two-week 'R and R' break. Sticking to the plan meant that companies were always under-strength. Tootal had tried to ease the strain on human resources by advocating abandoning a permanent presence in Now Zad, but had been overruled. On the plus side, he could look forward to some reinforcements. On 10 July it was announced that a 125-strong company group from the Royal Regiment of Fusiliers would be sent from Cyprus to Helmand to garrison Now Zad.

The commanders told themselves that, despite the problems, the direction that events had propelled them in was producing some unforeseen but nonetheless beneficial consequences. The vigorous reaction of the Taliban to the arrival of the British had forced a 'break-in battle' which the Paras and their comrades were winning. The Taliban were taking a beating. Intelligence assessments spoke of many wounded fighters retreating across the southern border to Pakistan to seek medical treatment. It was also claimed that they were having problems finding men to take their place. Local males were reported to be increasingly unwilling to join what looked more and more like the losing side.

These alleged successes were unquantifiable, however. The difficulties of keeping men in the field and supplying them with food and ammunition were serious and seemed likely to get worse.

Musa Qaleh and Now Zad, moored on the northern fringes of the battle group's area, posed particular problems. A British reconnaissance party had visited Musa Qaleh in late May. They had gone there on the insistence of Governor Daoud, who claimed that the government's forces were enduring vicious Taliban attacks. A Pathfinder patrol confirmed that this was no exaggeration. 'There were bloody huge rocket strikes, holes in the walls,' said Major Nick Wight-Boycott, the Pathfinders' OC. The Pathfinders are an essential element of 16 Air Assault Brigade, the formation built around the Paras. Their job was to go ahead of the main force, by land or air, to scope out the territory in which it would be operating. That meant gathering information about landing sites and drop zones. Thereafter they were to act as the brigade's reconnaissance arm. They were also expected to contribute to the brigade firepower, launching diversionary attacks if necessary. Despite their small numbers – there were only about thirty of them – they punched well above their weight. They were known as a 'force multiplier'.

The Pathfinders operated at distances of up to 200 miles from base. Six-man teams cruised around in WMIKs. Each team had a commander, a second-in-command, a medic, a signaller and sniper and a demolitions expert. Each member also had cross-training in another skill – such as forward air controlling. The Pathfinders were tough, versatile and extremely engaged and motivated. Their selection process has been described as 'P Company on speed'. It is a masochistic endurance test culminating in a 40-mile march across the Brecon Beacons staggering under a ligament-tearing burden of kit. That is before they start throwing themselves out of aircraft. Trainees do HALO and HAHO jumps. HALO stands for High Altitude Low Opening. 'That is up to twenty-five thousand feet,' explained Wight-Boycott. 'With full kit. So it's oxygen masks, rucksacks, rifles, going out the door and free fall for two minutes then pull your parachute. It requires quite a lot of determination to do that.' HAHO stands for High Altitude High Opening. The advantage of this type of jump is that men can be dropped far away from the target zone and fly in at high speed on their parachutes undetected, checking on GPS until they get to the landing point. Most Pathfinders come from the Parachute Regiment. They are augmented by specialists from the Royal Signals and the Royal Electrical and Mechanical Engineers.

The Pathfinders arrived in Helmand in mid March with the task of establishing 'ground truth' – discovering the lie of the land for the benefit of the rest of the brigade. They started off in Gereshk. On 6 April they patrolled up to Now Zad in eight WMIKs and two Pinzgauer troop carriers. As they arrived in town they were attacked from several positions. They returned fire and withdrew. While they were falling back, one WMIK overturned. Despite their reliability and manoeuvrability the vehicles were often seriously overloaded, which could make them dangerously unstable. The Pathfinders managed to destroy the vehicle with an anti-tank missile to deny it to their attackers. In the meantime they called in an A-10 to batter the enemy positions, and were told to hold their fire. The gunmen were in fact ANP. A few hours later the Pathfinders and ANP held a mini-*shura* and the medics patched up some of the Afghan wounded. The British soldiers were somewhat bemused to find that the Afghans seemed to bear them no ill will. 'They were all smiles and gave us tea and tangerines,' said Sergeant Major Andy Newell. Demonstrating a chutzpah that the Pathfinders could only admire, they also asked for an ammunition resupply to replace the bullets they had fired at their allies. The reasons for the incident were never properly established – the ANP claimed they thought the new arrivals were Taliban – but it gave the Pathfinders vivid proof of the confusing and treacherous environment in which they were operating.

A few days later they had another bad experience. They were tasked to provide security for a Canadian convoy near Sangin. As they drove along in single file one of the WMIKs rolled over a landmine left behind by the Russians. The vehicle was flung into the air and Lance Corporal Damien Manning and Sergeant Dave Burton, who were inside, were injured. Manning lost his leg.

The Pathfinders spent five days in Musa Qaleh late in May before handing over to an American force. The American deployment was only a temporary measure, however. Someone would have to take responsibility for the place. The question was, who? Early in June the Pathfinders were ordered to go there and hold the place for forty-eight to ninety-six hours, after which they would be relieved by 'A' Company of 3 Para. Wight-Boycott, who had just taken over command, thought it unlikely that their stay would be so brief and his scepticism was duly justified. As it turned out, 'A' Company got stuck in Sangin and the Pathfinders got stuck in Musa Qaleh.

Despite the supposedly limited deployment period the Pathfinders took no chances. Wight-Boycott loaded up with as many stores as his six WMIKs could carry, as well as sandbags and barbed wire to shore up the district centre's rudimentary defences. He was careful to take an extra .50-cal machine gun and tripod mounts so they could be dismounted from the vehicle and used to defend the base. The Pathfinders were supposed to leave on 11 June. Before they set off, they rehearsed drills and test-fired their weapons. When it came to the .50-cals it was clear something was badly wrong. 'They fired one round and then they would stop,' Wight-Boycott said. The problem was passed up the line. The answer came back that the guns had probably not been properly cleaned. The Pathfinders insisted that this was not so. Then it emerged that machine-gunners in other units were experiencing the same trouble. Wight-Boycott, after consulting with Andy Newell, said he was not taking his men out until the problem was resolved. The .50-cal machine gun was probably the gun the Taliban feared most. It had a range of more than 1 mile and fired, at a blistering rate, a thumping shell that tore through walls and trees and made mincemeat of human flesh.

Tests revealed eventually that the ammunition was faulty. There was not enough propellant in the rounds, and therefore not enough gas to recock the weapon. The batch was junked and a new supply bought from the Canadians at a cost of £30,000.

The Pathfinders left for Musa Qaleh in the early hours of 14 June, travelling for six hours off-road. The last stretch was through the dense vegetation of the cultivated zone to the west of the town. This close country was dangerous. The Pathfinders preferred the open desert where they could see for miles. They drove with pistols in hand to guard against the Taliban bushwhacking them from the trees and bushes scraping the sides of the WMIKs.

The handover from the Americans lasted a few days. Even once they left, the American forces would not be far away. They had established an FLE (Forward Logistic Element) about ten miles to the north, which was equipped with a battery of 105mm guns that could be called in to support the base if it came under attack.

Musa Qaleh lay at the confluence of two wadis running north–south and east–west. The district centre was bang in the middle of town, in between two bazaars. The compound contained a police headquarters, a prison and a clinic, built by the Americans. There were thirteen prisoners languishing in the lock-up, awaiting trial on charges ranging from rape and murder to failure to pay their debts. Some had been on remand for a year. They were likely to have to wait a long time for justice. The local judge and magistrates had fled to Lashkar Gah to escape the Taliban. Many of the inmates had malaria, as did many of the police. But the ten warders who guarded the prisoners treated them humanely and fed them well.

There were about eighty police in the compound. Only a quarter of them had uniforms, which they were not inclined to wear, preferring their dishdashas and flip-flops. They looked little different from the Taliban. On any night about ten ANP would put in desultory stag duty on the corners of the compound. Wight-Boycott noted that they tended to go to sleep.

The compound was like all the other district centres in Helmand, a cluster of low buildings, coated with cement and mud. It was surrounded by a 10-foot wall, topped here and there with razor wire. The buildings were widely spread out. The Pathfinders took over one in the centre of the compound. It had five rooms on the ground floor. They became the ops room, a clinic, a signals post and two small dormitories. There was more accommodation in the clinic. One of the Pathfinders, Corporal Tom Blakey, set up a make-shift café with the cheery slogan 'come in for a brew, stay for the slagging.' It was 'morale central' according to Andy Newell.On the roof was Sangar Two. Sangar One was at the north-west corner of the compound, on a two-storey building known as the Outpost which lay just outside the compound walls and was reached by a rickety, twenty-foot-high walkway. Sangar Three pointed out towards the rat-infested bazaar, which stretched westwards out of the town and led to the cultivated area and the wadi.

The prison complex was nicknamed the Alamo. It dominated the compound and the area around it, and was a good place to mount machine guns, whose arcs of fire could sweep in all directions. There were doubts about how much weight the roof could take, so for the time being only one .50-cal was mounted there. At the south end of the complex just outside the walls was a multi-domed mosque.

There was a big front gate made of haphazardly welded sheets of rusty steel, hanging off its hinges, which opened on to the bazaar to the west. Directly in front of it was a minaret-like tower which the troops called the 'obelisk'. The ANP's policing of the gate was inconsistent, and it was often left ajar. The town beyond the walls was a drab jumble of mud walls and unfinished concrete dwellings, with skeins of power and phone lines straggling overhead. It reeked of poverty and privation. What money there was in the town came from drugs and smuggling.

From the Pathfinders' point of view, the outstanding fact about the Musa Qaleh base was that it was completely surrounded by streets, alleyways, houses and compounds. Sangin had broad open spaces on three sides. Here the buildings lapped at the walls of the compound, providing excellent cover for attackers.

The town had considerable strategic importance. It lay along the main north–south route linking Baghran to the Sangin valley. As the attacks in May had shown, the town was high on the Taliban target list. They had already successfully created a climate of fear among the civilians. Anyone who cooperated with the foreigners could expect to be murdered. The school had been closed for four months after all the teachers fled to Lashkar Gah. There were signs, though, that the Taliban were reluctant to launch another major attack on the place as they had in May unless they could be sure of success. The damage that attack had caused had won them no new friends in Musa Qaleh. Most of the population had little reason to love the

Taliban. But as in Sangin, they doubted the value of foreigners' promises. Wight-Boycott's first meeting with the locals was not encouraging. The leaders were looking for tangible proof of good-will. One obvious way of demonstrating it was to replace an electricity transformer that had been destroyed in the Taliban attack. It would cost about £5,000. The money, and the transformer, eventually arrived.

The Pathfinders started off patrolling the town. '[We were] trying to build up a rapport, which was pretty difficult,' said Wight-Boycott. 'You were walking along saying, "Hi, *salaam aleikum*," and they would just blank you.'

As elsewhere in Helmand, the local population were continuously being forced to decide between the lesser of two evils. They had been happy at the overthrow of the Taliban in 2001. The tribal elders warned the local Taliban not to start a guerrilla war against President Karzai's forces and their foreign backers and told them to leave the area if they did not want to live in peace. But reports that the Karzai's regime was also seeking to destroy their livelihood reduced their enthusiasm for the new order. They were now ruled by people who seemed as brutal as the Taliban. In one incident in 2003, the then governor of Helmand, Sher Mohammed Akhunzada, sent forces into the village of Akhtak to chase out Taliban fighters. About eighty people were killed in the raid, most of them civilians. When the villagers demanded compensation a price was agreed but the governor never paid. There were other broken promises. The aid that was meant to pour into the region failed to arrive. Sher Mohammed had since been ousted from office, at NATO's demand. But there was no reason to believe that Governor Daoud would be any better. In the meantime, the Taliban had an opportunity to present themselves as patriots and protectors who would defend the local people against an alien force that brought fire and explosions in its wake.

It was unfortunate for the newcomers that they were visibly on the same side as the ANP. In Musa Qaleh, the police were as loathed by ordinary civilians as they were everywhere else in the province. The Pathfinders tried to teach the ANP some low-level skills. Despite their name, the ANP saw themselves as more of a militia than a police force, and the mundane business of operating vehicle checkpoints, searching cars and conducting arrests did not come easily. Their mentors also attempted to instil some basic drills. Muster parades were held in the mornings when their chief would inspect their kit and check that their weapons were clean.

The police chief for the Musa Qaleh district was Abdul Wulley, a smiling, bearded joker in his late forties who had at one time or another allied himself with virtually all Afghanistan's scrapping factions. Everyone, Afghan and Brit, called him Coco. Wight-Boycott was nearly twenty years his junior, but despite the age gap they hit it off. Neither could speak the other's language but they made each other laugh. 'He was a menace and he was a great guy,' said Wight-Boycott. 'He was funny. I used to have lots of great chats with him every afternoon when we drank tea together. He had fought the Soviets and the mujahedin. He had fought for the Taliban and now he was the chief of police.' As a result, his former friends in the Taliban now hated him. 'They used to sing songs about Coco. One of the famous quotes was "the Taliban would forget God before they forgot Coco"'. The enemies kept in close touch with each other. The Taliban would 'phone him up and say, "Hey, hey, Coco, what are you doing?" and start slagging him off. Likewise he would phone them and start slagging them off. Just like children. It was a very, very interesting dynamic.'

The behaviour of Coco and his men was a reliable source of amusement. The other policemen's gay proclivities were the object of horrified fascination. On Thursday nights the ANP had a social evening dubbed 'man love night' by the Pathfinders, when they walked around wearing mascara and holding hands. In one of his chats with Coco, Wight-Boycott explained that things were different in Britain. '[Coco] replied, "I hear in your country that you love your women and that is very strange. I have been married for twenty, twenty-five years and my wife and I meet in the night and fuck like strangers."'

Apart from his entertainment value, Coco was extremely useful. He seemed to have inside knowledge of all the Taliban moves and gave regular, accurate tip-offs about the insurgents' dispositions, impending attacks and state of morale.

The information was passed on to the other allied elements operating in Helmand, but was not necessarily absorbed. Two weeks after their arrival the Pathfinders were told that an American convoy would be passing through their area.

They warned the operational base at Kandahar to which the Pathfinders reported that the Americans should not be routed through Musa Qaleh as they would certainly be ambushed. As the Americans approached, the Pathfinders picked up intelligence that the Taliban had spotted them and were preparing to attack. They tried to radio the convoy but were unable to get through.

The Taliban struck about a mile to the south of the Musa Qaleh base. Wight-Boycott had only twenty-five men with him. If they sallied out to the rescue there was a big risk that if the insurgents chose to attack they would overrun the Afghan defenders at the base, so the Pathfinders were forced to stay put. The firefight went on for more than three hours, during which the compound also came under attack. Eventually an American B-1 bomber was called in and dropped a bomb on the attackers, allowing the convoy to extricate. One of the Americans was wounded in the firefight and a casevac helicopter was called in. The now battered convoy moved to an area next to the 'green zone', to wait. This was the area of trees, ditches and high-standing crops to the west of the town that the Pathfinders had driven through on the way in. The foliage and irrigation channels provided excellent cover, which the Taliban were to make full use of.

Before the convoy got there the American quick reaction force that had arrived from the FLE to rescue their comrades conducted a 'clearance by fire' – drenching the area with heavy machine guns and grenades from rapid-fire Mark 19 launchers. 'It was like a scene from *Apocalypse Now*,' said Wight-Boycott. 'The green zone just erupted in flames.' To everyone's astonishment green tracer flowed out from the trees and orchards where the Taliban crouched. The insurgents were still there and firing back. Wight-Boycott conceded that this was 'all credit to them. You have got this amazing scene.

There was a Chinook and an Apache coming in firing from its thirty-mil [cannon] trying to clear the zone, and rounds coming back towards the Chinook as well.' The casevac helicopter eventually abandoned its mission and the casualty was removed only when the Americans shifted to another landing site and a Black Hawk managed to get in safely.

When the Americans returned the following day to destroy their abandoned vehicles they were ambushed again and a few more potshots were aimed at the Brits in the base. The violence had a profound effect on the town. 'The next day all the Afghans in Musa Qaleh fled,' said Wight-Boycott. 'You could see people running over the hills.' The soldiers were trained to look out for 'combat indicators' – signs that fighting was imminent. Musa Qaleh was now a living example of one of them – the 'absence of the normal and presence of the abnormal'. Intelligence suggested that the Taliban were closing in and had thrown a 500-yard-deep ring around the base. They were, it seemed, preparing to attack, and had warned the townspeople to move out.

But, for the time being at least, apart from the odd burst of misdirected fire, the assault did not materialise. It seemed that the insurgents were still getting the measure of the defenders. To reinforce any Taliban doubts about the wisdom of attacking the base, aircraft flew ear-splitting, low-level runs over the town. The Pathfinders believed that these had an effect in dampening the Taliban's enthusiasm. When reinforcements arrived in the form of twenty men of 6 Platoon, 'B' Company, 3 Para – the Guards Parachute Platoon – it freed the Pathfinders up to increase the strength of their patrols, while the Guards secured the base.

The sight of the patrols seemed to both deter the Taliban and reassure the departed civilians. By 1 July, many had drifted back and business was starting up again in the shops and bazaars. By day, the Pathfinders walked through the streets trying to create an atmosphere of security. By night they patrolled around the base searching for likely launching points for Taliban operations.

Wight-Boycott believed in a vigorous, confident approach. During the American convoy episode, fire had been seen coming from a building about four hundred yards away, from where it was possible to see into the compound. Men had been seen apparently observing the base from the roof. He decided to mount a cordon-and-search operation to check it out. He took a chance with the Afghan police by including them in the planning and giving them the main role in the mission. The Pathfinders would provide the outer cordon. The Afghans would set up the inner cordon and carry out the search, accompanied by a British mentor. 'Coco and I drove out with his boys,' said Wight-Boycott. 'They had done a good job for the inner cordon and I said, "Right, you are going to go in there and search the building." They said, "We are not ..." I thought, "Great."' It was left to Wight-Boycott and another Brit to kick in the doors. They discovered three Pakistanis behind one of them. Their story was that they had come to Musa Qaleh because they couldn't find work at home. No one believed them. But in the absence of any incriminating weapons or communications equipment, nothing could be done.

Coco and his Musa Qaleh cops seemed bemused by the whole episode. 'He thought we were crazy,' said Wight-Boycott. 'So they had no understanding really.'

Like the other platoon houses Musa Qaleh was largely reliant on choppers for its resupplies, and one of the Pathfinders' most vital, and contentious, activities was securing the helicopter landing sites when they came in. The RAF were unhappy about flying into the base. There was plenty of landing space at a site directly to the north of the compound. The Pathfinders believed they could easily pro-vide security by pushing out a patrol, and would be able to sup-press any attack with fire from the sangars around the camp if things turned nasty. The RAF's preference was to put down in the wadi, half a mile away to the west of the town. This meant that the Pathfinders had to drive past the green zone, favourite haunt of the Taliban, to get there. They also feared that the predictability of the arrangement would increase the chances of a helicopter being shot down – some-thing that intelligence reports suggested the Taliban were itching to attempt.

Nick Wight-Boycott and his men were having an interesting and eventful time in Musa Qaleh. But it was not what they were in Afghanistan to do. The essence of their function was mobility. Their purpose was to roam the province, searching for the enemy, reporting on their actions and intentions and, when appropriate, shooting them up. What they were certainly not intended to be was a holding force. Yet this was what occupied them. It was extremely good news, then, to be told that they were about to relieved by G Battery, 7 RHA, the Paras' airmobile artillery support unit.

The plan was that the relief convoy would just drive in. The first attempt to break through was made on 6 July. The column was coming from the west. That meant passing by the green zone. By now the Taliban were well set up there and intelligence reports suggested they knew about the operation and were planning to disrupt it. Despite his previous experience, Wight-Boycott decided to include the Afghans in the operation. For all their shortcomings, they could hold and fire rifles. And one of the main objects of the deployment was supposed to be to involve the Afghan forces in securing their own country.

The Pathfinders set off from the base and lined up their WMIKs on the approach route, providing a battery of .50-cals to give supporting fire. The Afghans were tasked with probing into the green zone. As soon as they moved in, a firefight erupted. The WMIK line was hit from the side and rear. Wight-Boycott had not been expecting too much from the Afghans. Their orders were basically to locate the Taliban. If they came under attack they were to extract themselves and let airpower or the American artillery do the job of crushing the Taliban positions. The Afghans, however, had other ideas. They were 'shouting, running and charging all over the place. Command and control basically broke down.' The Pathfinders had to stay put to cover them, enduring Taliban fire, until the Afghans finally withdrew. 'It was quite dicey taking it until they got out,' said Andy Newell. Wight-Boycott learned a 'massive lesson ... trying to do an attack where you have got Afghans doing the attacking and Brits doing fire support doesn't work very well. In fact you are probably best just letting them crack on with their own objectives, rather than trying to do a coordinated attack.'

The relief operation was abandoned. Another attempt was made the following day, but this also failed. Eventually, some fresh troops were flown in and the Guards Platoon were flown out. The Pathfinders, however, stayed put. At least Wight-Boycott now had twenty gunners from I Battery, RHA, ten Afghan army soldiers and fifteen engineers at his disposal. They were all extremely welcome. The engineers were put to work shoring up the Musa Qaleh defences. The Pathfinders had done what they could, buying cement locally to beef up the sangars, and wood to build ladders and walkways to the rooftop positions.

The sappers could also carry out some much-needed improvements to the sanitation situation. 'We were basically crapping into a cut-off oil drum and burning it out with diesel every day,' said Wight-Boycott. The facilities for ablutions amounted to one dodgy shower. Security for the base was handed over to 7 RHA. The Pathfinders were still desperate to leave. By now they had been in the field for four weeks. Wight-Boycott worried that his men were reaching the end of their endurance. Their equipment was also starting to degrade – the radios were overheating. Above all, stuck in Musa Qaleh they were not able to do their job. Wight-Boycott argued that with the arrival of the reinforcements and with the ANP presence, he and his twenty-five men were no longer needed. Their departure would also reduce the strain on the overburdened supply helicopters. He asked for the Pathfinders to be withdrawn to FOB Price, where they could get on with their long-range patrolling activities. The appeal was turned down. The Pathfinders were staying put.

Wight-Boycott accepted the decision gracefully and turned his attention again to taking the fight to the Taliban. On the week leading up to 11 July he had been mounting patrols every night, creeping around the wadi trying to set up ambushes. The Pathfinders' freedom of action was extended by a change in the rules of engagement which came into force on the following day. This had major implications for how the Pathfinders went about flushing the Taliban out from their lairs in the green zone. The new rules applied to all forces deployed north of Highway One, the ring road that swept through southern Afghanistan. That meant everything beyond Gereshk – Sangin, Now Zad, Musa Qaleh and Kajaki.

On 16 July, Wight-Boycott decided to send out two patrols at one o'clock the following morning. Beforehand, he ordered the .50-cal that was normally sited on top of the Alamo to be mounted on the Outpost to support the ambush. They waited until darkness to move it, to avoid being spotted by the Taliban. At 11 p.m., he got a call from his sergeant major, Andy Newell, who was on stag at the Outpost with Sergeant Adie Summerscales, a transport expert attached to the Pathfinders. Through his night vision equipment Newell could see shadowy figures moving in a wooded area to the west. He also picked up a couple of figures on a rooftop, pointing in the direction of the base. It seemed that the Taliban were preparing to take advantage of the bright moonlight to launch a major attack. Wight-Boycott told Newell to take extra precautions and lay down on the floor, hoping to snatch some sleep before setting off on the early morning ambush.

Newell resumed his guard duty. Suddenly the night was pierced by 'a flash and the first of the RPGs flew towards me'. The sergeant major opened up with a GPMG as the grenade swished overhead, exploding harmlessly in the compound. It was followed by three or four others, and a wall of green tracer streamed towards the base, slowly at first, almost floating, then whipping up speed alarmingly as it got closer. Wight-Boycott leapt up and stumbled into the compound. Most of the fire was coming from the area opposite the Outpost. Three of the Pathfinders grabbed their kit and ran across open ground swept by fire, up a ladder and along a 30-foot makeshift bridge that led to the roof of the Outpost. They began returning fire. Among them was Lance Corporal Tony Robinson, an Australian on an exchange posting. Robinson was keen to fire the 51mm mortar located on the Outpost, something he had never done before. He dropped a bomb into the barrel and it soared off into the night. But there was no explosion.. Someone asked him whether he had removed the safety pin. He replied, 'There's a safety pin on these things?' The collective shout of 'Knob!' could be heard over the gunfire.

A group of Taliban were spotted going into a building in the green zone near the wadi. The American FLE base was contacted and an artillery strike requested. The building they had sheltered in turned out to be a mosque. It was badly damaged in the shelling, and a large number of insurgents were killed.

Coco learned that three vehicles laden with Taliban had set off from the Sangin area to join the action. An aircraft was already over-head. It peeled away and soon found the convoy, driving without lights along the wadi road towards Musa Qaleh, and destroyed at least one of the trucks. The rest disappeared into a built-up area and the aircraft returned to base.

The sangars stayed fully manned all night with the sentries taking it in turns to sleep. The Taliban, though, were still restless. During the night, a vehicle appeared in the bazaar to the west of the base and was engaged from Sangar Three, while two more fighters were spotted creeping up to the Outpost and were immediately killed with fire from the .50-cal.

It had been a hard night. 'Hopefully we have given these fuckers a bloody nose,' said Wight-Boycott in a report to Kandahar. That seemed to be the case. Intelligence revealed that the Taliban had 'left many friends behind'. The operation appeared to have been ordered and controlled by Taliban commanders in the south and reinforced with fighters from the Sangin area. Some of the Musa Qaleh ele-ment did not seem to know the people they were fighting alongside. In the morning the smell of burning wood drifted over from the bazaar to the west of the base. Tracer had set the flimsy wooden shacks and stalls alight.

Wight-Boycott had no doubt that despite the 'bloody nose' the Taliban would soon be back. In fact they took only two days to regroup and try again. On the afternoon of 19 July, intelligence picked up that they were moving stocks of RPGs around the town. As darkness fell, the defenders settled down for another long night. It was not long before all the lights in the town went out. The Taliban had cut the electricity. Over to the west the sentries could see the insurgents signalling to each other across the wadi with red and white lights.

The mortars fired 'illume' rounds to light up the ground. All was still. Wight-Boycott ordered an artillery strike on the wadi, even though the Pathfinders were under close scrutiny following the shelling of the mosque. The Canadians had sent up a UAV the following day to carry out a battle damage assessment. Wight-Boycott felt that the shelling had been justified. They had not known it was a mosque, and the Taliban had been carrying weapons when they entered it.

On this occasion, the brief barrage delivered by the Americans did little damage. It did, however, frighten the Taliban. Two shells had landed very near one of their positions. There were also aircraft about, flying over Musa Qaleh on some unconnected mission. At 11.18 p.m. the lights of the town went on again. It seemed the insurgents would not be attacking that night and another game of cat-and-mouse came to a close.

The Pathfinders were approaching exhaustion. They were getting only intermittent resupplies and were supplementing their rations with food bought from the few locals who were left. Mostly it was spaghetti and tomato paste and nan bread. One day some of the gunners bought a goat and made a stew. Wight-Boycott was 'on about three hours' sleep max. That was an hour's sleep at first light and two hours at night.' Andy Newell, whose ten years' experience in the Pathfinders had been invaluable to the OC in his first weeks of command, was getting the same.

On 16 July they had been told, once again, that they would shortly be relieved. The Danish reconnaissance squadron serving with the coalition forces had agreed to take over the Musa Qaleh garrison. A small advance party of five men had already flown in with the engineers. The rest were to arrive on 21 July, guided in by Newell. They were due to break in from the west. The Pathfinders watched them arrive. Through his binoculars Wight-Boycott could see the Taliban running into their ambush positions. He called in an air strike. A Harrier appeared and dropped a 500lb bomb with lethal precision on the insurgents. Most of them were killed. The others fled. The Danes decided that they did not have enough troops to clear the green zone on foot while the vehicles passed through. They broke off the insertion and drove back out into the desert. They had been within 1,000 yards of the base. Newell was frustrated and disappointed. He knew how badly the resupplies they were bringing were needed. 'I was going nuts at this point as the blokes had run out of batteries for their night vision devices and were low on ammo and food,' he said. The mood inside the base was bleak. 'You can imagine the morale of the blokes,' said Wight-Boycott. 'They had been there six weeks at that stage. We were meant to be there ninety-six hours and we had been told on three or four occasions, "You will be relieved tomorrow."'

Wight-Boycott had been left to his own devices for much of the time. Now he got a call from Ed Butler asking him how much longer he could hold on for. He replied, stoically, that they could hang on for another five to seven days, giving the Danes another chance to drive in.

Before they could do so the Taliban launched their heaviest attack so far. Since 17 July they had been mounting small, harassing attacks every evening as the light started to fade. This time there was no feinting or probing, but a full-on assault.

On the morning of 24 July intelligence picked up information that the Taliban were moving weapons around, a sign that an operation was imminent. The attack began in the afternoon. It opened, spectacularly, with two RPGs hitting the sangar on the Outpost and destroying it, and demolishing the western edge of the roof, which collapsed on to the ground below. It took with it the 50-cal., the GPMG, a sniper rifle, two radios and a night vision sight. There were two Danes from the advance party on the roof at the time. It seemed to Wight-Boycott that they must both be dead. But when the smoke cleared, one of them could be seen doggedly trading fire. The other, Lieutenant Thomas Rydahl, had fallen two storeys into a pile of rubble below the sangar where he lay, armed only with a pistol, in direct line of sight of the attackers. One of the Pathfinders, Private Mark Wilson, together with a medic, Corporal Johan Wessels, and the Australian, Tony Robinson, ran under fire along the walkway connecting the compound to the Outpost to help.

When they arrived they saw that the man in the pit was hurt but alive. Wessels threw down a field dressing to him then took over a GPMG and with Robinson began driving the attackers back. Mark Wilson, meanwhile, went to the Dane's rescue. According to Wight-Boycott he 'got over there, looked down, said to himself, "I can do something about this"'. There was an old bedstead lying on the roof. Wilson hung it over the side and, ignoring the incoming fire, shinned down to where the wounded man lay, bleeding from the head and with a broken leg. Wilson retrieved a ladder from among the debris and shoved the Dane up and out. He was to win the Military Cross for his courage.

Musa Qaleh was under attack from all sides. It was reckoned later that as many as three hundred fighters had taken part in the assault. The defenders had called for air support but it was a long time coming – it was ninety minutes before they heard the aircraft engines. This was the first time the base had been subjected to such a concerted effort. It seemed miraculous that the defenders had suffered only three wounded.

The attack seemed to indicate that Musa Qaleh had moved yet higher up the Taliban's target list. Wight-Boycott reckoned that by now there were about ten Taliban units in the area, each with a strength of 10 to 20 fighters. They had proved to be good at using cover and – as the Outpost incident showed – firing accurately. They had coordinated well and would have mounted an even heavier operation if reinforcements they had called in from Now Zad had not been intercepted by the Danish force still deployed out to the west, waiting to insert.

The convoy bringing the full Danish recce squadron finally arrived at 1.30 on the morning of 26 July after a forty-eight-hour trek from Bastion that involved a long detour and an attempted Taliban ambush. They approached the town from the east. Before they got there, aircraft dropped six 1,000lb bombs on known Taliban areas. There was no opposition when the 1,000-yard-long chain of vehicles arrived in town. The only casualty was the redoubtable Andy Newell. The Danes had been cautious about advancing through the dark, silent town up the road leading to the district centre's main gate. Newell had gone ahead to lead the way.

About forty yards from the gate there was a burst of automatic rifle fire and Newell felt an impact and fell forwards. He had been shot in his right arm by one of the ANP guards, who had panicked after being woken up by the sound of the convoy. Newell picked himself up and carried on into the base. His arm was completely numb. The single bullet had shattered bone and destroyed nerve tissue. It was the end of the war for Newell. He was casevacced back to Bastion then on to Britain for treatment.

The following night the Taliban stayed away. While the Danes were bedding in, the political situation in Musa Qaleh was soured by an accident of war which depleted drastically what goodwill remained among the local people towards their self-declared saviours.

One afternoon during an air raid on a Taliban position, a bomb was mistakenly dropped on the mosque adjoining the district centre. The building was empty, but the blunder created fury among the town elders. The normally genial demeanour of Coco the police chief vanished. It took all the diplomatic skills of Major Lars Ulslev, the Danish officer who had now taken over command of the base, to convince him that the mosque was not the intended target. Eventually Coco was persuaded, and set about explaining to both his men and the remnants of the population that the bombing was an accident and that the soldiers would repair the damage.

The Danish OC requested a *shura* to apologise directly to the town elders and promised that Coalition money would fund the rebuilding. They asked him whether those who were left should leave town and let the Taliban and the Coalition force slug it out. Ulslev replied that they should stay. However many chose to ignore the advice and over the next weeks the remaining population of Musa Qaleh slipped away, leaving it eerie and empty, save for the Taliban.

By the end of July the town and its surrounds were, in Wight-Boycott's opinion, the Taliban's 'centre of gravity in the region'. For this reason it was all the more important not to abandon the base. He suggested to Ed Butler that a battle group operation should be launched into the area to close down the insurgents' main supply routes either side of the town. Inevitably, this would suck in Taliban forces from outside, who could then be destroyed on ground of the Coalition forces' choosing. He also emphasised that this 'kinetic' operation should be balanced by a peaceful initiative – rebuilding the bomb-blasted mosque.

The deadly danger the Taliban posed to any battle group movement in the area was demonstrated on 1 August when a patrol of D Squadron HCR was ambushed in a village near Musa Qaleh as it attempted to relieve some of the Taliban pressure on the town. It was commanded by Captain Alex Eida, who was serving with 7 RHA. He was travelling in a Spartan light reconnaissance armoured personnel carrier when it was blown up by a roadside bomb. The vehicle was then hit by RPGs and heavy machine guns. Eida was killed, along with Second Lieutenant Ralph Johnson and Lance Corporal Ross Nicholls of the HCR.

A Scimitar light tank managed to escape the ambush and turned back to go to the aid of the stricken Spartan. It too was soon hit by several RPGs and ran into a ditch. The commander, Corporal of Horse Michael Flynn, ordered the crew to dismount and shoot their way out. As they passed the smoking wreck of the the Spartan it seemed that everyone in it was dead. But Lance Corporal of Horse Andrew Radford, twenty-five, who was some way from the ambush site, could see that the driver had managed to get clear. In what was described in the citation for the Conspicuous Gallantry Cross he later won as an 'almost superhuman effort', he ran 70 yards while under grenade fire to rescue his badly burned comrade and carry him to safety. He was helped by Corporal Flynn, who was awarded the Military Cross for his courage. 'B' Company were then sent to recover the bodies of Eida, Johnson and Nicholls and to destroy any sensitive equipment.

Eida had been a particularly popular officer. Major Gary Wilkinson, the 7 RHA battery commander, was his superior officer and a good friend, and went on the mission to recover his body. 'He was an exceptionally competent captain among the strong bunch that I had,' he said. 'He was very outgoing and extremely popular with the soldiers.' Even by military standards he stood out as an adventure sports enthusiast. 'He was big on skiing, big on climbing, big on every outdoor pursuit, so a real dynamic, larger-than-life character.' Wilkinson found it 'the most difficult day of the tour for me'. He could not let his feelings affect his performance. 'You get on with it,' he said. 'You do it. You're a professional soldier and you grieve when you get home.'

The Pathfinders did not finally leave Musa Qaleh until 6 August. They had been there for fifty-two days. It took a full-scale battle group operation, code-named Mar Chichel, 'Snakebite' in Pashto, to get them out and a relief force in. The newcomers were from the 1st Battalion, The Royal Irish Regiment (R IRISH). Some of its men were already serving with their fellow Irishman, Paul Blair, in 'B' Company. Calls from the field for more manpower had resulted in two more platoons and a mortar section being pulled off leave and dispatched to Afghanistan, almost all of them volunteers. Tootal went along to command the operation. The plan was for the resupply convoy, together with R IRISH's Somme Platoon and mortars and the Paras' Patrols Platoon, to drive through the night to a lie-up position to the west of Musa Qaleh. At dawn they were to secure a landing zone in the wadi and set up mortar lines overlooking it for 3 Para's 'B' and 'C' Companies to air-assault in. The companies would then clear the ground up to the green zone. A Canadian unit mounted in light armoured vehicles would punch through the green zone and secure a wadi on the other side. There, the Danes would meet the reinforcements and bring them into the base.

R IRISH's 81mm mortars were commanded by Corporal Danny Groves. The Royal Irish came from both sides of the island but Groves was a Brummie. He was efficient, cheerful, optimistic and observant, all of which is revealed in the diary he kept of the exploits of his eighty-five comrades, the 'Band of Musa Muckers'. Groves set up his mortar barrels on high ground overlooking the town while Somme Platoon moved out to secure the landing zone. While this was going on, a Taliban target was identified. The mortars of the Irish opened up. It was, as Groves proudly recorded, the first high-explosive round the regiment had fired in anger since the Korean War.

The battle group was supported by helicopters and bombers. The move into town opened with the dropping of a 500lb bomb at the start of the operation, 'giving the Taliban the good news', as the grim joke had it.

'B' and 'C' Companies then started moving through compounds to secure either side of the road that led through the green zone, using explosive 'mousehole' charges to blast through mud walls where they came across them. Once the road was in the Paras' hands, explosive experts from the engineers combed the route into town for IEDs.

While this was going on the Pathfinders were preparing to leave. It was the Danes' job to secure a 300-yard stretch of the road that led westwards up to the wadi and the landing zone. It took them three-quarters of an hour longer than planned to do so. When they finally succeeded, the Pathfinders drove out. They were saying a thankful goodbye to Musa Qaleh. When the time came, Groves and the mortar team descended from the wadi and joined their mates. The Canadian armour pressed forward to lead the way and the Royal Irish crammed into Pinzgauers and set off behind them. It seemed incredible that any Taliban fighter could still be alive in the green zone. But as the first wave of resupply vehicles returning from the district centre crossed back over the wadi, a gunner from the Royal Logistics Corps (RLC) who was mounted on one of the WMIKs protecting the convoy was hit in the neck by a rifle bullet and was killed. Private Barrie Cutts was a member of 13 Air Assault Regiment, a specialist unit of the RLC trained to provide firepower and protection for the logistics convoys in Helmand. He was nineteen years old, a quiet, well-liked man whose passions were his local Nottinghamshire football team and his family. He had been planning to join the Paras. His CO, Lieutenant Colonel Neale Jouques, said later: 'He died doing what he was good at – protecting his comrades. He was a brave and exemplary soldier.'

His death cast a pall over what had otherwise been an extremely successful operation. The delay in securing the route from the district centre to the wadi had allowed some of the Taliban to move into firing positions again. It was a sombre flight back to

Bastion. Barrie Cutts's body travelled with the departing Paras.

As the helicopters left, the Royal Irish were settling in. Danny Groves immediately set about scouting for the best fire base. He chose a site that offered decent protection, good communications and 360-degree arcs of fire, and began bedding in the barrels.

They had been there for only two and a half hours when the Taliban attacked. Groves regarded this as 'the perfect opportunity' to begin adjusting their fire to achieve maximum accuracy. He recorded in his diary that 'it also gave us the opportunity to send out a clear warning to the Taliban: "Don't fuck – the 81mms are in town"'.

12

Operation Augustus

In addition to trying to battle the Taliban in the district centres, the Paras were also expected to do their bit for Operation Mountain Thrust – the continuing US mission to track down and kill Taliban and al-Qaeda honchos. On 8 July Stuart Tootal was visited in Bastion by Major General Benjamin Freakley. He was head of the Combined Joint Task Force – 76, the American formation charged with counter-terrorism operations in Afghanistan. As such, he was Tootal's 'two up' superior, one above his Canadian commander, and yet another boss to answer to in the Coalition's tangled command chain.

Freakley was there to discuss an upcoming mission, which had fallen to 3 Para. It was called Operation Augustus, and its purpose was to seize a senior Taliban commander who was thought to be operating out of a madrassa – an Islamic school – in a cluster of compounds at a location near Sangin. Freakley told Tootal that 'by disrupting the Taliban's command chain and killing and capturing the core leaders and fighters we will [persuade] the less committed that there are better alternatives than supporting the insurgents'. Tootal was partly convinced. But he still firmly believed that a major 'kinetic' operation like the one proposed had to be balanced by development projects that produced a tangible result. Not enough effort, he felt, was going into that side of the plan.

Freakley seemed a sympathetic soldier. He talked to 'A' Company about the loss of Damien Jackson, whose death was still casting a shadow. Jackson's body was flown back to Britain early on the morning of 9 July. The coffin was carried up the ramp of the C-130 by six men of Support Company. Tootal, together with the new RSM, John Hardy, followed it into the aircraft to pay their last respects. Tootal was glad to see Hardy. He had lost one good man when the old RSM, Nigel Bishop, returned to Britain after being promoted. Bishop and Tootal were close. They had served in Northern Ireland and Iraq together. But he was getting an equally stalwart replacement. Hardy was 'the right man ... considered, robust and straight down the line, telling you how it is and how it should be'. Hardy was a reliable guide to the men's feelings. He had decided against asking 'A' Company to provide the coffin-bearers, in order to spare their emotions. The 3 Para party paid their last respects, a bugler played the Last Post, and Damien Jackson was gone, though far from forgotten.

'A' Company were 'understandably shaken and absolutely knackered' after Sangin, in Tootal's judgement. But they would get only a day or two of rest. They were needed for Augustus. After more than two years in command of the company, Will Pike was due to return to Britain to take up a new appointment, but was anxious to lead his men into what would be his last operation. Augustus was going to be big. 'C' Company were also taking part, as well as a Canadian company mounted in eight-wheeled LAVs.

'This was probably the most serious one-off thing we had done since we had been there,' said Pike. 'It was certainly the thing that carried with it the highest risk ... we all knew what was happening now. We had all seen it at close quarters. No one was under any illusions about what might happen.'

The target was a cluster of compounds about 3 miles north-east of the Sangin district centre. The plan was to place an FSG on high ground to the east of the compounds. 'A' and 'C' Companies would then assault in by helicopter as close to the Taliban base as possible. The thinking was that by doing so the risk of getting caught on open ground on the approach was reduced. It might be difficult to break into the compounds. But once inside, they would have the advantage of the cover that the buildings and walls provided, and have a launch pad for the next objective.

'A' Company were to land first and capture the first compound, code-named 'Tiberius'. This was believed to be a Taliban stronghold. Then 'C' Company would leapfrog over them to the next compound, 'Claudius', which was believed to be the Taliban command post. 'A' Company would then jump forward again. So it would go on until all the ten or so compounds were secured and the Taliban chiefs inside them captured or killed. The LAVs, which were to move up from the south during the night, would link up with the troops and secure their flanks.

It was thought from the beginning that the Paras would meet strong resistance. 'We were pretty sure we would take fire in the landing zone,' said Pike. 'It was that sort of place.'

Five Chinooks took off from Bastion in the early hours of 14 July. Each one carried about forty paratroopers and one quad bike and trailer. They would have plenty of company in the air. The Paras had the protection of a Spectre gunship with a radar-guided 105mm artillery piece and 30mm cannon, a Predator UAV equipped with Hellfire missiles as well as its spying equipment, a modified Hercules fitted with jamming equipment to block Taliban communications, and Harriers and Apaches to provide close air support.

Chris Hasler was piloting one of the Chinooks that was due to arrive in the first wave. He had decided to load on 200 kilograms of extra fuel to give him more 'loiter' time in the target area. As he strained to get airborne he felt he might have made a catastrophic mistake by doing so. The engines dipped into emergency power, something they could only sustain for twelve seconds before they burned up. But finally he reached flying speed and they turned southwards, executing a feint to fool any Taliban spies on the ground.

They reached Lashkar Gah and turned north, then dipped down to low level, going into a holding pattern in a valley while awaiting the order to go in.

The Chinooks had expected to be held for only one or two orbits, but they were kept there for ten minutes, watching their fuel gauges sinking alarmingly.

The target area had been quiet the previous night. Now reports came in that the Predator UAV was picking up signs of intensive activity. There were figures up on the compound roofs overlooking the landing site, in a hedgerow that ran alongside it and on the site itself. It seemed certain that an ambush was being prepared.

Stuart Tootal was in the third wave, aboard a UA-60 American command, control and communications helicopter. It seemed to him that either the mission should be aborted or suppressive fire called in. The Coalition air force had been cued to strike as soon as the fighting kicked off. But even with the new rules of engagement, it was not legal to blast positions unless the men in them could be positively identified as holding weapons.

Tootal was unable to see the video feed from the Predator for himself and radioed back to the JOC for an update on what was coming in. The picture was unclear. He ordered one of the escorting Apaches to make a final sweep. The pilot reported back that there was no sign of activity. Tootal gave the order to press on.

The Chinooks left their holding pattern and raced into the landing zone. Hasler was in the third ship, behind his boss, Wing Commander Mike Woods. As he approached, the situation on the ground seemed quiet and the radios were silent, 'a very good situation indeed'. However, 'the good fortune was not to last'. As Royal Navy pilot Lieutenant Nichol Benzie put down the first Chinook, the shooting began.

'All hell broke loose around the aircraft,' said Will Pike, who was in the lead chopper, sitting next to Benzie. The sky was laced with tracer from heavy machine guns and rifles and with the fiery trails of RPGs. Hasler thought he could make out five or six positions on one side of the dry river bed where the landing site was located and four or five on the other. 'They were definitely dug in, definitely ready for us,' he said. 'They didn't just pick up weapons when the aircraft came in. They were there.'

There were yells of 'Abort!' coming over the radios but it was too late. Benzie was calmly settling his Chinook into the middle of the flurry of fire zipping across the landing site. The thirty or more Paras aboard were desperate to get off and away from the chopper, charging down the back ramp and jumping out into the darkness, which was now stitched with glittering tracer. The ground was boggy and rutted, entirely unlike what they had been led to expect. While they searched for cover an RPG exploded just below the Chinook as it lifted away.

Looking down from the second Chinook, Hugo Farmer saw the pyrotechnics and was comforted by the thought that the helicopter escorts were laying down suppressing fire. 'Then I oriented myself and could see that the rounds were coming in my direction. I thought, "All right, here we go again."' When they were 40 feet off the ground he heard the whang of rounds bouncing down the fuselage. 'I was just standing there, making myself nice and small.' Everyone was desperate to get off. The bottom of the aircraft was armoured but the protection ran only a few feet up the side. Private Steven Jones was one of the last in the queue surging down the ramp. Just as he got there a round pierced the side, hitting him in the shoulder. It was a lucky wound, missing all veins, arteries, bones and joints. His first response was to shout, 'I've been shot!' Then, according to Martin Taylor, who was next to him, he started to struggle down the ramp. 'I told him he was going straight back to Bastion but he wouldn't have it,' Taylor said. 'He was shouting, "I'm coming with you, I want to come with you."' Taylor ordered him to stay aboard. The others scurried through the swirling dust and dived into a ditch 25 yards away.

As Chris Hasler came in to land the third Chinook, he 'wanted nothing more than to pull in power and get away from that place as fast as possible'. But the first Paras were now on the ground. He realised that 'if I didn't put my own troops on the ground to bolster their strength they would surely be cut to ribbons'.

He continued his approach 'for what seemed like years. There was so much incoming fire and balls of tracer that he 'didn't realise how fast I was going until it was almost too late'. In order to slow down his helicopter he had to flare back while only a few yards from the ground, hauling the nose upwards so the belly acted as an air brake. It was a highly dangerous manoeuvre, running the risk of the aft rotor hitting the ground if the angle was greater than 26 degrees. Hasler 'managed to check the nose forward to just under twenty-five degrees, half a second before we touched'. It was a hard landing but they were down. Hasler felt 'jubilation that I hadn't killed everyone on board'.

A heavy machine gun was pouring bullets at them from a

position on the left, about a hundred yards away. One of the crew-men was trying to return fire from the Chinook's door guns but 'was having a tough time ... the enemy had sent out groups of women and children ahead of them while they fired over their heads at us'. However cruel the tactic, Hasler though it was 'quite effective as the enemy know British forces will not fire into a crowd of civilians and the Taliban seem not to care whether or not they hit their own'.

Before they set off the crews had been told that if they found themselves on the ground for more than thirty seconds they were to lift off, even if there were still troops aboard. Hasler now saw he had been down for more than a minute. His crew and co-pilot were urging him to go and he began to lift. Unbeknown to them, Flight Lieutenant Matt Carter, the principal forward air controller, together with Colour Sergeant Stuart Bell and Sergeant Webb, were still on the tailgate, struggling to unload mortar bombs. Rather than stay aboard and fly back to safety they all leapt into the darkness. Bell fractured one of his legs and Webb broke his hand. When Carter recovered from his jump he set about calling in fire from the Spectre gunship.

As the last soldier departed Hasler poured on the power and the Chinook lifted 'like a cork', pursued by 'big green bulbs of tracer swishing past my co-pilot's head at what seemed like only inches away'.

On the ground, Will Pike made a rapid assessment of the situation he and his men had landed in. It seemed to him to be vital to break into the compounds as quickly as possible so as to 'secure this baseline, dominate the landing zone and the area around so we could then have a stable foot on the ground that would then enable whatever else was going to happen to happen'. Hugo Farmer was commanding 1 Platoon, and Andy Mallet 2 Platoon. Pike sent Mallet and his men to the southernmost of the two compounds and Farmer to the northern one. The easiest way of breaching the compounds was by blowing a hole in the wall. They had arrived with combat engineers armed with 'mousehole' charges. These were simple devices – two bits of plastic cabling in the form of a cross with ten sticks of P4 plastic high explosive on the ends. The plan was to blow two holes in each compound wall. That way the defenders would not know which one the attackers were coming through.

The engineers set the forty-second fuses and retired. In UK exercises the safety distance for a ten-stick mousehole charge is 1,000 yards. Hugo Farmer was about three yards from this one, crouched in a trench. He shouted to his men to cover their ears. Then came the explosion. 'I wasn't in danger from flying debris or anything but I hadn't counted on how strong the shock wave was,' he said. 'It knocked the air out of my lungs and I felt dizzy, light-headed, and for a brief moment I saw stars.'

On recovering Farmer jumped out of the ditch, threw a grenade into the compound and ordered the first pair of men through the door. There was still some sporadic fire coming towards them. but the compound itself was empty. They moved through, methodically checking the outbuildings scattered around the courtyard. To the south, Andy Mallet and 2 Platoon were doing the same thing.

Apart from the odd incoming round the initial Taliban resistance had died away. The air over the target area was now buzzing with A-10s, Apaches and the Spectre gunship, which blasted any sign of insurgent activity. The two Chinooks carrying 'C' Company had stood off for what seemed to its OC, Paul Blair, like a long ten minutes before putting down. By the time they landed the firing had subsided. They moved through 'A' Company and on to their objectives. When they entered their first target compound they found a small group of civilians. If Taliban fighters had been there before, they had now gone. Blair decided that 'rather than us charging in' he would send forward a section of anti-tank troops attached to the company 'to try and find out what was going on and try to reassure them that we were not there to rape and pillage'.

By now the Paras had been joined by the Canadian company in their armoured vehicles. The senior Taliban commander they were there to capture was reported to be hiding in one of the remaining compounds. Supported by the Canadian LAVs, Blair and his men moved to check it out. In one compound they found a vehicle loaded with two 107mm 'Chinese rockets' of the type that had killed three men at Sangin two weeks earlier. They also found half a dozen RPGs. These were put in a pile to await destruction by the engineers. The vehicle with the rockets was blown up from the air by an Apache. It took three shots before a Hellfire missile finally connected.

In some of the compound buildings Blair found twenty beds crammed into a space meant for only six. 'A lot of people had moved in there pretty quickly,' he said. Whether they were farm workers getting out of the way of the insurgents or the insurgents themselves was not clear. But he reckoned from 'the look and the feel of the area it was clear that a Taliban presence had been there'. If so, they were no longer around. There was no sign of the 'high-value target' that had prompted the exercise.

By mid-afternoon there was nothing left to be done. It had been a long day. As they pulled back to the south to await the helicopters Farmer saw a big explosion south of their position. 'It turned out that even though we hadn't found much at the target location, the action had flushed out a number of enemy leaders who had gathered in a building three kilometres south of Sangin. The Canadians levelled this with two missiles.' If Augustus had been an anticlimax it had at least 'achieved this side effect ... even though what we were looking for wasn't there, it had the effect of high-lighting them in another location'.

The 3 Para battle group had certainly done what was asked of it. American gratitude for their efforts was slow in coming, however. Eight days after Augustus General Freakley arrived in Lashkar Gah for a meeting with the Canadian commander, David Fraser, Charlie Knaggs and Stuart Tootal. Daoud and his security chiefs were also present, and it was the governor who started the proceedings. He said he was worried that the Taliban were gaining the upper hand and that the feeble grip the government had on Helmand was in danger of being prised loose. Freakley then turned to the others and asked them what they were going to do to answer Daoud's concerns. In the opinion of one who was present the American gave an 'emotive and bombastic' performance. He made it clear that, in his view, the British were not doing enough. In fact, given their superior numbers and weight of equipment, they were doing less than any of the other Coalition partners in the province.

Tootal rose to the challenge. He replied that by answering the governor's demands the British had gone far beyond the task they were originally given and had dangerously stretched their resources. It was still possible to do more, but only if compensating reductions were made on their existing responsibilities in the platoon houses. By that, he meant pulling out of Now Zad.

13

Eating Dust

While the commanders were meeting in Kandahar, the defenders of the Now Zad platoon house were enduring yet another day of attacks. The district centre, 40 long miles to the north of Bastion, had become the hottest spot in Helmand. The town was empty except for the fighters, and Now Zad was an eerie arena, where a sinister silence alternated with the eruption of gunfire and the earth-shaking detonation of bombs. Inside the compound, 200 yards square, twenty-five Gurkhas pitted themselves against scores, some-times hundreds, of Taliban, who attacked with relentless determin-ation. In the week leading up to the commanders' conference, Now Zad had been attacked thirty-five times. On 16 July, an average day, the fighting opened at breakfast time with sniper shots which continued throughout the morning. In between, the Taliban fired mortar bombs into the base. In the afternoon they sneaked into a clinic 20 yards from the southern wall and opened up from there. Shortly afterwards, they launched a volley of RPG fire at Sangar Three, on the south-east corner of the compound, before signing off with a last firefight as dusk descended.

Now Zad had become a classic example of the unintended conse-quences of the platoon house strategy. It had been the first outpost the Paras had reinforced in answer to the pleas of Governor Daoud. When 'B' Company arrived there on 22 May, it seemed that his con-cern that 'the black flag of Mullah Omar' would shortly be fluttering over the district centre was exaggerated.

Now the threat was serious. Whether that was due to the arrival of the British troops or would have happened anyway was a question that would never be answered. But the fact was that, while the deployment may have asserted the government's authority in the area, it also presented a challenge that the Taliban appeared unable to resist. Afterwards this would be presented as a positive development. The platoon houses were candles on which the insurgents seemed fatally eager to burn their wings. That was not how it struck the beleaguered force at Now Zad. The defenders of the compound felt vulnerable and isolated. Worst of all, they were stuck, fixed, unable to manoeuvre. The situation favoured the attackers. By the beginning of July the Taliban had the run of the town and were able to strike when they liked. Their objectives were limited and seemed achievable. By killing one Coalition soldier they could claim a minor propaganda victory. By killing thirty or forty aboard one of the helicopters that had to fly in to sustain the garrison – always a real possibility – they could significantly undermine Britain's willingness to sustain the platoon house strategy. Looking at it coolly, the Gurkhas concluded that, given the choice, they would rather be in the attackers' boots than their own.

The Para deployment in Now Zad had been brief. Giles Timms and his men moved out after a few days and a platoon of the Gurkhas' 'D' Company moved in. The local Taliban had been hit hard during Operation Mutay at the beginning of June, and the town stayed quiet for the rest of the month. But as the month wore on the Gurkhas began to notice some ominous changes. Initially, life flowed along, placid and unmenacing. The local people took little notice of the newcomers. A few were openly hostile. Most were indifferent. The pick-up trucks, loaded with crops and goods, came and went to the weekly open-air bazaar, which stretched along the town's main north–south road. But as the weeks passed, there were fewer and fewer people on the streets. The bazaar closed down. Then, on 28 June, the Taliban fired a mortar at the ANP post on the top of the hill south of the compound, causing no injury but marking the start of hostilities.

'ANP Hill', as it became known, was a key point for attackers and defenders alike. It looked out over the base and the town, giving anyone who held it a strong tactical advantage. It also dominated the patch of desert to the south-west of the district centre, where the helicopters came in.

The district centre was on the western edge of town, about a thousand yards from the hill. Inside the walls were a main building, a prison, a mosque and some offices and storerooms that could be used for accommodation. There were heavily sandbagged sangars at each corner, with one each on the main gate and the back wall. The ops room was in the main building in the centre of the compound. Each time the shooting started the OC and his team moved up from the ops room to a position on the roof known as the Control Tower to follow events more clearly. On 1 July, the Gurkhas' 10 Platoon were relieved by 11 Platoon. For the next month they would hold the fort, together with twenty ANA soldiers, overseen by an OMLT, and a mixed contingent of policemen.

'D' Company was commanded by Major Dan Rex, a quiet, courteous thirty-four-year-old who seemed to have a particularly warm relationship with his men. His father had run away from school when the Second World War began to fight in the Indian Army against the Japanese, before becoming a tea planter in Assam. Rex was born in India and grew up wanting to join the army. He first came across the Gurkhas when he was a cadet at Sandhurst and 'felt a real affinity for the soldiers'. He had spent his career with the Royal Gurkha Rifles and spoke fluent Nepali, perfected during a year spent building schools in Nepal.

'D' Company had been put together at very short notice. The Gurkhas were told only in January that they were Afghanistan-bound. They arrived in April, charged with providing protection for Bastion. The plan soon changed, to the satisfaction of the soldiers. 'We really wanted to go to the front line, rather than doing the force protection job,' said Corporal Khailash Khebang Limbu, a twenty-five-year-old who had followed his grandfather and uncle into the British Army. 'It's quite boring just standing in a sangar. I wanted to fight with the enemy. All the Gurkhas wanted to fight the enemy.'

By the time 11 Platoon arrived in Now Zad it was clear that their wish stood every chance of being fulfilled. By now the exodus of civilians was in full swing. 'It was rather a miserable sight seeing people in donkey carts loaded with their belongings, just clearing out,' said Rex. He had invited the local elders to a *shura* soon after his arrival. He had worked hard building up a picture of local politics and identifying those who wielded power and influence. The elders came to the compound and listened politely to Rex's 'passionate' speech about peace and reconstruction. He 'told them what we were there for, and I really made the point that we were not the Russians. I said to them, the last thing I want to do is use aviation against you'. He mentioned some possible QIPs that would benefit the town. Their response, though, seemed to him to be 'really ambivalent'. The locals knew that the British presence would guarantee trouble with the Taliban. As at Sangin and Musa Qaleh, they had no way of knowing which would be the winning side, and were cautious about deciding which way to jump.

One of the elders' main concerns was the conduct of the police. There was a mixed force of policemen in the base. A small number were from the National Directorate of Security. They carried out intelligence duties and were from outside Helmand. Rex found them more reliable than the ANP, who were local and therefore intricately involved in the area's opaque and complicated politics.

The elders wanted guarantees that the soldiers would force the police to wear their uniforms. This seems to have been so they could be more easily held accountable for their misdeeds, and also to identify them to the Taliban. As the British were finding everywhere, the ANP were hated, feared and despised. The Now Zad elders accused the local force of arresting boys on false charges and demanding ransom money for their release. Rex had found a young man in the compound prison when he arrived 'and released him because there was absolutely no reason why he was there'.

The alliance with the robbing, oppressing ANP did serious damage to British claims to be on the side of the local people. The Taliban, on the other hand, set themselves up as avengers of the ANP's crimes. One of the Taliban's first acts while infiltrating Now Zad had been to start a campaign to starve and frighten the ANP out. They intimidated the local bakery into stopping supplies of bread to the base and took potshots at the policemen when they left the compound to patrol. As a result, the ANP had stopped going out and were effectively prisoners inside the district centre.

The ANP's relationship with the Taliban was complicated, however. Some policemen had taken out an insurance policy by volunteering their services as spies in the British camp, and regularly tipped the insurgents off about the Gurkhas' movements.

Rex had told the elders that he had no desire to bomb Now Zad. But he was equally clear that if the Taliban attacked, they would be hit hard. There was no problem about getting the message back to them. Two of those present at the *shura*, he suspected, were Taliban spies who were taking advantage of the invitation to get a good look at the compound from the inside.

The insurgents made thorough preparations before starting their campaign in earnest. It seemed, from the pattern of their attacks, that they had carried out careful reconnaissance and knew the strength of the Gurkha force. They mounted small, probing attacks designed to reveal weaknesses in the compound's defences. At nightfall the defenders noticed the chink of steel on masonry. The Taliban were burrowing through the walls of the surrounding buildings to set up close-quarter firing positions. They also used underground irrigation channels, which were dry in the summer months, to move men and equipment around.

The first big attack started in the early hours of 12 July and lasted for six hours. It was intended to be a decisive action that would drive the British out of Now Zad. The fighting had begun late the night before when an ANP patrol surprised a Taliban team who were moving stealthily up the main road towards the base. In the firefight one of the policemen was wounded. The main assault was launched just after the Taliban had extracted themselves. Sangars One and Three on the eastern side of the district centre and the Control Tower on the roof of the main building were hit by rifle and heavy machine guns and RPGs. The Gurkhas' two .50-cals were on top of the main building and next to Sangar Three. Their heavy-calibre bullets were devastatingly effective in suppressing enemy fire, but the Taliban knew the exact locations of their positions. 'They had red-hot rounds bouncing off them, so to get on the .50-cal was bloody difficult,' said Rex. The pattern was repeated in subsequent attacks, and by the time the Gurkhas left Now Zad both guns had been hit so many times that their barrels were beyond repair.

For a while, all 'D' Company's men were pinned down and unable to fight back effectively. It was time to call in the aircraft. The Gurkhas had a Joint Tactical Air Controller with them, Sergeant Charlie Aggrey of 7 RHA, who requested help. Soon afterwards, American A-10s came in low, strafing Taliban positions amid some trees to the east and in a former school to the north-east with cannon shells and rockets, before dropping a 500lb bomb on the building.

Despite the pounding and the continued presence of aircraft, the insurgents returned to the school and resumed the attack. Rex was impressed. 'I thought, you're brave boys to do that.' Another 500lb bomb struck the building and the shooting, at last, stopped. The attackers had still not given up. A Predator UAV overhead sent back pictures of two Toyota Corollas, the pick-up trucks used by all Afghan fighters, drawing up close to the school. Yet another bomb was dropped. The defenders watched the vehicles catapult into the air and the attack at last subsided.

Any hopes that the Taliban had exhausted themselves were dispelled the following night. There was a full moon. Corporal Khailash Limbu was on Sangar One, peering into the streets and alleys to the north-east of the base, where most of the shooting had come from the previous night. In the moonlight he glimpsed four men 'leopard-crawling' along a pathway about a hundred yards away, steadying themselves with one hand and holding their weapon in the other. Limbu alerted his men. As they moved forward they opened fire simultaneously, killing three of the approaching attackers and knocking over the fourth.

For a quarter of an hour, quiet descended once more. Then the base shuddered as salvoes of RPG and heavy machine-gun fire hit it from several directions. Corporal Khailash's sangar was rocked by several RPGs that arrived in quick succession. 'They wanted to destroy one sangar so they could break in through it,' he said. 'When it happened, I thought at first we were all going to die.' The temptation to fall back was strong but the men in the sangars fought it. 'We were thinking about our grandfathers, about the old generations,' said

Khailash. He and his men held their ground. It was impossible to see what was happening. At one point he felt sure the Taliban were at the foot of his sangar and jumped forward to throw two grenades over the wall.

For twenty minutes an unbroken stream of Taliban fire cracked and thumped into the compound. Movement was almost impossible. Then, slowly, the Gurkhas began to regain the initiative. For those in the sangars it was a question of summoning up the courage to get into a firing position and shoot back, forcing the attackers to take cover themselves, creating a few seconds' grace that would allow another soldier to join in, increasing the weight of fire incrementally until they were winning the firefight. The shooting went on and on.

Inside the compound the atmosphere between the British and their supposed allies was rapidly curdling. Rex's suspicions of the ANP had hardened to the point where he had accused them of communicating with the Taliban. As the din grew louder, the police started 'behaving extremely suspiciously and fingering their weapons'. Rex took the precaution of removing the police chief's radio and 'politely' putting him under guard.

It was only after two and a half hours that the battle faded out. An American A-10 arrived to drop a 500lb bomb and shoot up the Taliban lines to the north. As the shooting died away Rex toured the sangars. He was astonished and delighted to find that no one had been hurt or killed. He wrote later, 'we lost some of our nine lives that night, and had the Taliban been more accurate with their RPGs we would have been in for a very close fight'.

The Taliban were extraordinarily bad shots and seemed to believe that weight of fire was more important than where they aimed their weapons. But there was no doubt that the defenders had been extremely lucky. They had done their best to build up the sangars and to site the guns to give the best protection, but there were still blind spots which the attackers recognised and exploited. The Taliban controlled the town. Rex reckoned it would have taken a battalion to wrest it from them, and with his tiny force of forty men there was no question of aggressive patrolling. The insurgents could attack when they wanted. The garrison was particularly vulnerable during a helicopter resupply. Half the platoon were needed to secure the landing site, leaving the district centre dangerously undermanned.

The defenders had the great advantage of air power. Most of the engagements ended with the drone of an approaching aircraft and the seismic thump of a huge bomb. The defenders took great pains to avoid collateral damage and to comply with the rules of engagement. The air controller, Charlie Aggrey, risked his life to get into a position where he could eyeball the intended target and make sure there were no civilians present. There was only one minor civilian casualty during the Gurkhas' time in Sangin. The victim was shot by the ANP.

Despite the mad courage they showed in returning to the school building after it had been struck by a 500-pounder, the Taliban feared their enemy in the air. They had sentries scanning the skies round the clock for approaching jets or helicopters. But it still took an average of forty minutes between a request going in and an aircraft appearing.

Initially resupply was fairly regular. There was a flat stretch of desert about a thousand yards to the south-west of the base, in the lee of ANP Hill, where the helicopters could get in. It was overseen by the hilltop post but still liable to attack. Early on in the Gurkhas' deployment, a mortar landed close to a Chinook during a resupply, causing it to break off the mission and return to Bastion with its cargo, including badly needed engineering supplies to build up the defences. Later, as the service became more erratic, stores had to be delivered by 'jingly-truck', which was always a risky venture. One was destroyed by a mine. Another was a week late arriving. Supplies of food, water and ammunition never reached critical levels, although at one point the Gurkhas had used up all but 20 per cent of their ammunition before they were resupplied.

As for the morale of the defenders, there were no signs that the Gurkhas were wilting. They were fighting not just to hold their position but for the reputation of a regiment that was as dear to them as were their families.

One attack started with the Taliban advancing up the road from the south. Rifleman Nabin Rai was one of the youngest soldiers in the compound. He had been in the army for less than a year. He was part of the quick reaction force, standing by in the compound, when the shooting began. Rex ordered him to reinforce the sangar where the fire was coming in. 'In order to get there he had to climb up two fairly lengthy ladders that were attracting a lot of fire,' Rex said. Nabin then took over the .50-cal that was adjacent to the sangar. Because of its size, it couldn't fit inside, so he didn't have the same protection as he would have had inside the sangar. Bullets were hitting the sandbags in front of him. One round hit the barrel of the .50-cal and ricocheted off, grazing his cheek. Nabin kept shooting until the weight of fire forced him to duck into the sangar. His face was smothered with blood. The sangar commander ordered him back down the ladder for medical attention. Nabin decided to stay where he was. Frustrated at being unable to return fire, he dodged outside again and started to shoot into the swirling smoke, dust, debris and flame with a Minimi light machine gun. Crouched down behind the sandbags it was impossible to see the attackers, so he got to his feet and carried on shooting until a bullet hit his helmet, knocking him on his back. He sat up, smoked a cigarette while he recovered his senses, then crawled back to the wall and resumed firing. 'It was only three and a half hours later that I could get him out of the sangar during a lull,' said Rex. 'And even then he was very reluctant to leave his team.'

The Gurkhas needed all their reserves of fortitude to deal with the daily routine. Life in the compound, and in the pounding heat on top of ANP Hill, drained stamina and grated nerves. Rifleman Yam Roka Pun wrote a poem about it.

> This is the place where rocks melt into sand
> And the bitch heat blows it into your face
> For minutes visibility is zero
> For days you eat dust
> And for months dust will eat you.

There was a further heavy attack on 16 July. The assault was launched from several points around the compound and one RPG struck Rex's post on the ops room roof. A bullet hit Rifleman Barren Limbu in the left thigh. The defenders radioed for help and thirty-three minutes later one of the British Apaches arrived and hit the Taliban with 30mm cannon fire, very close to the Gurkha positions. The attackers managed to reach an abandoned clinic only 20 yards from the southern wall of the base and opened fire on the sangars from there. The Apache swooped in to shoot up the position, hovering 60 feet over the compound and showering empty shell cases on to the heads of the Gurkhas below. One of the rounds went astray, narrowly missing the 11 Platoon commander, Lieutenant Angus Mathers. The defenders then hurled grenades into the clinic from the compound walls, and the Taliban firing stopped. Later still a helicopter came under fire from an anti-aircraft gun sited in a building 100 yards from the district centre. It sent a Hellfire missile into the position, silencing the gun.

That evening, Rex received welcome reinforcements. 12 Platoon flew in with a small-fire support group from 'A' Company of the Royal Regiment of Fusiliers, who had just arrived from Cyprus. The Fusiliers were equipped with two mortar barrels and two GPMGs. Dan sent them up to ANP Hill, where the mortars could provide a significant addition to his firepower.

The Taliban continued their determined attacks until the evening of 22 July, when there were simultaneous assaults on both ANP Hill and the district centre. They were repulsed by a bombing and gun run by an A-10. After that the insurgents changed their tactics. Even the Taliban had limits to how many casualties they could take before they became disheartened.

Towards the end of the period of heavy fighting, Rex had tried to get the Taliban commanders to see sense and back off. He sent a message via an interpreter: 'I said to them, "Look, you have two paths here." I suggested that we'd been quite lenient so far and I was going to take the gloves off next time. Actually, we were being hammered.'

On another occasion he used the fact that Taliban routinely tried to eavesdrop on radio traffic to trick the insurgents into identifying themselves. One night, a convoy of pick-up trucks appeared on the edge of town with their headlights blazing. 'It was extraordinary,' said Dan Rex. 'Like the M25.' It seemed obvious that they were Taliban, but the rules of engagement did not allow an attack without a positive identification. Afghan police were manning the observation post on ANP Hill. Rex got them to ask over their net whether anyone had seen the lights of the Taliban vehicles. The headlights were promptly switched off. The Fusiliers then targeted the convoy with their 81mm mortars.

Throughout this time the Taliban continued to harass the base and ANP Hill with mortar and sniper fire. The mortar bombs were haphazardly aimed and caused no casualties. After 13 July, however, the aim of the Taliban improved markedly and carefully bracketed rounds started landing in the compound. The suspicion was that an outside team was now operating the barrel. On 19 July, three rounds landed inside the district centre. Later 12 Platoon, sitting up on ANP Hill, spotted the mortar position and strafed it thoroughly. There was no more trouble from mortars during the rest of the Gurkhas' stay.

The Taliban snipers were professionals. Their positions were well concealed and set back deep inside buildings behind walls that had holes cut in them to allow good arcs of fire as well as offering protection. The snipers used high-velocity Dragunov rifles. They moved around from position to position, keeping the garrison in a permanent state of anxiety. To minimise risk, Rex ordered a stop to all unnecessary movement in daylight. One day Corporal Jack Cook, the OC's signaller, decided to repair the field telephone used as the secure line from the sangars to the ops room. He was immediately hit in the back by a sniper round, and had to be casevacced out.

The Gurkhas responded to the sniper threat by bringing in their own marksman. Corporal Imbahadur Gurung played a long, lethal game of hide-and-seek with his counterparts. He would lie up for hours in an elevated position inside the compound, watching the known sniper points and waiting for one of his opposite numbers to appear. He succeeded in killing three of his opponents, but

192 • PATRICK BISHOP

gunmen kept returning to the positions and were not deterred by regular blasts of machine-gun fire. In the end the firing points were destroyed by air strikes.

Close air support was fundamental to the Gurkhas' defence. They knew that they could usually rely on attack helicopters to come to their rescue when a situation began to slide into precariousness. That did not mean that their requests were answered without question. Rex once received intelligence that a senior Taliban commander had established his headquarters in a building to the northeast of the compound and requested a pre-emptive air strike. The request went all the way back to Permanent Joint Headquarters (PJHQ), the highest level of command, at Northwood before being rejected. No reason was given.

'D' Company left Now Zad on 30 July, to be replaced by the Fusiliers. Stuart Tootal mounted a 3 Para battle group operation to carry out the relief. The Gurkhas were thankful to go. In their time there they had fired more than 30,000 rifle rounds, 17,000 machine-gun bullets and had thrown twenty-one hand grenades. They had also called in numerous air strikes. As a result, they had killed about a hundred Taliban, while suffering only three low-level injuries themselves. This was a stark imbalance. The Taliban had thrown all the violence they could muster at their enemy, showing extraordinary courage and determination. The attacks eventually tailed off but never quite stopped. Throughout August, the Fusiliers would have to contend with intermittent mortar and small-arms attacks. The big fights had achieved nothing except the destruction of large areas of the town and the flight of much of the population. The Taliban had nothing to show for their efforts and sacrifices. The Gurkhas could commend themselves on their fortitude. The fighting they had been through was as vicious as anything seen in the district centres and they had stood firm. But whether their efforts had done anything to advance the original aims of the mission was another matter.

14

Hesco

In Sangin, the Taliban had mounted a different sort of siege. With 'B' Company's arrival on 3 July, the district centre started to look like a proper fortress. The ever-mounting piles of sandbags and the tangle of razor wire were unlikely to be breached by direct assault. For the next two months, the insurgents would test the defences night and day. But it was less in the hope of overpowering the occupants than in sapping their willingness to stay.

Giles Timms's men spent their first days making constant improvements to the fortifications. On 7 July, they filled sandbags and humped them around the compound, building up a 'super-sangar' on a building on the eastern side of the base. While they were on the roof, an RPG whizzed overhead from the direction of the bazaar. They fired back but the attackers had disappeared. Further 'shoot and scoots' continued throughout the afternoon. One RPG hit the building that 4 Platoon used as a dormitory, but fortunately the men were all on the roof at the time. As the Paras changed stag duty at 7 p.m. they were shot at from the orchard to the south of the base. They called in an artillery strike from FOB Robinson and shells crashed into the ground 100 yards from the compound.

The Taliban had been using the built-up area to the east to fire on the district centre. One building, which lay on the far side of the orchard, was a particular favourite. That evening, 7 July, Timms decided that enough was enough. He called in an air strike and shortly afterwards an A-10 appeared carrying a JDAM-equipped 500lb bomb. Joint Direct Attack Munition was a bolt-on guidance system which transformed an old-fashioned gravity bomb into a 'smart bomb'. The desired coordinates were fed into the on-board computer and, once dropped, the bomb directed itself to the target. It was accurate and inexpensive. Each kit cost £10,000, which put it in the bargain basement of the high-tech munitions supermarket.

Harvey Pynn, the regimental 'doc', sat huddled in helmet and body armour with the rest of the garrison to watch the show. The bomb landed 'with a flash and a bang covering our compound with dust'. He noted that 'it was great to witness such destruction close at hand, but it's not exactly what we're here for'. The ruins became a point of reference in the geography of the Sangin battlefield – the 'JDAM building'.

This was a drastic measure. In other respects, though, Timms favoured a less forceful approach. His inclination was to reduce the volume of fire pumped out from the base. This had the doubly beneficial effect of limiting damage to the town and the risk of caus-ing civilian casualties, as well as preserving ammunition stocks and reducing the necessity for dangerous helicopter resupplies.

He also wanted to avoid, where he could, the physical and psy-chological wear and tear on his men that came with the static busi-ness of manning a fort. During the (by now routine) Taliban night attacks, everyone was ordered to stand to. Timms tended to stand them back down again soon after the shooting subsided, rather than keeping everyone on high alert for long periods. This consideration was very welcome. The constant nag of anxiety was debilitating, as was the heat. It was stifling in the airless rooms of the compound. Some men preferred to kip outside, reckoning that the possibility of a slight breeze outweighed the constant attentions of the mosqui-toes and the occasional alarm caused by a 107mm rocket or an RPG hurtling overhead.

The Taliban had not repeated their success of 1 July and the Chinese rockets they fired resumed their customary inaccuracy. There was more confidence now that, thanks to the improved defences, if the insurgents got lucky again the results would not be as devastating. They certainly seemed determined to keep trying. Giles Timms thought they were 'on a bit of a high' after the rocket strike.

'It was pretty full on,' he said. 'We were in contact four or five times a day. Some days there were only a couple. Some days it would be six. The Taliban were obviously pretty buoyed up by their success.' He suspected the ANP in the base of passing the news of the deaths of Hashmi, Thorpe and their interpreter to their supposed enemies.

But on a couple of occasions the Taliban crept up close under cover of darkness. One night they got within 15 yards of the compound wall and had to be driven off with hand grenades. The defenders placed claymore mines in front of their positions. These were banana-shaped, flat metal boxes that sprayed shrapnel over a wide arc when detonated by a command wire. On the night of 6 July, as many as ten Taliban fighters were killed by claymores after they were spotted creeping up to the compound walls.

Mostly, however, the Taliban now chose to attack at a distance of several hundred yards, from the cover of the urban fringe or the cultivated land to the south. The Paras responded with .50-cals, GPMGs, mortar and sniper fire, the occasional artillery barrage from 7 RHA's guns at FOB Robinson or an air strike when the Taliban were particularly threatening. Some of the firefights lasted just a few minutes. Some could go on for forty minutes.

The snipers operated in two-man teams from the roof of the FSG tower. Craig Mountford, the thirty-six-year-old sergeant who had been frustrated at not having seen what he regarded as real operational duty, was getting his full share of action in 'lawless Helmand province'. He commanded a platoon of about twenty men, which was split into three sections of six when R & R was taken into account. Each section was made up of three sniper pairs. Within each pair, one sniper would man the gun, the other the binoculars, telescope or night sights.

The snipers' job was little understood outside the army. The primary role was, in Mountford's words, 'to take out key enemy personnel like commanders, radio operators, mortar crews, anything that is going to pose a threat to friendly forces'. But the teams spent most of their time working as observers, as 'an extra set of eyes for the commander'. They scoped out the ground, passing on information about suspicious movements. They were also trained to call in mortar and artillery fire if needed.

The British Army sniper rifle fires a 8.59mm round. This is considerably larger and heavier than the 5.56mm bullet that comes out of the standard SA-80 infantry rifle. It is equipped with powerful Schmidt and Bender sights and is clinically accurate up to 1,000 yards. Because of the tight rules of engagement, the snipers had to exercise great care before engaging targets. They were allowed to fire warning shots when they saw what looked like suspicious behaviour. After a while, the snipers worked on the principle that any movement on the edge of town after dark was suspicious. By now most of the ordinary folk of Sangin had left and the night belonged to the insurgents.

'Any light within the market square at night-time we kept an eye on,' explained Mountford. 'Sometimes we put warning shots down to stop people.' Occasionally, during daylight, heads would pop up unexpectedly on rooftops. 'Now you can't just go shooting people's heads off unless there is a definite threat there,' he said. 'It happened on a couple of occasions that you would see them, and the next thing an RPG would come whanging towards you. They were getting up, having a quick look, then getting back down and coming up with an RPG.' Mountford insisted on telling his men, 'Right, if you see any heads, just fire warning shots next to them. Don't shoot them.'

One day Corporal Andy Key was manning a sangar when he saw shapes moving behind a wall about five hundred yards away. Looking through his sight he could see a gunman in a black turban taking cover behind a wall. 'I just took him out,' he said. 'His mate was behind the wall and he engaged us with RPG and then ran off.' He felt some satisfaction at killing the would-be shooter, because 'obviously it stopped him shooting you or any of your friends. But nothing bad about it. Nothing like that. No way.' None of the snipers ever knew how many of their opponents they killed. A lot of the time they were fighting in darkness, shooting at muzzle flashes.

The enemy had become depersonalised. No one thought very much about the motivations of 'Terry Taliban'. They were too busy trying to stay alive. Someone wrote a poem on a scrap of cardboard from a box of rations and stuck it up on one of the sangars on the FSG tower.

> Watch out Terry, we're hunting you down
> There's nowhere to hide in Sangin town
> You shit yourself when the .50 cals are fired
> No point in running, you'll only die tired
> Got A-10s on call for brassing you up
> No food or water, we don't give a fuck
> So do one, Terry, you've plenty to fear
> We run this town now. The Paras are here.

The sentiments were shared by many in the battle group. The soldiers did not underestimate their enemies but they held them in contempt. 'We had no respect for them,' said Private Craig Sharp, a twenty-one-year-old from Portsmouth who served in Sangin with 'A' Company. 'Some of them weren't even from Afghanistan but had gone there simply to cause trouble. We all wanted to hammer them so we could put an end to the fighting, or at least make it easier for those who would have to follow us.'

Life at the base was uncomfortable and loaded with stress. The snipers often kipped on the roof of the FSG to save time running up the stairs when they came under fire. 'We didn't have luxuries,' said Craig Mountford. 'We just slept in what we wore, wearing our body armour … when it came to first light we would go downstairs and try and recuperate, have something to eat and go down to the river. Then try and get a couple of hours' sleep so that when it came to that night we were full-on.' There was nothing to do in the brief periods of downtime. Sometimes they played cards. One or two had brought along books. Otherwise the reading matter was restricted to half a dozen well-thumbed copies of *Zoo* and *Nuts* and some old newspapers.

Daytime duty was an ordeal. It was exhausting, constantly scanning the bazaar and wadi, the pharmacy area and the garages, scrutinising every movement, trying to establish who was innocent and who was not. The men stretched ponchos and khaki-coloured camouflage netting over the top of their sangar to try to soften the pounding of the Afghan sun.

The mounds of sandbags around the snipers' position got thicker and thicker. The sniper sangar attracted particular attention from the Taliban, who seemed to understand it was a prime observation post. One night Mountford was on stag with another sniper, Steve Hurst, when a protracted firefight broke out with a Taliban team who were firing from the bazaar area. At one point an RPG hit their sangar, bursting against the sandbags they had arduously installed that day. For a moment, the danger was forgotten as the pair of them peered over the front, oblivious to the rounds zipping past them, earnestly inspecting the damage to their handiwork. All of a sudden, the ludicrousness of the situation struck them as hilarious. It was not the first time that soldiers had dealt with the weirdness of battle by falling about laughing. 'If you tell someone who doesn't know about it, they think you're crackers,' said Mountford. 'But at the time it was quite funny.'

Laughter, behavourists say, is a classic response to fear, and there was plenty of reason to feel it in Sangin. 'What sticks in my mind', said Andy Key, 'was the constant shooting at you. Even when you went to the river to have a wash, the next thing you heard was a "whoosh" or the "click, click, click" of rounds and you thought, "Let's have some peace for once." But no, you had to grab your weapon, put on your shorts and helmet and body armour and go running up to the roof, still with the soap sticking all over you. It was just non-stop.' After he was nearly hit by the same RPG that struck the sniper sangar he thought, 'I really don't want to go on this roof any more, but I had to, because everybody was in the same shoes.'

Alex Mackenzie, the FSG commander who was sent into Sangin as 'A' Company pulled out, found that the constant danger ended up having a numbing effect. The first night he mounted the FSG tower a contact started straight away and 'it had been quite tasty'. But after a few days, he found he was getting 'slightly blasé'. By the time he finished his three-and-a-half-week stint he was thinking, 'we

Captain Alex Mackenzie (*front*) and Piers Ashfield having a brew at Sangin. The mug is made from a 'greenie' mortar bomb case.

BELOW: Corporal Jay Jackson on stag in Sangin.

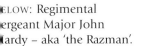
ELOW: Regimental ergeant Major John ardy – aka 'the Razman'.

RIGHT: Lieutenant Ollie Dale gets his head down n Sangin, surrounded by spent cartridge cases from a recent firefight.

ABOVE: The Pathfinders at Musa Qaleh. Their OC, Major Nick Wight-Boycott, is the tall man in the middle with the beard.

MIDDLE: Company Commanders Jamie Loden (*left*) and Paddy Blair on the roof at Sangin. The blast hole behind them is from the rocket that killed Corporals Pete Thorpe and Jabron Hashmi and Daoud, their translator.

RIGHT: Sergeant Major Mick Bolton in front of the Sangin district centre, carrying the standard SA-80 rifle. It was hard to keep clean but reliable and effective.

A mortar team at Sangin fires in support of patrols on the ground.

The tensest moment of any airborne operation. A Chinook takes off from Sangin under fire.

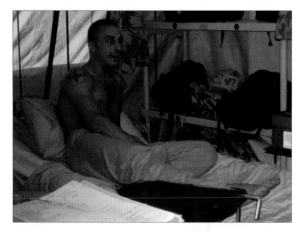

Private Pete McKinley recovering from shrapnel wounds in the base hospital. McKinley was not the most disciplined of soldiers at home, but he was a hero in the field.

BELOW: Corporal Bryan Budd on patrol in Sangin. Budd later died winning the Victoria Cross.

Rifleman Nabin Rai, one of the youngest Gurkhas in Helmand, after a contact with Taliban in Now Zad.

(*Left to right*) 3 Para's 2-I-C Major Huw Williams, Captain Nick French and a signaller at Musa Qaleh.

A .50-cal heavy machine gun inside a well-reinforced sangar at Sangin. This was probably the gun the Taliban feared most.

Lieutenant Colonel Stuart Tootal in the desert near Musa Qaleh. Whenever possible he led the battle group from the front.

ABOVE: Heading out to the helicopter landing site after a successful resupply operation at Musa Qaleh.

LEFT: 'Giving the Taliban the good news'. Watching an air strike go in outside Musa Qaleh.

BELOW: Sergeant Christopher 'Freddie' Kruyer, Easy Company's intelligence expert and all-round Mister Fixit.

TOP: Dinner at Bastion.

ABOVE: Major Adam Jowett, OC of Easy Company, chats with local elders. After fighting a long, fierce battle, his diplomatic skills cemented the Musa Qaleh agreement.

RIGHT: Hugo Farmer on patrol in Gereshk in full kit. Patrolling on foot in full body armour, carrying a weapon, a radio and ammunition, was hot and heavy work.

LEFT: Private Dave Prosser (*second from right*) and other members of Mortar Platoon. Prosser was badly wounded in the Kajaki minefield accident that killed Mark Wright.

BELOW: A *shura* in Sangin, under the big tree where councils with the locals were held.

Brigadier Ed Butler on the day of the official battle group photo – the first and last time the whole battle group was together – congratulating soldiers on a successful tour. The next day, companies began to fly home.

need to turn people around now. I need to go back because I have had X number of RPGs fired at me and they have missed every time, so every time I duck a little bit less'. The first time on the roof he had been crawling around, not daring to stand up. Towards the end he 'saw a bloke with his helmet off and people walking around and I thought, "Fellas, you only need to be unlucky once and the chances of that happening up here are high"'.

Mackenzie had noticed the effects of a protracted stay on the 'A' Company men before they left. 'It was attritional,' he said. 'People were psychologically, physically, mentally and emotionally run down.' The same process was working away at the mental stamina of their replacements.

The patrols that 'B' Company pushed out were no longer conducted with any intention of providing security, or demonstrating to the people of the town that they were in safe hands. By now, many of the inhabitants had left or moved away from the western fringes, where most of the nightly mayhem occurred. The sorties were intended as a show of will, a signal to the Taliban that the Paras' resolve was as solid as ever.

The patrols ventured no more than 500 yards beyond the compound walls. Inevitably their appearance would draw Taliban fire. 'It was an advance to contact, it wasn't a patrol,' said Mackenzie. His duties kept him on the roof of the FSG tower. But he watched with admiration and sympathy as the soldiers left the base, loading magazines, their thumbs flicking in anticipation at the safety catch of their SA-80. 'Younger soldiers were shaking with fear, every time they went out,' he said.

Like many, Mackenzie found that the worst part of being shot at was the anticipation of being hit, and the antidote to fear was the thought that you would be seen to be failing to do your job. 'The one thing I felt, as soon as it started, was "am I going to let my blokes down here?" I wasn't at all worried about getting shot. I think that everybody felt the same way, but particularly the blokes in a position of responsibility.'

Yet despite the danger and the exhaustion and the hardship there was something strangely satisfying about life in Sangin. Mackenzie thought it was 'the happiest I have seen the blokes'. At one point, the Taliban attacks slackened off. 'There were three or four days when there was no contact. I had never seen the blokes so depressed and bored. And then we got hit again and there were blokes cheering, whooping – absolutely ecstatic! It was amazing.' This was, after all, what they had signed up for.

But their situation was still precarious. The dangers of resupplying the base meant there were shortages of food and water. On 12 July the men of 'B' Company were down to sixteen boxes of rations, 'enough to feed one man for sixteen days', noted Tootal, 'but there are over a hundred to feed!' They were also reduced to one bottle of water per man per day. They supplemented this with water from the river. They boiled it and added sterilising tablets but it was hard to stifle the thought that the river had flowed past several thousand Afghan families and assorted livestock before it reached them. The daily food ration consisted of two boil-in-the-bag hot meals. The choices included bacon and beans, corned beef hash, Lancashire hotpot, curry and chicken-and-mushroom pasta. The Paras could also snack on brown biscuits and pâté, and chocolate bars that melted in the 40- and 50-degree Centigrade heat.

Tootal had toyed with the idea of a parachute resupply. It was a nice idea, but experience taught that getting the goods to land where they were supposed to was a difficult business and the exercise was likely to benefit the Taliban as much as the Paras. To get the supplies in that the garrison would need to sustain itself for a reasonable period would require a road convoy, with all the dangers that entailed. Plans for one got under way.

Despite the privations, when Tootal visited Sangin on 15 July he found 'B' Company in good spirits. It was the day after Operation Augustus, and the Paras' purpose now was to lay on a show of overwhelming force to persuade both the locals and the Taliban that the British were determined to stay.

The town was saturated with battle group troops. The Paras of 'A' and 'C' Companies and Patrols Platoon were joined by Canadians mounted in LAVs and 2 Troop of the HCR. When the Taliban saw the dimensions of the operation they prudently withdrew, falling back across the Helmand river to the north and south of Sangin. For the first time in weeks, the Paras were able to patrol in peace.

They carried out a clearance of Taliban positions and found a few RPG warheads and some bomb-making equipment. The insurgents seemed to have taken their stores with them. The exercise had proved that given enough soldiers, it was possible to scare the Taliban away. The problem was that there never were enough soldiers.It would have taken all of 3 Para battle group's resources to secure Sangin alone, creating the conditions that would allow reconstruction – or *construction*, as the realists preferred to call it – to take place. No one doubted that once the reinforcements departed, the Taliban would be straight back. Hugo Farmer believed that they would have returned no matter how many troops were present.

'Frequently, when something changed markedly, whether we had a different way of operating or we had different assets or more people, the Taliban would sit and watch. So I'm sure that if we had stayed with that number of people, they would have come back at us somehow.' For the moment, though, they 'were just standing off and watching'.

Tootal spent the evening of 15 July preparing for a *shura* with the local elders. It had been designated as a 'super-*shura*', a high-level affair, to be attended by Governor Daoud, Ed Butler, Charlie Knaggs and the Foreign Office representative, Nick Kay. Daoud had been reluctant to come, and it had required a certain amount of arm-twisting to secure his presence. British patience with Daoud was wearing thin. It was he who had pressed for the battle group to expand into the district centres. By agreeing to this approach, Butler had put himself in conflict with the Americans and in particular Ben Freakley, who was firmly against the notion of immobilising troops in fixed positions. The two men did not get on. Freakley disliked Butler's confident manner and determination to do things his own way. After one fractious meeting, the American told another senior US commander that he had come very close to landing up in Fort Leavenworth, the military penitentiary, so tempted had he been to 'punch that guy's lights out'. The British viewed Freakley as an outstanding tactical commander. But they doubted his ability to see beyond war fighting and to grasp the political and cultural complexities of the Afghanistan mission.

Butler had stuck his neck out for Daoud. Now he was expecting the governor to deliver his side of the deal and make a serious Afghan contribution to the effort of maintaining the British presence.

Before the meeting, Butler gave Daoud a warning. British and Canadian blood had been spilt on the governor's behalf and if he failed to cooperate, he could expect the UK task force support in Helmand to be withdrawn.

At the meeting, the elders complained about the continuous violence and the damage it was doing to the trade that sustained the town. Tootal could only agree. Sangin, he thought, was in a dreadful state. 'The town is a slum,' he wrote, 'rubbish and animal parts strewn everywhere.' The need to fulfil the promises of non-military help that had been made so frequently was acute. But, as always, nothing lasting could be achieved without security. An ITN news crew had flown up with the *shura* team. When interviewed, Tootal took the opportunity to try to counter the perception that was growing back home that the Paras were desperate, demoralised and on the point of defeat. This had partly been created by alarmist newspaper reports on the ration shortages in the district centre.

The supply problem was about to be solved, at least for the time being. A convoy was on the way, carrying enough provisions for thirty days. It was also loaded with engineering supplies to provide proper, top-specification protection for the district centre. Instead of sandbags and mud and breeze-block walls, the base's defences would be bolstered by Hesco Bastion. This was a British invention that was used at military bases throughout the world. It came in flat packs of steel mesh which were easily erected. They were lined with heavy-duty plastic sheeting and could be filled with sand, gravel or dirt. A 2-foot thickness would easily stop rifle bullets or shrapnel, though it was reckoned that 5 feet were needed to guarantee protection from an RPG.

The operation to protect the convoy went ahead without the

Canadians. Their LAVs were being withdrawn to combat a Taliban offensive that was developing in the south around Garmsir. The ANP who were defending the town were reported to have fled, leaving it to the insurgents. Tootal was sad to see the Canadian armour go. The LAVs were robust. They had eight wheels and were mobile and fast, capable of 60 miles an hour. They were also well armed, with a 25mm cannon, and were feared by the insurgents.

The convoy arrived in two waves on 18 July and got in and out without trouble. The Taliban watched it arrive but were dissuaded from attacking by the numbers of soldiers on the ground. The extra presence was clearly having an effect. Tootal decided to leave 'A' Company in place for a while to boost 'B' Company. It was unlikely, though, that they would be able to stay for long. The situation in Now Zad was becoming critical. The latest reports said that the Taliban had complete freedom around the platoon house in the town and that the Gurkhas who were manning it alongside the Afghan police were under enormous pressure. 'A' Company might have to go to their aid. There was also, however, another call on their services. Tootal had been warned by the Canadians that they might be required to reinforce the effort in Garmsir. The pressure to retake the area was coming from President Karzai. Yet again, the battle group's resources were being stretched in several different directions at once.

To add to Tootal's problems, concerns were now floating down from on high about the amount of ammunition his troops were expending. One communication from PJHQ in Northwood queried the need to have an artillery battery in Helmand. By the end of July more than four hundred shells had been fired in defence of the platoon houses and in support of operations. The news of Northwood's anxieties caused some bitter amusement. Did they think the soldiers in Helmand were firing their weapons for fun?

In Sangin, though, things were going better than at any time since the deployment. Patrols were able to penetrate parts of the town that had been off limits for weeks without fear of attack. 'I don't remember any shots being fired at all,' said Hugo Farmer. Some commercial activity was taking place. On the other hand, the attitude of the local people seemed to have turned to one of indifference or hostility. When they first appeared in Sangin the Paras had distributed leaflets printed with a Union Jack with Pashto text explaining who they were and what they were there for. 'Initially people would take them,' said Farmer. 'They were a funny novelty.' Later on, he 'would be handing them out as we were going around and some people would litereally throw them on the ground and I would think, "Ah, well, that's the attitude now is it?"'

'A' Company stayed a week without trouble. The Taliban might not be shooting, but they were still around and, on occasion, visible. Farmer was eager to counter them by mounting a deliberate ambush along a route that the insurgents used across a cornfield to the north-east of the district centre. It was a tricky operation. It was difficult to hide a platoon of soldiers for long. If you lay up, waiting for your victims to arrive, you risked being stumbled upon by a local farmer, or spotted by the Taliban themselves. The trick was to establish an OP that would give a last-minute warning of the insurgents' approach, allowing you to get into position fast.

The ambush was scheduled for the night before 'A' Company were to leave. 1 Platoon were all set to go when it became clear that the Taliban had got wind of the operation. Farmer was all for going ahead anyway but the decision was made to call it off and the platoon withdrew to the base.

By the time they left, said Farmer, 'Sangin had really quietened down. Things were looking up. It was still clear that people didn't like us and the damage had been done and we weren't equipped properly to change that … we weren't winning hearts and minds by any stretch of the imagination but we were dominating the ground by force.'

Harvey Pynn had done his best to show the Afghans the human face of the battle group operation. He had made use of the lull to provide a much-needed medical service for the town's depleted population. Sangin's one, shabby hospital had closed and most of the general practitioners had departed. 'There was no healthcare provision at all from what I could make out,' he said. Pynn put the word out through the base interpreters that he would provide basic medical care for anyone who needed it. He set up an open-air clinic by the front sangar. 'We saw a handful,' he said, 'not many, because there just weren't many people left in Sangin except our "enemy"'. Patients were searched on the way in. Among them were a couple of guys who came in complaining of 'global' body pain. Pynn could find nothing wrong with them; he gave them some vitamin pills and sent them on their way. He reckoned they were 'fairly blatantly enemy fighters who came in just to have a little recce'.

Pynn had another patient, however, whose injuries were all too genuine, and whose situation was a reminder of the civilian suffering that the fight the Paras were engaged in entailed. He was 'a young lad who came in who'd taken some shrapnel in the lower leg and then some nasty grazes and burn-type injuries. We brought him back every day for a week. We sent him away with sweets and he'd come back, have another dressing and some more sweets, so we treated him reasonably well. Poor guy. We'd obviously mortared a position in the town and he'd taken some shrapnel from that'. At least he was alive. Pynn believed that the same attack had 'killed several members of his family'. The fighting in Sangin and Musa Qaleh resulted in a number of civilian casualties caused by British fire. Such incidents were 'isolated', according to Stuart Tootal. 'That does not mean that they are not very serious,' he said. 'Unfortunately in close-quarter fighting in complex terrain there's always a risk.' The British certainly took the rules of engagement seriously and there were a number of occasions when they broke off engagements with the Taliban because there were civilians in the vicinity, or called off air strikes because they were not sure whether non-combatants were in the area. Nonetheless, every killing or maiming of an Afghan innocent dented the battle group's credibility and its claims to be a force for good.

Pynn left Sangin at the end of July, with his ideals intact, if a little bruised by their collision with the realities of Afghanistan. 'I deployed with a romantic notion that we could make inroads into security and reconstruction but I failed to grasp the conditions that make Helmand province such a difficult place to work,' he wrote. What he did take away with him was an enduring affection for his comrades. Medical Officers occupied a special position. They were outside the structure of the command and their healing vocation often gave them a privileged glimpse of what their charges were feeling. 'Working with the blokes so intimately at this level, one gets a very good idea of what they think and what makes them tick,' he wrote. 'They are a close knit team who work hard for each other. All they want to do is see this through together and get out the other end intact.'

15

Attrition

As it turned out, 'A' Company had only a few days to recuperate before they returned to Sangin on 27 July. They had not, after all, been required in Now Zad. Instead, they were back in their old stamping ground, replacing 'B' Company. It had changed a lot since they had first gone there. But despite the improvements to the fortifications, the place was just as dangerous as ever, as they were to discover on the very first day of the new deployment.

They arrived under a new commander, Jamie Loden, who had taken over from Will Pike. Loden had the Parachute Regiment in his genes. His father, Ted Loden, was a career soldier who won a Military Cross with 1 Para in Aden in 1967. 'I grew up living that life, in various nice places around the world,' Jamie said. 'By the time I was fifteen, I decided I wanted to join the army. To me it was a profession that offered you a challenge in three dimensions. It was physical and mental and there was a moral and leadership dimension in there too.' By now he was thirty-three, with a string of impressive appointments behind him, including a stint, post-9/11, in Afghanistan, as a staff officer with an American brigade.

Loden reached Helmand only on 23 July. He was strongly aware of his newcomer status. 'I was taking command from a very good friend of mine, and that company had already been through quite a lot,' he said. 'I would have had great sympathy with any soldier who said if I tried to suggest a way of doing something, "What the fuck do you know?"'

In fact the transition was smooth. 'He had a lot of humility,' said Hugo Farmer. 'He would say to me, "What do you think about this, what do you think about the other," and that was something I was not at all used to.'

The battle group operation in Sangin had strengthened the Paras' determination to deny the insurgents control of the town. Loden intended to patrol aggressively, using expanded platoon groups with beefed-up firepower. Unlike the Gurkhas in Now Zad, the Paras in Sangin felt they had the strength to close down the Taliban's freedom of movement. The aim was to find and destroy them and to dominate at least the area around the district centre.

The new OC wasted no time in putting the intent into practice. 1 Platoon under Hugo Farmer were sent out on patrol on the afternoon of the day they arrived, and Loden went with them to familiarise himself with the town he had heard so much about. The Paras set up a few vehicle checkpoints, walked through the bazaar, then moved on into the centre of town. It was relatively quiet as they tabbed through the streets. Mid-afternoon was the hottest part of the day and the inhabitants usually went indoors for a siesta. Among the patrol were a Pashto-speaking intelligence team who stopped twice to chat with locals.

By now, the Paras' nerves started tingling if they spent more than a few minutes in one place. The conversations seemed to take ages and they began to get impatient. Farmer sympathised, but was keen to know what was being said on the streets. Eventually, they resumed patrolling. The plan was to circle through the town, taking in all the points of interest, and exit by the pharmacy. Then they would turn south-west and head across the bazaar to the safety of the base. As they approached the bazaar, everyone noticed an ominous quiet. 'It was totally silent,' said Farmer. 'There were never usually that many people cutting around but it was totally dead. I had never seen the town totally abandoned before and this was eerie.'

Pete McKinley was famous for his eyesight. Now he spotted two figures on the pharmacy roof, clutching rifles and 'running along like monkeys'. Farmer ordered Corporal Bryan Budd to take his section, including McKinley, towards them. They had gone 50 yards when McKinley saw two gunmen dart out of a doorway by the pharmacy. 'I brought my weapon up to my shoulder and dropped the first one,' he said. 'I shot at the second one but I don't think I got him. The next I knew, two other blokes popped up behind us. The fire was coming in from two places and me and Bry were in the open.' They both started to shoot back. In the firefight that followed, Private 'Eddie' Edwards, who was a stand-in from 2 Platoon, was hit twice in the leg.

Dan Jarvie was still in the main street towards the back of the patrol when he heard the shout of 'Casualty!' Jarvie was one of the most popular men in 3 Para. He was thirty-one years old, from a small mining village near Dunfermline in Fife. His father had been in the Black Watch. His brother joined the Parachute Regiment when Jarvie was eleven, 'so obviously that was where I wanted to go after that'. He had been a Para since he was sixteen. He looked tough and spoke loud. His confidence was reassuring. But what made Jarvie so popular was the paternal warmth he showed to everyone, officer and Tom alike.

Together with Corporal Stuart Giles, the medic on the patrol, he now ran forward towards the front of the patrol. 'It was like the gun-fight at the OK Corral,' he said. 'There were rounds whizzing by us, rounds hitting the dirt at your feet.'

Edwards had been pulled into cover. It was appalling what two rifle bullets could do. They had 'basically opened the top of his leg from his thigh to the knee ... from my initial assessment I thought, "Fuck, he is going to lose it"'. Giles applied a tourniquet. Jarvie and Hugo Farmer held the wound together while the medic patched it with field dressings, injected Edwards with morphine and splinted his bad leg to his good one. There was a short wait until the Samaritan, an armoured ambulance belonging to D Troop of the HCR, arrived. Jarvie tried to take Edwards's mind off his injuries. 'Eddie,' he told him, 'there will be no more fucking tap dancing for you for a couple of months.' Ten minutes later Edwards was in front of the new MO, Captain Phil Docherty.

After the first contact, Budd and McKinley had kept advancing, driving the Taliban back and creating a space in which Edwards could be treated and evacuated. As they moved forward, McKinley suddenly found himself lying on his back. He had no idea what had happened. Budd pulled him to his feet and they carried on fighting. Budd forced some of the gunmen back into a shelter used as a public toilet and lobbed in a couple of phosphorus grenades in an attempt to smoke them out. The interpreters reported hearing someone screaming, 'I'm burning!' As Budd kept coming, the remaining fighters fled, running across an open field under fire from the rest of the section.

McKinley was starting to think he had been hit. He called to Dan Jarvie, who examined him. 'I pulled his body armour down at the back and sure enough there was a fingernail-sized piece of RPG shrapnel in his back.' By now the fighting was dying down and McKinley was driven back to the base and, against his wishes, casevacced back to Bastion that evening.

Stuart Tootal and John Hardy went to see both men in the medical centre. Edwards's left femur had been shattered and the bone splinters had ripped the muscle from knee to pelvis. He would keep his leg, but recovery might take a year. He was sedated when they visited. McKinley was very much awake. Before the deployment Tootal had known him mainly for his record of indiscipline. Now it was his courage which attracted the CO's attention: at Now Zad during Operation Mutay, during the rescue of the ambushed American convoy on 14 June, and lately for the alertness and aggression he had shown in Sangin.

The Paras continued to push out patrols over the next few days, and invariably provoked a Taliban response. On 30 July two patrols came under attack. The following day another was shot up as it fell back to base. That evening, the district centre came under fire yet again from the roof of the pharmacy. A request was made for the building to be bombed flat, and duly granted. A few weeks previously Harvey Pynn had worried that the pharmacy, which also served as a GP's surgery, might get damaged in the crossfire. Now it was a smoking ruin.

Loden had to balance high-risk patrolling with the Paras' duty to protect the camp and offer some security to the Royal Engineers as they went about their work of building up the defences. The sappers were often called on to guard the district centre themselves when the Paras were out on the ground, and on many occasions were swept up in the firefights around the base.

'A' Company theoretically had the resource of the Afghan forces lodged at the district centre at their disposal. But, as elsewhere, their services turned out to be of very limited value. A platoon of ANA soldiers and half a dozen policemen were based at Sangin. The British were expected to work alongside them in as visible a fashion a possible, to give an 'Afghan face' to operations. The Afghans were often reluctant partners, however. The police refused to join patrols or even to wear uniform.

The thirty ANA soldiers had recently undergone training by Coalition instructors and were under the eye of an OMLT sergeant. They did not appear to have gained much from the experience. The Afghan platoon commander was given cash to pay his men but preferred to spend it on drugs for himself, which he bought in town. His men disliked and distrusted him and the platoon split along tribal lines into quarrelsome factions. 'They were going feral and threatening to shoot each other,' said Hugo Farmer.

Initially the Afghan soldiers were prepared to stand to when the base was attacked and mount the occasional patrol in town, where the Taliban seemed to leave them alone. When the engineering work required extra protection, Loden would send them to check on people traversing the wadi route that ran through the centre of town. They made use of their authority to 'take little boys off the street and round the corner and then go and wash themselves in the river. It was blatant. There was no disguising what was going on'. Most of the soldiers had no particular problem with the Afghans' sexuality, but the abuse of minors appalled them. Eventually the platoon commander was sacked. But if the soldiers performed poorly, the police were no use at all. There were further promises from Governor Daoud of new, better-trained and more reliable police. Their loyalties had never been clear, however, and in the first half of August half of them fled into town while the rest joined the Taliban.

This confirmed the low opinion the Paras had formed of their Afghan allies. Circumstances demanded that they try to get along with the ANA and ANP but it was hard to trust them, particularly the policemen. In Farmer's experience, 'every other hour someone would come up to me and say, "Boss, we are being dicked by this guy there on the roof, signalling to people over there"'.

It seemed to the Paras that they were now fighting a different sort of enemy. At the ouset, the Taliban had appeared to be a hybrid force. It was led by what were called the 'Tier One' Taliban, committed ideologues, who had a degree of military skill. Their footsoldiers were the 'Village Taliban', local youths who were attracted to the insurgents' ranks by the pay of 10 or 12 dollars a day, rather than puritanical religious zeal. Intelligence reports suggested that as time went on, the top tier found it increasingly difficult to keep the youths' allegiance. The insurgents' losses were painful. No one was able to establish exactly how many were killed and wounded. The Taliban carried their dead away and had a basic casevac system by which casualties were passed back to rear areas or over the border to Pakistan for treatment. But if British estimates were correct, sixty-three were killed in Sangin in the first week of July alone. Suffering on that scale made money an insufficient motivation, especially as the Taliban were making no visible progress in their aim of dislodging the foreigners, something they had boasted they could accomplish in days. The word being picked up by intelligence was that elders in the towns where the fighting was going on were starting to tell the commmanders that their young men were no longer available to fight.

As a result, Taliban leaders were having to bring in replacements from outside. Some were from other parts of Afghanistan, and a smaller number from Pakistan and elsewhere. Punjabi speakers were heard on occasion. The newcomers were militarily far more experienced and tactically smarter than the hired guns, whose marksmanship was poor. They knew how to fight, as the British were to discover.

Between 7 and 11 August, 1 Platoon patrolled every day. The idea of walking into town filled everyone with foreboding. 'No one really wanted to go because of the high risk of ambush on the relatively few routes in and out of the bazaar,' said Hugo Farmer. 'You could say they were reluctant. There were all sorts of arguments being raised about how it was not the right thing to do.'

The younger Toms were beginning to wonder what the point of being in Sangin was. 'They would say, "We are not having any effect here, we are going out for the sake of it, people are dying, there is no clear benefit." It is those sorts of negative attitudes that start eating away at the whole thing.' Farmer regarded himself as 'not the sort of commander that stamps on discussion and tells people to shut up … I would much rather they told me what was on their mind than going, "Yes, boss, yes, boss," and blabbing off to someone else'.

With Loden, Farmer explained to the men that 'we couldn't develop this siege mentality. We had to go out, we had to dominate the ground and not just hand them the initiative. We couldn't just be reactive.'

The men listened, but it was 'difficult to persuade the blokes when whenever they go out the gate they get ambushed, people are getting seriously injured, people have died and they start thinking about their R & R and home'.

On 12 August the Taliban carried out one of their most daring attacks to date, ambushing a 2 Platoon patrol led by Andy Mallet when it was only 40 yards from the front gate. The lead section were already home when a group of four or five insurgents popped up from behind a wall about twenty yards from Mallet and his radio operator and opened up on them with rifles and RPGs. 'That was a defining moment for me,' said Mallet. 'I was the commander on the ground and I had been ambushed.' They had taken every precaution, but the insurgents had 'still managed to catch us on the hop'. He and his section scrambled into cover behind a wall and he radioed the mortar fire controller for help. Once the 81mm mortars started landing the Paras returned fire, gradually subduing the ambushers. A Household Cavalry Scimitar light tank emerged from the base and began firing its 30mm cannon, covering the Paras while they hurried to safety. Hugo Farmer saw Mallet come in. 'He had the "thousand yard stare" look in his eyes and I think he was counting his lucky stars,' Farmer said.

Spirits were low that day. There had been another death. Corporal Sean Tansey of the Life Guards was killed when an armoured vehicle fell on him while he was carrying out routine maintenance. He was twenty-six years old, and the fourth to die in the time that 'A' Company had spent in Sangin.

The Paras also were having to endure repeated strikes on the base with 107mm Chinese rockets of the type that killed three men on 1 July. They were mostly fired from a treeline to the north, which the men nicknamed 'Wombat Wood'.

They improvised constantly to improve their security. The path into town was blocked at several points by thick mud walls, which dictated which route the Paras took when they went out on patrol. This made their movements predictable and liable to ambush. They tried to solve the problem by blasting holes through the obstacles using bar mines, to create new approaches. Bar mines were five times as powerful as mousehole charges. They needed to be, as the mud-brick construction was incredibly tough. On 14 August Farmer led a patrol to clear a new route. He asked the engineers to blow a gap in one wall 'big enough to drive a vehicle through'. They decided to use three bar mines. They set the fuse and everyone took cover. The marketplace appeared to be empty, then suddenly Farmer noticed two men on a motorbike driving towards them. 'I stood up and shouted at them to stop,' he said. 'They didn't understand at first but then they did stop and just stood there watching us.' All of a sudden there was 'the biggest explosion … a massive boom and you saw the shock wave go through the valley and the dust kicking up'. The two men were knocked off their feet by the blast, to the amusement of the Paras. If they had come any farther they would almost certainly have been killed.

The engineers' activities building up the camp inevitably attracted the attention of the Taliban, who would harass them with fire. During August the sappers built the Hesco wall, complete with sangars, around the base. To the south, they cut back the corn and maize fields surrounding the helicopter landing site to a distance of 100 yards, robbing the Taliban of cover. Despite this, the HLS was still vulnerable, and on 17 August Loden ordered a dawn patrol to clear the area. The objective was to deter the Taliban from hiding weapons in advance of any helicopter resupply. One of the attackers' techniques was to cache rifles and RPGs in buildings and fields along likely patrol routes. This gave them the freedom to move around unarmed, pick up the weapons, carry out the attack, then drop the arms and assume the guise of civilians.

By now, the Paras had a reasonable idea of how their enemy were organised. It seemed that they operated in sub-units of about ten men. In the course of the fighting that summer the Taliban had evolved more sophisticated tactics, firing simultaneously from several angles and using a variety of weapons. Above all, they had developed very fast reaction times. Any patrol was 'dicked' immediately. If the Paras stayed still for more than ten minutes they could expect to be ambushed – hence the short times allowed for vehicle checks and intelligence-gathering encounters with the locals.

To counter the increased threat, patrols were now often more than forty strong. At three o'clock on the morning of 17 August, 1 Platoon tabbed to a lying-up position in the green area to the south known as the Gardens and regarded as 'Taliban Central'. At first light, a troop of HCR moved out west to the gravelly, scrub-covered flood plain of the Helmand river, to provide them with covering fire. Once they were in place, 1 Platoon began their patrol. The plan was to walk along a lane that cut through the fields, back to the district centre, searching compounds as they went. Before they set out they received an intelligence report saying the Taliban knew they were there. As soon as they started they saw two young men on a motorbike who appeared to be dicking them. Farmer ordered their arrest. They were grabbed, masked with blacked-out plastic goggles and handcuffed prior to being taken back to the base. While his men were dealing with the prisoners, Farmer glimpsed, through a gap in the crops, another pair of men walking along a path about seventy yards away. 'I didn't know who they were at first,' he said. 'I thought they were farmers.' They were 'laughing and joking, just two of them walking along'. Then, as they got closer, he saw 'webbing, AKs, RPGs, and not only that. I saw five guys behind them with exactly the same kit'. He turned to warn Sergeant Carl Lane, who had taken over as platoon sergeant after Dan Jarvie returned home on R & R. As he did so, the Taliban saw them, and the firefight began. Farmer called in the mortars and 1 Platoon started moving forward.

'Whenever we got in a fight with the Taliban, I always made a point of forcing them back,' said Farmer. 'Taking the initiative, showing them that if they are going to take us on conventionally then they are not going to win.' Things started well. 'This was a nicely coordinated, satisfying attack. The covering fire was going in well, the mortars were going in well, sections were moving well and it was all good.' When they reached the Taliban position the Paras found they had 'bugged out along a little covered route. We exploited beyond that, trying to find them and looking for blood trails, etc., but there was not much to see'. The Paras were 'a bit pissed off. But we had made the point. We had won, we had pushed them back and given them something to think about.'

The Taliban had not given up, however. During the fight, the two prisoners the Paras had seized were killed, apparently caught in the crossfire of the initial contact. One died on the ground, the other was shot dead as he ran away. The incident was looked into by the Royal Military Police Special Investigations Branch, who were in camp to investigate the death of Lance Corporal Tansey. They determined that both men had been killed by Taliban fire and found no evidence of wrongdoing on the part of the Paras. Farmer had not heard that the prisoners were dead until the time came to extract. It seemed to him that the Taliban did not know either. 'It was pretty clear that they thought we still had these prisoners with us and they relentlessly pursued us for a kilometre into camp,' he said. 'They were obviously keen to get back the detainees they thought we still had.'

The pursuing Taliban had been reinforced with fighters from the town. Other groups began shooting towards the Paras from several different directions. They were now about a thousand yards from the safety of the base. It was a long way in the circumstances. 'We were a big unit and we stuck together so they could target us quite easily,' said Farmer. 'There was a lot of dangerous ground to go through. If we got a casualty we were going to be in a lot of trouble.' The Paras dropped back, firing and manoeuvring, and called for help from the air. Two RAF Harriers appeared overhead and the team back at the district centre tried to guide them on to the Taliban position. But the pursuers were hard on the Paras' heels and the chances of a deadly cock-up were high. The Harriers were too fast-moving to get more than a glimpse of the ground as they swooped over. They did, however, open fire, at one point hitting the Hesco walls of the base. Farmer tried to help by marking his location with a coloured smoke grenade, but this only gave away their where-abouts to the Taliban and drew their pursuers towards them.

Farmer decided to set up a snap ambush. The platoon peeled off and turned to face their enemy. As the Taliban advanced up the path they were hit with fire which inflicted some casualties and slowed down the pursuit.

By now everyone in the base was involved in the drama. The engineers had stopped work and were manning two WMIKs, mounted with .50-cals, which emerged from the base to provide supporting fire. The guns of FOB Robinson joined in with salvoes of 105mm shells. The HCR had moved their armour to a better position to cover the withdrawal, but in the process a Spartan threw a track and could go no farther.

After a second snap ambush the Paras were able to break out of the vegetation and into the scrubby dry river bed to the east. The pursuers chased them right to the edge of the wadi. The sight of the disabled Spartan distracted them and they began to spray it with RPG and small-arms fire. The crew were still inside. As the Paras fell back, everyone in and around the base concentrated fire on the Taliban while an HCR Scimitar raced out to rescue their comrades and retrieve sensitive equipment from the stricken Spartan.

Once everyone was safely back in camp, the Harriers came over again, dropping two big bombs which put an end to what had turned into a very long engagement. As on so many occasions, everyone had been very lucky. Farmer thought to himself that it was 'an absolute wonder that no one died that day'.

By now they were wondering how long this could last. The Taliban were becoming more tenacious, more daring and more skilful. Their numbers did not seem to have gone up but the quality of the fighters had. It appeared that the Pakistani newcomers had more experience and imagination than their local allies.

It was essential to unbalance the enemy by coming up with new approaches. Intelligence reports suggested that the Taliban were preparing to plant IEDs on the Paras' well-trodden routes into town. The need to find new ones was pressing. On 20 August, 1 Platoon set off to find a new path through the area north of the base. It meant blowing holes through a series of compound walls. 1 Section, led by Bryan Budd, pushed ahead into cultivated land to the north and east of where the demolitions would take place. 3 Section, commanded by Corporal Andrew Waddington, and supported by a WMIK, moved out to the north and west. Together they would screen 2 Section under Corporal Charlie Curnow and the engineers who set the charges.

Budd was leading from the front. As he pushed through a field, shoulder high with maize, he saw a group of Taliban about thirty yards ahead. He used hand signals to warn his men and to prepare them for a swift attack. They started to move stealthily round in a left flanking movement. As they did so, however, the WMIK with 3 Section came under fire. The element of surprise now vanished. Alerted by the shots, the Taliban spotted the advancing Paras and began firing. The gunmen were invisible, hidden by the thick maize. Budd charged into the oncoming fire, followed by his section. Immediately, Corporal Guy Roberts spun back, hit in the shoulder. Private Andy Lanaghan was struck in the upper arm and the face. Craig Sharp took a bullet in the chest plate of his body armour, which knocked him over. 'I heard the buzz of the round a fraction of a second before and then it was like being hit by baseball bat.' His chest and stomach were burning. He put his hand under his vest, expecting to feel blood, but there was none.

Three of the eight-man section were down. If they stayed where they were, they might all die. Budd made a decision that cost him his life, but saved those of his men. By now he was close enough to see the gunmen, only 20 yards away. He ran forward, crashing through the vegetation, firing as he ran. That was the last time he was seen alive. His self-sacrificing action had succeeded. The enemy fire slackened and the rest of the section crawled back to a drainage ditch 25 yards away.

Hugo Farmer had been with Charlie Curnow's section, but moved forward when the shooting began and met up with Budd's men. When he learned that their commander was not with them, he and Curnow led 2 Section towards where the 1 Section commander had last been seen. 'We tried to move forward and it was clear there were enemy all over the place and it wasn't going to work,' he said. They tried a different approach, moving south, then flanking right and following the stream northwards.

As they advanced along the bank they saw 'Taliban bodies ... I could see two from where I was quite clearly. Someone had tried to patch them up, or maybe they tried to patch themselves up because there was cotton wool and medical equipment lying around.' There was no sign of Budd and no possibility of going farther, as the section came under intense machine-gun fire. The bullets were 'hitting rock, hitting chest plates and they were splitting'. Farmer got 'shrapnel in my boots, shrapnel in my chest plate and shrapnel in my arse'. Curnow was hit in the leg.

Back at base it was clear to Loden that 1 Platoon were 'now in a fairly sticky plight'. He had three men badly injured and another missing. He called Bastion for air support and was told that two Harriers were just arriving and Apaches were on their way. By this time, Bryan Budd had not been seen for forty-five minutes. Loden needed more men on the ground but was running out of soldiers. He had already dispatched a quick reaction force under Tam McDermott to secure the casualty collection area. He now scraped together a second platoon, plundering every unit that was attached to the base. He stripped out the sangars, leaving each one manned by a single engineer. The HCR troop commander and seven of his soldiers made up another section. The third was formed from four engineers, two members of the sniper team and the two military policemen who were still in camp. They hurried out of the district centre, led by Andy Mallet.

Their task was to advance to where Hugo Farmer and his men were pinned down and stop them being cut off from behind. The Harriers had arrived, but the air controller was unable to see the enemy and direct the pilot on to the target. Then an Apache appeared and the Paras' fortunes began to improve. Loden spoke to the Paras first then passed them on to Farmer, who was able to talk directly to the crew. 'I asked them to strafe the enemy positions on the other side of the stream and very soon after that they started forcing them back,' Farmer said.

The Paras were at last able to move up to where Bryan Budd had last been seen. They found his body lying on the sun-baked earth at the edge of the maize field, where the crops thinned out. The bodies of three Taliban lay around him. Four of his comrades carried him back to where a medic and quad bike were waiting. At first the medic thought he could feel a faint pulse, but it was wishful think-ing. They loaded Budd on to the quad and collapsed back into the base, while the Taliban harassed them with mortar and small-arms fire.

The engagement had lasted more than an hour. The death of Bryan Budd sent a chill through his comrades. The tempo of the fighting was relentless yet the high attrition rate the Taliban were suffering did not seem to wear them down. Every firefight, every contact, increased the chances of death or injury. Farmer found himself thinking, 'Right, I have had enough of the army now. I am going to sort this mess out and then I am just going to see my time out because I don't want this any more.' He knew what he was supposed to do: 'get the blokes to agree that they are going to carry on as per usual. They are going to keep on doing the job. That this is part of war fighting and no one said it was going to be easy, so let's just crack on.'

But at the back of his mind he was wondering, 'Next time I go out, is it going to be me? Is it going to be more of the blokes? Are we going to get into a real state and start getting a number of people killed?' Bryan Budd had seemed indestructible. If he could die, anyone could. 'His blokes had a belief in him,' said Dan Jarvie.

Budd was twenty-nine years old and a newcomer to 'A' Company, having just arrived in June. Before that he had served with the Pathfinders. He shared most of the qualities that made a popular soldier. He was, according to Jarvie, 'outrageously fit, outrageously switched on, with a mega sense of humour and very, very helpful'. But he had a noticeably gentle side. He was devoted to his wife

Lorena and their daughter Isabelle, and could not wait for the birth of a second girl, who was due in September.

The section commanders in 1 Platoon were 'very much the big brothers', said Hugo Farmer. 'They weren't heavy handed, they would mould the guys. It was a bit like a family, and Bry fitted in with all of that.' Budd was also outstandingly competent in a culture that prized professionalism. Farmer 'remembered a time we were being mortared and everyone went down to the basement to get away – quite rightly so. But I decided to go up to the top of the [FSG] tower to see where the mortars were coming from to try and locate it and pass it on to Major Loden who would call in air if needs be.' When he got there, 'who was there, already doing exactly what I was going to? Bryan Budd. That was typical. He thought above and beyond his immediate safety and about the bigger picture.' He was notably brave amongst men for whom courage was the norm. 'He would always be happy to go forward. There would never be any questions, any indications that he was scared and didn't want to do it.'

But what he was finally remembered for was his devotion to his life beyond the battlefield. 'He was different,' said Farmer.

> Every now and then he would come up to me with pictures in his hand of his family and he would say, 'Boss, this is my little girl, this is my wife, we are expecting another baby.' Whenever he put his bed down he would put up pictures of his family. No one else did that. They would have their magazines, books and ration packs strewn about the place, but he would have a nice, neat bed space and a picture of his family, and that is what he wanted to talk about most.

Budd seemed destined for a long, successful career. He was due for promotion to platoon leader. He was 'an outstanding soldier', in the judgement of Stuart Tootal. 'He died doing the job he loved, leading his men from the front, where he always was,' he said. 'He was proud to call himself a paratrooper and we were proud to stand beside him.'

An investigation was carried out into the circumstances of his death. There were suggestions that he might have been the victim of friendly fire, though these were not substantiated. A subsequent ballistics investigation could not confirm a match with any of the Paras' weapons. What was certain was that Bryan Budd had sacrificed his life for his men in an act of selfless heroism that thoroughly merited the Victoria Cross he was awarded four months later. 'It was rare to see the enemy when a firefight began,' said Craig Sharp, who was a few yards behind Budd when he ran forward. 'Bryan saw the gunmen and knew it was going to turn very nasty. He acted in the best interests of his men. He decided to precipitate the attack in order to save our lives.'

Hugo Farmer was due to fly out for a fortnight's R & R but offered to stay on after Budd's death. Loden told him to go and get some rest. 'A' Company, who prided themselves on their toughness and resilience, were feeling bruised and haunted by doubt. 'The company was at its lowest ebb,' said Andy Mallet. 'We had lost an extremely talented NCO, but also a magic guy as well. He was a big character and he was missed by a lot of the blokes.'

Mallet prepared himself to deliver the inevitable 'crack on' pep talk. He told the men: 'Right, you are probably not going to want to hear this right now, but we have to go out again. We have to find these guys. If we don't go out they have won.' He could see in their faces that 'probably all they wanted to do was go home. But over the next twenty-four to forty-eight hours they managed to find it within themselves to carry on with the job that needs to be done'.

There might be no patrolling the next day and perhaps the day after. But they were going to have to go out again. He told them: 'When we next patrol I need you to be on the ball, I need you to be focused on what you are doing. And they looked at me and said, "Yeah, when are we going out, boss?" For an eighteen- or nineteen-year-old kid to say that to you after some of the stuff we had done was completely humbling. That's when I realised that these blokes are a bit special.'

Their reaction, he thought later, was a fine demonstration of the Para ethos. It was the supreme manifestation of the spirit that they had shown in P Company in the boxing ring, and when they threw themselves, heavily laden, out of aircraft at night. 'At that moment, every man was milling something,' he said. 'They were milling their consciences or milling their fear, but every man found it in himself to jump when the green light went on, day after day after day.'

But the Paras, like everyone else, had their limits. The worst aspect of the fighting was, as Mallet said, the repetition. Conventional wars tended to be a succession of intense encounters. They were terrifying and exhausting but they were separated by firebreaks of time which allowed recovery, and a dimming of the memory of what was involved. The soldiers of the battle group were fighting a different kind of war. They were fighting day in, day out, facing danger over and over again, experiencing a lifetime's worth of trauma in a week.

Inevitably there were psychological casualties. 'Battle shock was an issue,' said Jamie Loden. 'There were guys who in the aftermath of particular incidents were very much shaken by what it had been like. As much as you could, you would try and rest them.' As a result it had been necessary 'to break up and mix sections together, partly because the wounded had removed the key commanders, but [also] because some people were being less effective ... in terms of asserting their command responsibility, and it became necessary to make changes in order to make things function properly'. Some of his men 'had made it pretty clear that they didn't want to go on. But twenty-four hours later they were a bit ashamed about saying that'.

'Blokes were saying, "What's happening here?"' said Private Craig Sharp. 'We were going out every day and getting hit, and some were wondering why we were doing this ... but it didn't last long.'

Commanders had a fine judgement to make when faced with a weakening of resolve. 'Leadership remains a balance of passion and grip,' said Loden. 'You have got to give them time to accept what has happened and then force them to get on with it.'

Only a few of the battle group experienced psychological difficulties during the deployment. But at dark moments, many suffered doubts about the value of the mission. This was not a war of national survival. The Afghanistan expedition was an aftershock of the earthquake the USA set in motion in response to 9/11. British soldiers felt little of the sense of outrage that burned in their American counterparts. As a result, said Loden, 'there were inevitably moments when some of them thought, "What the fuck am I doing here." I think that happened at every level.' The only answer was to crack on, not out of any belief in the purpose of the War on Terror but from a sense of duty to your mates, your unit and your regiment. It was the spiritual cement that had held soldiers together throughout history.

On 29 August a full battle group operation was mounted to get a logistic convoy and an air-portable bridge into Sangin. The bridge was to span the Helmand river and open up a safe route to the west. Operation Baghi was conducted by 'B' and 'C' Companies and the HCR. When it was over, 'A' Company would come out and 'C' Company would stay on.

It would be a potentially hazardous operation. In recent days, the Taliban had shown they were still determined and aggressive. They also appeared to have improved their fighting skills. The planning was detailed and maximum resources were mustered to ensure success. The HCR were to escort the convoy in. It would arrive from the east. On the final route in they would have to cross the open patch of land between the western edge of Sangin and the district centre. It was at this point that it would be at its most vulnerable. The plan was to swamp the area with troops to prevent the Taliban from infiltrating and attacking. 'C' Company would push down to the south of the town. 'B' Company would take care of the north.

That meant securing three buildings that the Taliban were likely to use as firing points. The most important was the 'Chinese Restaurant', so called because of its garish, pagoda-like decor. The other two lay slightly to the east. The job of taking the Chinese Restaurant was given to Lieutenant Ollie Dale, who had arrived with 3 Para only in May. He had joined the Paras as a soldier and had put himself forward for officer training. He was now commanding 4 Platoon. They flew in at first light and moved out of the compound a few hours later. Despite the recent fighting, there was still life in the town. 'As we moved out, very aggressively and all kitted out to fight, there were still guys walking about, going to the market,' Dale said. 'It was quite surreal.' He and his men waited by the ruins of the pharmacy while 5 Platoon from 'B' Company and 8 Platoon from 'C' Company moved out to the east. Before they had got very far, all three groups came under fire. Most of it seemed to be coming from the Chinese Restaurant and a wall that ran behind it.

'B' Company's OC, Giles Timms, was with 4 Platoon and requested an air strike. Shortly afterwards, a JDAM bomb thumped into the Chinese Restaurant. This was followed up with a strafing attack by two Apaches. Artillery rounds and mortars were also landing on the Taliban position, but to Dale's astonishment 'they were still firing'.

The objective lay across a daunting stretch of dusty, ridged open field. 'There was no way round it,' said Dale. 'We tried to put smoke into it, but it was still exposed.' The Paras staggered into cover in a compound by the side of the Chinese Restaurant and prepared for the final assault. When they reached their objective they found that the Taliban had gone. 'There were a couple of weapons and some rags but we didn't find any bodies.' The fighters had pulled back and taken cover behind a wall, giving them a good view of the Para lines. The Taliban knew what they were doing. 'They had prepared their positions well,' said Dale. 'They kept bobbing and moving around. One of my soldiers was rueing the fact that he couldn't zero in properly. This guy kept popping up his head but he couldn't make the shot count. They were behind a wall a couple of hundred metres away and we were shooting at them, trading blow for blow.' As always, the insurgents demonstrated an ability to use the ground to get in behind their opponents, so that even when the Paras cleared a position they could still expect to be fired on from all angles.

By now 5 Platoon had moved up towards the Chinese Restaurant to support Dale's men. Lance Corporal Karl Jackson and his section had taken up a position to the south-east. He could see a group of Taliban moving through a field to attack 4 Platoon. 'They didn't know we were there,' he said. 'The blokes opened up on them and destroyed quite a few of them.' The rest disappeared into the cover of the crops.

For a time the shooting died away. Jackson checked on his men then went to report to the platoon sergeant, Paddy Caldwell, who was lying up on a low roof with some others. 'As I went up to see them, they were all looking over the side. The Taliban were about forty metres away, moving up through an irrigation ditch sheltered by trees.' The insurgents had not seen them. There was a move to hurl grenades at the Taliban once they were in range but Caldwell stopped it. 'Paddy got on the net and organised 81mm mortars to hit their location,' said Jackson. 'Once he had called in the fire mission he said, "Right, as soon as the eighty-ones go in, we will open up on them as well."' The first mortars hit the ground and the shooting began. 'As soon as we started firing there was a crack which just whizzed past me,' said Jackson. 'I flinched and as I did I saw Paddy slumping back, like in slow motion, folding back.'

Jackson helped to drag Caldwell down from the roof and carry him to an irrigation ditch, where he applied first aid. 'He was grey, his lips had gone purple, so straight away I thought he was looking pretty bad.' The men struggled to undo his chest rig and remove his body armour to try to find the wound. There were two, one in the shoulder and one in the neck. They applied pressure to them while they waited for him to be evacuated.

The fighting was still going on and it took some time for the medical team to arrive. Eventually Caldwell was loaded on to the trailer of a quad bike and driven off in a Scimitar to the base. Stuart Tootal saw him in the aid post. Caldwell complained that he had no feeling below his neck. A casevac helicopter was called in and he was flown back to Bastion.

Operation Baghi had achieved its objectives. The convoy arrived safely and the prefabricated bridge was all ready for the engineers to install. It was time for 'A' Company to leave Sangin again. As they boarded the helicopters, everyone hoped that, this time, it was for good.

16

The Musa Muckers

The competition for the title of worst platoon house in Helmand was fierce. All the outstations were bad, but each was bad in its own distinctive way. The soldiers who had to defend the Musa Qaleh district centre were convinced that they had the grimmest job of all. It was partly a matter of geography. The base was claustrophobically sited in the middle of town, hemmed in by streets and alleyways full of lurking Taliban. The location made resupply exceptionally difficult. Securing a landing site was a risky operation. Musa Qaleh felt very isolated, and not just because of its distance from Bastion. It often seemed to the defenders that their plight was not understood by the folks back in Bastion. They were tasked with unrealistic missions. 'They would say go and secure this landing site,' said Danny Groves of the Royal Irish Regiment. 'But the buildings in between you and the location might easily hide a hundred Taliban. I don't think they had a full grasp of the situation.'

Groves arrived in Musa Qaleh on 6 August with his mortar section and Somme Platoon of the Royal Irish. They were there to replace the Pathfinders and reinforce the 1 Danish Light Reconnaissance Squadron. Denmark was supporting the ISAF mission and had agreed to lighten some of the battle group's load. By 8 August, there were about 170 troops in the base. The increase in numbers and the extra firepower the Danes brought with them did not appear to deter the Taliban, however.

At about 12.30 that afternoon Groves was talking with his friend Patrick Brannigan, the Somme Platoon sergeant, when 'a loud whoosh went overhead followed by a massive thud and a loud detonation'. He ran to his mortar line and heard that the mortar fire controller's OP had taken a direct hit from an RPG. The three men inside were 'a little shaken but OK'.

Groves was the odd man out among the new arrivals. There was not a drop of Irish blood in his veins. He came from Birmingham and worked as a landscape gardener, until 'one day I thought to myself, I don't want to be doing this sort of shit for the rest of my life. I want to go out and make a difference and do something worth talking about'. The local army recruiting office had steered him towards the Royal Irish, an amalgam of some of the historic regiments of the Emerald Isle. Its men came from both sides of the border, and although it was a new formation it had a strong identity and spirit.

The Danish squadron – known as the Griffins – were Copen-hagen's contribution to the NATO effort in Afghanistan. They were well equipped and lavishly provided for. They were 140 strong and were mounted in forty-six light armoured 'Eagle' vehicles, many carrying .50-cals. They also had a twelve-strong medical team with them.

The Griffins were specially trained for mobile operations and dis-mounted patrolling. Yet here they were, virtually stationary. Before they arrived, the Royal Irish had been told by their Para briefers not to expect much from the Danes. 'The impression we got was that the Danish would not be very aggressive and they were sitting on their hands,' said Groves. They arrived 'expecting to find a force who were going to be giving parcels to people and maintaining community relations. What we found was a force that was under siege.' The Danes were 'getting whacked every day' and could not move out of the compound. The attacks were so frequent that they gave up recording the minor ones.

The Irish and the Danes hit it off. 'Somme Platoon had a real natural relationship with them,' said Brannigan, known to everyone as 'PJ'. They shared their rations, which were much more lavish than the British ones, and also their abundant kit. 'They would give us their night vision goggles to go on stag with. There were no dramas at all.' The fraternising did not extend to 'Combat Barbie'. This was the nickname given by the Pathfinders to Anna, a notably efficient

.50-cal machine-gunner who was the sole woman on the base. It was said that she never made eye contact with a single British soldier for the entire duration of the deployment.

The inhabitants of the Musa Qaleh base were in a permanent state of tension. They could expect to be attacked at any time of the day or night. They were hit with every weapon the Taliban had: they were sniped at, mortared, hit with recoilless rifles, RPGs and Chinese rockets. The allies' best defences were the .50-cals and the mortars. Everyone in the battle group loved the .50-cal. 'Even a single round exploding over your head has a hell of an effect,' said PJ Brannigan. The Danes had eight of them mounted on the sangars. They also built ramps so they could drive the armoured vehicles up them and shoot over the walls. This created an all-round field of fire that had a marked effect on the insurgents' enthusiasm.

The Irish had two 81mm mortar barrels with them. This did not sound like much but they had an effect that was out of all proportion to their numbers and their low-tech specification. They were particularly useful in the special conditions of Musa Qaleh. The attackers were often invisible, hidden away in the compounds and narrow streets that crowded up against the walls of the base and out of reach of the machine guns and rifles. As in Now Zad, they had also burrowed through walls and cellars to creep up close to the base.

Mortar tubes delivered indirect fire. They could lob their bombs up almost vertically to crash down on advancing fighters. Being on the end of mortar fire was unnerving. 'It's horrible,' said Groves. 'You know it's been fired because you can hear it going up in the air, but you don't know where it's going to come down.'

Groves's team could easily manage ten rounds a minute, grouped in a pattern to create a 'beaten zone' which would kill everything for 40 yards around. The mortars had a definite deterrent effect. 'If you get ten of them in the air, in the general direction of the enemy, and they're landing, CRUMP, CRUMP, CRUMP, CRUMP, if it doesn't kill them, it's going to get them to stop.' The Irish mortars were to kill many during their stay in Musa Qaleh. By the time they left they had fired 851 rounds, one quarter of all those expended by the entire battle group.

But the Taliban kept on coming. Two days after the Royal Irish arrived on 6 August, Sergeant Ally McKinney was badly wounded by a sniper. Another soldier, Ranger Ricky Armstrong, was also injured. The shoot was followed up by small-arms fire, which was silenced by the mortars. After dark the base was hit with sustained heavy machine-gun fire. The mortars were in action again. 'As usual the Taliban shit themselves and hastily withdrew,' Groves wrote in his diary. The mortar team's day was not yet done, though. Reports came in of movement in the green zone, the lush land to the west, which was seething with Taliban. The mortars fired sixteen 'illume' rounds to light up the landscape for the benefit of the Irish and Danish snipers.

There was no respite. The next morning Groves recorded that the 'Taliban must have woken early because they RPG'd the Alamo watchtower [the OP on the compound's main building] ... I was already awake writing my daily sitrep and again I heard the whoosh-thud and saw it hit the Alamo.' Groves thought he could identify the direction it had come from and responded with five rounds of high explosive and two of white phosphorus. 'We then sat down to breakfast,' he wrote. 'Sausage and beans. Mmmm.' In the afternoon they came under mortar attack themselves. A duel followed which the Irish won. Intelligence recorded 'some poor Abdul flapping that he had been on the receiving end of some very accurate and heavy mortar fire ... Goodnight, Abdul!'

Groves had made it a point on his previous deployments to read up the history and background of the places he was going to. Whereas the rest of the platoon were volunteers, he had been called off leave to go to Afghanistan and had not had the time to do his research this time. He had no respect for the Taliban's aims, but a reluctant admiration for their courage. Like many soldiers who had fought in both places, he made a favourable comparison between Afghan and Iraqi insurgents. 'In Iraq, they didn't have the balls to come out and confront you,' he said. Their preference was for roadside bombs. The Taliban, however, 'kept on attacking and attacking and attacking. We were dropping one-thousand- and two-thousand-pound bombs on them, firing at them with Apaches and they came back again and again.' A story went round afterwards that a mass grave had been found near Musa Qaleh containing 200 dead fighters. That seemed feasible to the men who fought the Taliban. 'It proves the resolve of these people,' said Groves. 'How do you get inside their heads?'

The truth was that, living on their nerves and anxious only to survive, no one had the time or inclination to try to divine the motives of the Taliban. 'I didn't really care, to be honest, especially when they're killing and injuring your friends,' said Groves.

The soldiers of the battle group took losses personally. The death of Damien Jackson gave a sharper edge to the Paras' efforts in Sangin. The wounding of McKinney and Armstrong had the same effect on the Royal Irish in Musa Qaleh. Late in the afternoon, three days after the incident, one of the sangars spotted some fighters moving into a known firing point and reported it to the mortar team. They cracked open boxes of ammunition for the 81mm and 51mm mortars. Then, wrote Groves, 'all we were waiting for was the word'. At 5.35 p.m. they got the command to fire, and 'unleashed our most vicious display of mortaring yet'. Sixteen high-explosive bombs from the 81mm and 'countless' rounds from the 51mm hit the position. Groves recorded in his diary that the men on Sangar Three who had alerted the mortar team saw the damage that was done and reported legs and arms flying in the air. It was hard to say how many were killed but it did send a clear message. Don't fuck with the Royal Irish. This one's for Ally and Ricky you bastards. The Danish guys came down and said: 'You Guys Rock!!' [It] was the most awesome display of accurate mortar fire they had ever seen. 'You ain't seen nothing yet,' said one of the lads. 'We've only been here five days and we're just getting warmed up.'

On this occasion the Taliban displayed lethal incompetence. But they were also capable of skill. The firepower available at the base was unable to stop their sniping attacks. Aircraft had been called in to bomb suspected sniper positions but this still did not solve the problem. One night the officer commanding Somme Platoon, Captain Mark Johnson, went out on a joint patrol with the Danes to clear some possible firing points. The Danes had explosives experts from their engineer detail with them who blew the back walls off suspect buildings to illuminate the rooms so that snipers could not shoot out of the cover of darkness. The patrol checked for shell cases that the shooters might have left behind but found none. Good snipers took any evidence away with them. The patrol did, however, discover a sheet hung across a doorway to mask the sniper's comings and goings from his position. It was only 150 yards from the Outpost. The discovery suggested that this shooter had not only craft but courage.

The Taliban were almost maniacally determined. The losses inflicted by the defenders did nothing to slow down the tempo of attacks. Nor did the regular pounding they were receiving from the air. The battle group's tenure of Musa Qaleh appeared to be achieving nothing other than the steady destruction of the town, and the risks involved in staying there were high. Casualties were mercifully low, given the weight of fire that was hitting the place. That could not last. As always, the dark prospect of a casevac or resupply helicopter being shot down hovered in the back of everyone's mind.

The miseries of Musa Qaleh might have been more bearable if those suffering them knew when they were going to end. On 12 August, the Royal Irish underwent one of the ritual experiences of those who had successively manned the base over the summer. Major Lars Ulslev, the OC of 'Camp Shit Hole', as the Royal Irish had come to call it, announced that the camp would be evacuated in four days' time. This buoyed everyone's spirits until the date came and went and they were still there. The newcomers had yet to learn the bitter lesson the Pathfinders knew so well. Leaving dates from Musa Qaleh were very elastic.

The precariousness of their situation was brought home on the evening of the 'departure' announcement when the base was hit by very accurate mortar fire. The snipers on the Alamo roof thought they had identified the firing point and two mortars were fired in response, but they had no effect. Five minutes later two more rounds came in. Groves decided to move his team away from the mortar line, which was stacked with high-explosive and phosphorus bombs and take shelter inside a shipping container while they waited for the location of the Taliban mortar team to be correctly identified. In the meantime an A-10 had arrived overhead so there was nothing for them to do. They amused themselves by writing on the inside of the container: '1 Royal Irish Mortar Platoon took cover here. We hid like cowardly dogs.'

The mortars were doing a great job, as the Danes recognised. Lars Ulslev passed on to them an intelligence report that said the accuracy of their fire against the Taliban teams had led the insurgents to bring in a 'high-profile commander' with thirty years' experience of mortars as well as 107mm Chinese rockets, which had a range of about ten miles. The enemy had fallen back on stand-off weapons because they were no longer comfortable attacking at close quarters, he said. Their firing points out in the desert would, however, make them more vulnerable to attack from the air. All this was a tribute to the efficiency of Groves and his team.

This was all very welcome. But the mortars' success had come at a price. A warning came through from Bastion about the amount of ammunition that was being used. Groves knew from 3 Para that in the previous four months their mortar teams in Sangin, Kajaki and Now Zad had fired more than a thousand rounds. He and his men had fired 100 in just a week. The pressure on helicopters meant that they could not rely on a steady resupply of ammunition. From now on, he would have this reality in the front of his mind whenever he ordered a fire mission. The Taliban were making sure that they needed every mortar bomb they could get. On 14 August, Groves recorded in his diary the outbreak of 'World War III'.

'We were woken early again at 7.30 with our ususal whoosh! bang! RPG alarm clock,' he wrote. 'Sangar 4 opened up and we began … to engage with the 81, neutralising a few enemy positions. Word was then passed that the Taliban were fanning out in the field to our east and there were a fair few of them getting ready for an all-out assault on the compound. By this time we were down to only 33 HE [high explosive] rounds per barrel on the mortar line.' Normally they would have chosen to engage with the 81mm rounds. Instead they relied on the smaller-gauge 51s, which did not have the same effect. They fired about fifty rounds but the Taliban were not deterred. The attack faded out with the arrival of A-10 bombers.

But an hour later, intelligence came through that another attack was planned. Groves wrote: 'Just as we were planning a strategy to defend ... and also to make the 81mm last longer, an RPG hit the Alamo watch tower.' The next thing they heard was the familiar whistle of an incoming mortar. 'Just as we were bracing ourselves for the loud crunch, all we heard was a thud as the round made contact with the ground. A blind [dud]! Thank fuck cos that was close.'

While Groves and his team were trying to plot the Taliban firing point they 'heard another whistling noise and the shout of "incoming!"' This time, the round landed and detonated, ten metres to the right of the mortar line and metres from the Danish ammunition compound and just missing our trailer which was stacked with HE, Illume and WP [white phosphorus]'.

One Dane was hit in the leg with shrapnel and one of the mortar men, Ranger Adam Dunlop, was wounded in the hand. The mortar team fired back but the Taliban continued to pound the base. 'As we were failing to identify where the rounds were coming from,' wrote Groves, 'we had no choice but to take cover in the container again until the fast air arrived and as usual the Taliban fucked off.'

After the attack subsided, a whisper of what appeared to be good news ran around the camp. Word had filtered all the way from Kabul to Musa Qaleh that the incoming commander of ISAF, the NATO-led force that had taken control from the Americans, 'had decided that the outposts were a bad idea for whatever reason'. Troops were to be pulled out of them. And the first withdrawal would be from Musa Qaleh within the next four days.

The ISAF commander in Kabul was General David Richards, a Brit who was well endowed with the multiple talents, military and political, that were needed to go to the very top. He had inherited the platoon houses when he took over on 1 August, and made it clear that he was unhappy with the legacy. But getting out of a bad situation was far more difficult than getting into it. It would be some time before the extraction could begin. And in the meantime, the defenders of Musa Qaleh would have to hold on.

It would take a while for that realisation to dawn on the inhabitants of 'Camp Shit Hole'. In the meantime, warmed by their illusions, they eagerly prepared to depart. Groves got the first inkling that the joy might be premature when he gave his daily sitrep over the net to the second-in-command of 3 Para Mortars, Colour Sergeant Stu Bell. Groves told him about his dwindling ammunition stocks but was reassured that resupplies would be flown in soon. Initially, Groves 'was pleased that we would be getting some more ammo as we desperately needed it, but then I thought, "why do we need more if we're out of here in a few days?"' His doubts were confirmed when he ran into PJ, who was supposed to have flown out with his platoon earlier that morning. Later they heard, via Lars Ulslev, the reason for the delay. 'The regional governor of Helmand Province had made a direct plea to the Prime Minister of Afghanistan not to let Musa Qaleh fall into the hands of the Taliban.' They would be staying 'for the foreseeable future'.

Groves, however,

> couldn't understand what he meant. As far as I was concerned, the town *was* in the hands of the Taliban. All we had was a 100 metre by 100 metre square dartboard, at which they threw darts in the form of RPGs whenever they fancied. We couldn't patrol and dominate the ground as the casualty evacuation plan was shit and there was no guarantee that they would get you out of here if you got hurt. Unless we got more ammo, more troops, guaranteed casevacs and a new strategy ... how could the situation improve?

Danny Groves's analysis was based on bitter, direct experience. Political considerations, however, weighed more heavily with the decision-makers than the truth on the ground. It was fortunate that the morale of the Royal Irish was so resilient. Groves and his comrades were bound by bonds that were remarkably strong even by military standards. They were the 'Musa Muckers', and they took the bad news with the same good-humoured resignation and determination to carry on that infused everything that happened to them in Afghanistan.

They needed all the fortitude they could muster. It emerged that the Musa Qaleh garrison would indeed be relieved. But this relief would not include the Royal Irish. The Danish government had decided it no longer wanted its troops in such a vulnerable spot. The Griffins were pulling out, and fast. They would be replaced by the Royal Irish's Barossa Platoon and a rapidly formed Company HQ made up of 3 Para personnel. The Musa Muckers, however, were staying put. Together they would be responsible for the defence of Musa Qaleh, under the command of Major Adam Jowett of 3 Para. The new force would be the fifth company in the battle group and therefore took the letter 'E'. It was soon known as 'Easy Company'.

There was to be no let-up by the Taliban before they arrived. They hit the camp with mortars, RPGs, Chinese rockets and recoilless rifles. As the date of the Danes' departure got closer the Royal Irish began to realise what they would be missing. They had hit it off brilliantly with the Danes, sharing danger, rations and a Northern, ironic sense of humour. Jan the quartermaster was especially droll. One day they were under a particularly heavy bombardment. They had requested artillery support from I Battery of 7 RHA, which had just set up in the area, but the fire was a long time coming. 'What the fuck are they waiting for?' one of the Royal Irish demanded. Slowly, calmly and in a serious voice, Jan replied: 'They are waiting … for authorisation … from the Queen in London.'

Nor, contrary to the view in Bastion, were the Danes short on aggression. Whenever word came through that a Taliban attack was imminent the OC would call a 'Winchester', a two-minute blast at known Taliban firing points with every weapon at their disposal.

Now those weapons were disappearing. When the Danes left, the .50-cals would go with them. The new arrivals would be bringing only two .50-Cals and nine GPMGs, which, though useful, did not have the same destructive power and psychological deterrent effect. The twelve-strong Danish medical team would be replaced by an MO and two combat medics. Groves and his mates were not happy. 'We were just about surviving, with more men, better weapon systems and better medical cover,' he said. 'We were getting worse weapons, lower medical cover and fewer men. We knew we would hold our own. But imagine the effect that had on the boys who had been in contact two, three or four times a day.'

The Danes left quickly. Adam Jowett had only two and a half days to prepare for the insertion. Jowett was soft spoken, warm hearted and exceptionally polite. His self-effacing manner belied a robust approach to soldiering. He had got out of a staff job in order to go to Helmand. He had spent a month in Sangin, so knew the reality of platoon house existence. In the scramble to organise the deployment he took special care over the medical arrangements and insisted on taking a Medical Officer with a surgical background. He was given Captain Mike Stacey. 'I wanted the best,' said Jowett. 'I found out from his chain of command that he was the best and I insisted on having him.' Jowett also demanded extra supplies. 'I then insisted on an enormous uplift to what we should have had – rubber gloves, saline, intravenous fluids, morphine, oxygen, antibiotics – anything like that, triple it.'

The reinforcements arrived before dawn. The Chinooks carrying them landed in the baked-dirt landing site close to the district centre. Among those on board was Sergeant Freddie Kruyer, who came in with the company headquarters team. He was a thirty-seven-year-old Londoner and had joined the Paras in the late 1980s, intending to serve for only three years. His real name was Christopher. He owed his nickname to the razor-fingered anti-hero of *Nightmare on Elm Street*. He had acquired it on his first day in the Paras and no one thought of him as anything else. He was now a member of the intelligence cell. He had heard all about conditions in Musa Qaleh when in Bastion, and had mixed feelings as the helicopter took off. 'I was looking out the back door and you could just see Bastion disappearing into the distance and I thought, that's the last time I will probably see that.'

When they piled off the back of the Chinook and into the base he was relieved to find that it was 'quiet and peaceful'. There were plenty of shrapnel scars and bullet holes in the scabby masonry. But what struck all the house-proud Paras was the mess the Danes had lived in. There were empty ammunition cases and boxes of rations all over the place. The Danes had lived outside, next to their vehicles, adding to the general air of untidiness. Worst of all, the sangars looked shoddy and inadequate. Only one of them had any overhead cover. Nonetheless, Kruyer thought, 'this is not too bad', as he set off to find himself a room.

The first task was to learn everything of value from the Danes before they left. As he stood chatting, 'all of a sudden the place just erupted. A couple of cracks, and then all the machine guns started opening up'. It was the first of six attacks that day. The Danes had greeted their replacements with the gloomy salutation 'welcome to Hell'. That had seemed to be a wind-up. Now the new arrivals were not so sure.

The Danish Reconnaissance Squadron left the following day. A full battle group operation with air support was mounted to get them out. Jowett felt relieved as the huge convoy passed the point where Easy Company would have to go to their assistance if they took casualties. Now he could concentrate on the daunting task he had inherited.

As the Danes left, a force of seventy ANP came in by road. Coco, the police chief in residence, who had caused the Pathfinders much amusement, had not been so popular with the Danes, who suspected him of collusion with the Taliban. He left with them, along with his men. The replacements were not Pashtuns but came from the north and were free of the tribal entanglements that made the local ANP such dubious allies.

Their numbers did something to allay the sense of emptiness that had settled on the compound with the Danes' departure. The extraction operation had been big and noisy. It had been closely observed by the Taliban. The intelligence reaching Easy Company suggested that the enemy believed they were watching a major pull-out and that the district centre was ripe for the taking. The early morning helicopter mission to insert the Paras and the Irish had looked insignificant. 'We had a very good feel for what their intentions were,' said Jowett. 'They had seen this big convoy go out and nothing really tangible had come in. There were four old pick-up trucks with Afghan National Police hanging off them and that was that.' Intelligence reports said the fighters were telling each other confidently that they would be 'drinking tea in the district centre tonight'.

Easy Company's first full day opened with the usual breakfast-time RPG. An hour later five grenades hit the camp. Just before 10 a.m. the Outpost was hit by a Chinese rocket. Another struck later but failed to explode. As yet there was no sign of an all-out attack. Early in the afternoon, a large convoy of Taliban was spotted lying up in a wadi in the south. It was assumed they were planning an operation. An air strike was called in which dropped two big bombs and fired nineteen rockets, destroying seven trucks.

The Taliban spent the first couple of days trying to gauge the defenders' strengths and test their responses. They would creep in close, so close that grenades were needed to drive them back. One night Easy Company's sergeant major, John Scrivener, hurled several at some gunmen lurking in the area of the disused mosque on the southern edge of the compound. After that, the Royal Irish nick-named him 'Michael Stone', a blackly humorous reference to the Loyalist fanatic who had killed three people in a gun and grenade attack on an IRA funeral in Belfast.

Occasionally the men ventured out of the compound to try to map the alleyways and rat-runs and to reset flares that lit up the night when tripped by an advancing gunman. But most of their time was taken up with preparing for and responding to the next action. Most of the intelligence they were getting was coming from inter-cepts. 'There was no contact with the public because there was nobody in the area,' said Freddie Kruyer. 'The town was completely deserted.' The Afghan police in the camp would venture out occa-sionally and come back with information. The police were from outside the area and Kruyer tended to take their reports 'with a pinch of salt. They were in the same boat as us and the fact that they walked outside the walls didn't mean that they knew more than we did.' They also 'had alternative agendas – like wanting to get out of there as quickly as possible'.

Conditions in the base were bearable. Nobody expected very much. There were two wells providing water that was potable when purified with sterilising tablets and blessedly cool, colder than what came out of the two freezers they had inherited. There were plenty of small rooms in the compound to kip down in. They slept four to a room on X-frame American-issue cots which previous tenants had left behind, underneath mosquito nets. When they were not sleeping or on stag, they brewed tea, smoked and chatted and played the occasional game of backgammon.

Freddie Kruyer, the platoon house Mr Fixit, rigged up a shower. The men had to pick their time to use it, if they did not want their ablutions interrupted by the Taliban. 'From about twelve to three was a good time,' said Kruyer. 'They would be getting their heads down because it was too hot for them. Then, after nine o'clock in the evening and before eight in the morning. It wasn't a hundred per cent, but they were the safest times to go outside.' The men crapped in communal 'thunderboxes', 55-gallon oil drums cut in half topped by a hardboard plank with holes in it. One of the least desirable jobs was burning them off with diesel every day. 'We were pretty house-proud and despite everything that was going on, that was a tidy old place to live in,' said Jowett.

Twenty days after they got there, Easy Company were subjected to a concerted effort to take the camp. The attack began on the evening of 26 August. Intelligence reports said that two groups were supposed to take part, but when one was late arriving the other started without it. Just before the OC's evening briefing the compound was hit from several different directions. The action died out after an A-10 was called in but resumed again just as the sun was rising. The new assault was the worst the defenders had yet faced. Village elders later told Jowett that 150 or more fighters were involved. 'They weren't all fighting at the same time,' Jowett said. 'It wasn't like *Zulu* where they line up on the crest and you can count them. But it was a coordinated, full-on attack.'

Easy Company were ready and waiting. Jowett had ordered his men to stand to at first light. Logically, this was the optimum time for the Taliban to launch an attack. The advantage the defenders had with their night vision equipment would fade with the coming of daylight. The men on the sangars would be groggy after a sleepless night, their alertness blunted by hours spent peering into the hostile darkness. On this occasion, though, the defenders were wide awake.

The whole company, together with the Afghan police, crept to their positions, giving away nothing that would alert the insurgents.

The Taliban started shooting at 4.55 a.m. 'It was like a Jean-Michel Jarre concert with the tracer and the noise,' said Jowett. The attack came in from all sides. The defenders had ten machine guns. Only two were .50-cals and the rest were GPMGs. With these they had to 'win the firefight, win that initial exchange ... we are trying to kill them and stop them ... very quickly [they] get the message that we are not asleep, that they are not just going to walk in. It's part of taking someone's heart out so they just don't want to continue'.

Jowett was on the headquarters building roof with the signallers who had come in with his company, 'tucked up behind a hip-high, shitty wall, taking effective fire and trying to suppress it'. Most of it was coming from the area of the mosque on the south-west corner of the compound. Jowett heard a shout of 'Medic!' One of the signallers, Lance Corporal John Hetherington, had been hit as he moved across the rooftop. Jowett checked his pulse, but could not find one. They carried him off the roof and put him on the quad bike to take him to Mike Stacey at the medical post.

The first thought was to call Bastion for a casevac helicopter, but it soon became clear this would not be necessary. John Hetherington was dead. The bullet had hit him close to his armpit, in a gap in his body armour.

The fighting stopped just after 7 a.m. when an A-10 arrived and strafed the Taliban positions, just a road's width from the Outpost.

It was a desolate morning. Hetherington's body was put in a room at the edge of the camp, and extracted by helicopter thirty-six hours later. The bodies of several Taliban were lying in the road in front of the main gate. There was an informal understanding that no attempt would be made to interfere with their recovery.

The Taliban would not be drinking tea in the compound that night. There were, however, seven more firefights that day. In mid-afternoon the base was struck by five mortars and six RPGs. An American B-1 bomber was called in and dropped a 2,000lb bomb. Calling in air power was a delicate business. Bomb strikes and gun runs killed many Taliban, but the close-quarters nature of the fight-ing meant there was always a risk of 'fratricidal' incidents. The skill of the FSG, which brought in air and artillery strikes, was vital in Musa Qaleh, as it was elsewhere. There were two considerations when giving the coordinates of a target. One was the possibility that there were civilians in or near the location. The other was whether the bombs, shells or missiles would pose a threat to the defenders. The FSG in Musa Qaleh was made up of Bombardier Ray Anderton, Lance Bombardiers 'Ginge' Pritchard and Paul Wright of 7 RHA and Corporal Abe Williams of the RAF Regiment. In training exercises, each weapon had a 'danger close' range. If you were within it, you risked death or injury. The 'danger close' limit for A-10 gun runs was several hundred yards. In Musa Qaleh it was not unusual to have cannon shells exploding 20 or 30 yards from the defenders' posi-tions. The safe distance for a 1,000lb bomb was more than a thou-sand yards. The jets were dropping them 140 yards from the base. The fact that no one was hurt in the scores of air strikes mounted in the area was a tribute to the skill of both the observers and the pilots.

After the failure of the two big efforts of 26/27 August, the Taliban reverted to stand-off attacks with rockets and mortars. The losses they had suffered in the effort to overrun the base seemed to have subdued them. They were also having difficulties with their resupplies, of men, ammunition and medical equipment. D Squadron of the HCR was now operating MOGs (Manoeuvre Outreach Groups) in the desert, small, fast-moving patrols that operated on the principles of mobility and unpredictability. They intercepted and attacked resupply columns of pick-up trucks car-rying reinforcements and stores. The insurgents could no longer regard the desert as a friendly hinterland where they had only the Coalition air force to worry about.

Morale in the base was strong. Everyone was a Musa Mucker now. They were all in it together. 'There was not a bloke who was tucked away in a storeroom,' said Jowett. 'There wasn't a single man who at some point wasn't returning fire, shooting at the Taliban from the rooftops.' He found there was no need for him to 'keep driving them on. They were chipper. They were up for it.'

On 1 September their resolve faced another, searching test. The day started slowly. Three mortars hit the camp around 9.30 a.m. Just before 10 a.m., I Battery of the RHA, which was now operating in the desert near by, landed some rounds from their 105mm guns on a Taliban OP. Then, a few minutes before 4 p.m., four mortars flew into the base. Two of them hit the Alamo, one landing on the roof with an explosion that kicked up a huge cloud of smoke and debris.

Danny Groves was on the mortar line when he heard the impact. Soldiers were running towards the Alamo carrying stretchers. 'Stomachs began to turn,' he wrote. 'There was panic everywhere and one soldier was brought down and stretchered across to the clinic, closely followed by another casualty shortly after.' Groves went to the clinic to get more information and ran into someone who told him that one man was dead and another severely injured. The dead soldier was Ranger Anare Draiva. The wounded man was Lance Corporal Paul Muirhead. Draiva was one of four Fijians in the Royal Irish contingent. 'D', as he was known, was twenty-seven, a big, smiling, friendly man, who belonged to the mortar team. He had served in Iraq and had been one of the first to volunteer for Afghanistan duty. 'Moonbeam' Muirhead was twenty-eight, from near Stratford-upon-Avon. He was a member of the Patrols Platoon and another volunteer. He and 'D' were friends. He acted as an older brother to some of the younger, less experienced soldiers.

When Groves broke the news to his mortar men, 'you could tell by the look in their eyes how shocked they were but I don't think anyone quite knew what to say so we just said nothing'. After a while the shock was replaced by anger. 'When something like this happens it's a natural reaction to want to lash out and get vengeance for the loss. I wanted it, I have to admit, and you could see in everyone else's face that they wanted it too. We were all wanting to fire and I don't think we really cared at what or who, just as long as it felt like we were doing something.'

By now, though, there were aircraft overhead, dropping JDAM bombs and flying gun runs. Danny Groves went up to the Alamo roof with his friend, the mortar fire controller Corporal John Harding, to clean up the mess before any of the other mortar men saw it. The casevac helicopter arrived at 7.30 p.m. Paul Muirhead was flown on to Oman for specialist treatment but died on 6 September. 'They always say when people die, "Oh, he was such a good guy"', said Adam Jowett. 'But they were, they genuinely were.'

Even Groves's optimism and good humour were sagging as he finished his diary entry for a black day. 'Surely,' he wrote, 'something good will happen soon.'

17

Peace of Exhaustion

There were to be more dark hours for the battle group before their tour was over. Throughout the summer, the soldiers at Kajaki had been living on hillsides, baking in the daytime heat and shivering at night, guarding the dam from continuing insurgent attacks. At about noon on the morning of Wednesday, 6 September, a patrol set off from the Observation Post called Normandy to investigate a sighting of the Taliban in the town below. The insurgents had set up a checkpoint on one of the roads and were waving down vehicles. It seemed they were forcing drivers to hand over money. With the heavy presence of civilians and children, there was no question of the Paras calling in a mortar strike. Instead, Lance Corporal Stuart Hale, after checking with Corporal Stuart Pearson of 3 Para Support Company, decided to get closer to the scene and see whether there was a chance of picking off the gunmen with a sniper rifle. Hale had gone about seven hundred yards when he reached a narrow dry river bed, and jumped over it. He then, as he told a reporter later, 'found myself hopping back. It was like I had hit a spring and I remember thinking, "That's strange. What's going on here?"' He fell flat on his back. He looked down and saw that he was missing a finger. His leg was twisted at a weird angle and there was a stump where his foot should have been. He had stepped on a mine.

High up on the hill, about a mile away, the men in the 'Athens' OP heard the explosion. Private Dave Prosser of 3 Para's Mortar Platoon thought little of it. 'You just got used to loud bangs going off all the time,' he said. 'You just didn't react to them.' Then Corporal Mark Wright began calling for medics and stretcher-carriers. A party of nine men hurried off down the hill to help.

When they arrived, Stuart Pearson directed them on a safe route to the casualty. They applied tourniquets, gave Hale morphine and attached intravenous drips to get fluids into his system. Mark Wright took charge. He decided that Hale was likely to bleed to death if he was carried back up the hill so he called Bastion for a casevac helicopter. Together with Stuart Pearson and some of the others, he prodded the ground for mines, to clear a path to a flat patch of ground about fifteen yards away, where they thought the helicopter could put down. They stretched warning tape along the route, put Hale on a stretcher and carried him across to the landing site.

Pearson then turned to go back along the cleared path to the spot where Hale had been hit and where other members of the group were still waiting. As he picked up a water container, there was another explosion. Private Jay Davis, who had helped carry the stretcher, watched with dismay. Now they knew that there were mines everywhere.

Everyone's first instinct was to help Pearson. He was only four or five yards away. But they also knew that if they took a step they risked further catastrophe. 'No one could get to Stu because obviously if we moved, other people would get blown up,' said Davis. Pearson, who, like everyone in 3 Para, had basic medical training, would have to treat himself. 'He put the tourniquet on himself, put morphine into himself and we just had to leave him.' They were 'standing stock still. Everyone was shouting orders. Then it calmed down a bit and we heard the choppers coming in'.

By now it was 1.30 p.m., more than an hour and a quarter after the first mine went off. The arriving Chinook was fitted with emergency medical equipment. But none of the battle group CH-47s had winches. The stretcher party marked the landing site with green smoke but the helicopter landed about fifty to a hundred yards away, in a cloud of dust and grit. The pilot ordered the medical team to stay on board because of the mine threat. The loadmaster was told to signal to the soldiers to bring the casualties to the aircraft. He stood on the ramp and gave a thumbs-up sign. But no one came forward.

There was no question of them risking the journey over ground that might be densely sown with mines. In fact, the soldiers thought the helicopter's presence itself was a hazard. There had been talk before it landed that its downdraught might dislodge rocks that could cause more explosions. According to Davis, before the Chinook landed 'Mark was trying to tell the pilot to fuck off just in case it set more mines off, because it didn't take a lot'. Then the loadmaster saw a bare-chested man dressed in boots and shorts make the letters 'T' and 'O' with his hands, which he translated as 'Take off'. He told the pilot and a minute after they had landed, the Chinook rose again in a swirling column of dirt.

The soldiers ducked down to shield themselves from the dust storm kicked up by the rotors. Jay Davis watched Mark Wright 'crouch down, just to get out of this down blast. He put his hand out and – boom'. Another mine went off. Wright was badly wounded in his left upper chest, arms, face and neck. The blast also caught Lance Corporal Alex Craig, one of the medics, wounding him in the chest. Dave Prosser went to help him. By now medical supplies were running low. Prosser improvised, taking off his T-shirt and using it as a bandage. Craig decided to take his chances and, despite his injuries, set off to walk up the hill to an OP.

He managed to make it to safety. But it was a rash thing to do. It was clear that the slightest movement could trigger another explosion. Yet despite the appalling danger another medic, Lance Corporal Paul 'Tug' Hartley, moved forward to help his comrades. He flung the medical pack he had carried down from the 'Athens' OP on to the ground in front of him, to detonate any mines in his path, then moved forward to stand on the patch where the kit had landed.

He reached Mark Wright without setting off any mines. As he got to him, Fusilier Andy Barlow, a machine-gunner attached to 3 Para who was standing near by, stepped back to give the medic room. As he did so, Barlow trod on another mine, which blasted shrapnel into his lower left leg. The explosion also blew Hartley to the ground and hit Prosser. In mine strikes, the debris on the ground around becomes almost as dangerous as the shrapnel. Prosser got 'bits of stone in my leg and in my ear, and a big bit of frag in my chest'. He had to 'start first-aiding myself with what I could find. I had blood pissing out of my chest and everywhere. I lay on my side. I remembered that if you have a bad lung, the one that's uppermost will still work because the fluid will drain into the lower one and if you lie on your back, the fluid will drain into both and knacker both lungs'.

Paul Hartley threw across a field dressing. Prosser 'put that on, but the blood started coming through that straight away so I got another one on. I basically scrunched up the field dressings, poked one in the hole and got another one, wrapped that round, tied it in a knot and lay on my side'.

When the first news of the mine strike reached Bastion, Stuart Tootal had asked his higher headquarters at Kandahar for an American Black Hawk helicopter, equipped with a winch, to go to assist, but was told that there would be a long delay. Three hours after the first mine went off, two Black Hawks were finally on their way.

The wounded and the stranded waited calmly for them to arrive. No one screamed, no one groaned, but Mark Wright talked, quietly. He spoke about his wedding plans. He was about to get married to his girlfriend Gillian. 'He was saying how much he loved her and how much he was looking forward to seeing her again,' said Jay Davis. 'He said he might have to call the wedding off because his arm was in clip and we were telling him not to be so stupid.' Wright made brave jokes about the amount of insurance that would be coming to him.

The helicopters were a long time getting there. To Dave Prosser, 'it felt like bleeding for ever, just lying there'. At last, they heard the throbbing of the rotors and the Black Hawks were hovering over them. They were from a rescue unit and had specialist American jumpers on board. Two of the jumpers were winched down with a scoop stretcher and started hauling the wounded to safety. Stu Hale went first, then Mark Wright. When the wounded were on board, the crew winched up the unharmed members of the rescue party.

Wright was flown off to the helicopter landing site at Kajaki Dam and loaded on to a waiting casevac Chinook, which took off immediately for Bastion. He died of his wounds on the way. Mark Wright was twenty-eight and had been a member of 3 Para Mortar Platoon since October 1999. 'He was a brilliant bloke,' said Dave Prosser. 'I went to the Mortars in January 2001 so I had known him a long time.' Wright would join in when they went for a drink and liked a game of cards. But he also had a quiet side. He was a dog lover who kept a picture of his black Labrador with him and went back to his home in Scotland every weekend from Colchester to see his fiancée.

Shortly after they got back to Bastion, news arrived of further casualties in the platoon houses. There were wounded men in Sangin and more in Musa Qaleh. It had been another hot day in Sangin. Since morning, the Taliban had launched four attacks with small arms, machine guns and mortars. At 5.30 in the afternoon they landed a number of mortars in the compound, in the orchard area, where a platoon orders group was taking place. Three men were injured, including Lance Corporal Luke McCulloch, one of the Royal Irish soldiers attached to the Paras' 'C' Company. He had been hit in the head by shrapnel and it was clear that his injury threatened his life. A casevac helicopter set off from Bastion, flown by Major Mark Hammond of the Royal Marines. When he and the crew arrived, shepherded by two Apaches, a firefight was still in progress. There was no way to safely land the Chinook, and Hammond reluctantly swung away and back towards Bastion.

In Helmand, a bad day still had a long way to run. Immediately after reaching Bastion, Hammond was told to prepare for a second mission. Another casevac would have to be flown to extract two wounded Royal Irish soldiers, Rangers Panapassa Matanasinga and Dominic Whitehouse, who had both been hit by shrapnel when mortars hit the base at Musa Qaleh, just after 5 p.m. Matanasinga had the more serious injuries. Mike Stacey, the MO at Musa Qaleh, had told Stuart Tootal in Bastion that he could keep Matanasinga alive only for six or seven hours.

When the Chinook arrived, the Taliban were waiting. The plan was to put down on the helicopter site close to the compound walls. It was a very dangerous place, in the middle of a complex of compounds and alleyways which provided ideal cover from which to mount an ambush. Hammond went in fast and low but was met by a stream of fire and had to turn away. One of the escorting Apaches saw a pair of RPGs swish 10 yards above and below the Chinook. Once again, the crew spent several hectic minutes returning fire from the door guns. When they got back to Bastion it was found that four rounds had hit the aircraft, one almost shearing off a rotor blade at the root.

Tootal decided to wait for dark before trying again. Another Chinook was found, and artillery batteries and aircraft were put on alert to batter Taliban positions around the two bases as the helicopter darted in.

Hammond, along with his three crewmates and the four members of the medical team, took off for Sangin once more. As soon as he touched down an armoured Spartan from the HCR raced out to the landing site and delivered the wounded. As Hammond lifted off, the Chinook came under fire from machine guns. The crew shot back from the door guns until they had reached safety height.

Back at Bastion, Lance Corporal McCulloch was pronounced dead in the ambulance on the way to the medical centre. The others would be all right. McCulloch was twenty-one years old and was born in Cape Town. He had already been in the army for five years. He was described by his CO, Lieutenant Colonel Michael McGovern, as a 'truly outstanding character' who was 'a delight to have around'.

There were still wounded men in Musa Qaleh. As the citation for Mark Hammond's thoroughly deserved Distinguished Flying Cross later stated, at this point he would have been justified in declaring that the threat in Musa Qaleh was too high and he would not be returning. Instead, he accepted the task without hesitation.

This time all available air assets were there to support him. There were Apache attack helicopters, A-10s and a Spectre gunship. Just before the Chinook made its final approach they pounded known Taliban positions. This time Hammond got in and out unscathed.

Wednesday, 6 September, had been the most testing date in the calendar since the battle group deployed. It was, as Tootal said, 'a day of days'. Once again, the helicopters had taken enormous risks. Once again, they had got away with it. But the deaths in Afghanistan were mounting up. Only four days before, all fourteen men aboard an RAF Nimrod reconnaissance aircraft had crashed while supporting a ground operation. The lengthening casualty list added to the growing perception in Britain that the mission was going wrong.

The odds were shortening all the time, as Hammond's first mission to Musa Qaleh had demonstrated. The shot that hit the rotor root could have brought the Chinook down. That prospect once again raised the question of what exactly was being achieved by holding the platoon houses, and in particular Musa Qaleh. Since the wounding and subsequent death of Paul Muirhead, the tempo of attacks there had remained high. On 2 September, six more Royal Irish were wounded, one of them, Lieutenant Paul Martin, seriously. Three days later, the Taliban had made another attempt to overrun the base. The attack was beaten back by the defenders, helped from the air by bombs dropped by Harriers and A-10 gun runs.

Easy Company were inflicting daily defeats on the Taliban but their position was tenuous, as was only too clear to Corporal Brian Price of 3 Para, one of half a dozen reinforcements who had been flown in to replace the battle casualties. Price had been in Sangin but Musa Qaleh had a far more sinister vibe. 'Sangin wasn't easy,' he said. 'But Musa Qaleh was hideous at times because of how close they got to the camp.' After the Hesco ramparts of Sangin, the base's defences looked flimsy. 'If the Taliban had the numbers I think they would have got in because some of the walls were six feet tall which were easily jumpable.'

Attacks at Musa Qaleh came out of the blue from all sides. One night Price was arriving for stag duty in Sangar Three, which faced eastwards, when the base came under rifle fire from the north. This, as it turned out, was just an artful preliminary. 'The way they did it was they fired small arms from one direction to get us to concentrate on that side, and then they would RPG us from another direction, which did catch us out.' As Price arrived at the top of the stone steps leading up to the sangar it took a direct hit from a grenade. The shot failed to penetrate the walls, 'but it was enough to knock me down the stairs and knock me out', he said. When he came round he struggled back up to the sangar just as another RPG hit. He

lurched in, semi-conscious, to see 'fire hitting the side. All the lads
were on the floor. We finally got everyone back up into position and
firing back'. They were getting hit from the north, east and west.
Then, to complete the 360-degree engagement, they started taking
fire from the south as well.

This level of violence placed a huge strain on the defenders'
morale. The Royal Irish felt deeply the deaths of their 'brothers' Paul
Muirhead, Anare Draiva and Luke McCulloch. They dealt with it by
carrying on with extra determination. Adam Jowett was a committed Christian and leant on his faith to keep going. He carried a card
tucked in his helmet printed with the Paratrooper's Prayer and the
following lines from Isaiah:

> Even youths grow tired and weary, and young men stumble and
> fall; but those who hope in the LORD will renew their strength.
> They will soar on wings like eagles; they will run and not grow
> weary, they will walk and not be faint.

But the defenders could only carry on if they had the necesssary
means, and supplies and resources were running alarmingly low.
There were enough men in the camp to defend it. The Afghan
security contingent was more reliable and skilful than its counterparts in the other platoon houses. The problem was equipment and
ammunition. The base had only two .50-cals, one of which had
been damaged by insurgent fire and put out of action. They were
reduced to mocking up a dummy in the hope it would have a
deterrent effect. They had no Javelin missiles as they did in Sangin.

Their biggest worry, however, continued to be the ammunition
stocks. In all of Easy Company's time in Musa Qaleh they received
only six deliveries, all of which came in on casevac helicopters. On
8 September the mortars had thirty rounds of 81mm left. This was
enough to last for one serious engagement. They had no link
ammunition left for the Minimi light machine guns, and had to
spend tedious hours pushing 5.56 rounds left behind by the Danes
back into the used links.

The shortages were all the more alarming as intelligence reports indicated that the insurgents were preparing another heavy attack on the base. The Taliban were suffering. In the first few days of September, information came through that a senior commander's son had been killed in a mortar attack. Later it appeared that it was the commander himself who was dead. More and more foreign voices were heard, apparently Pakistanis who had been drafted in to replace the local casualties. Fighters were complaining to each other that they were starting to feel the cold at night and missing their families.

The Taliban appeared to be reaching the limits of their determination. They spoke, according to the intelligence reports, of 'the final sacrifice' and the 'end of the story'. A new commander had been brought in to take charge. It seemed that one last attempt to overrun the camp was imminent. The defenders almost welcomed the development. 'In many ways I think we all hope it is soon,' wrote Danny Groves. 'We hate the indirect fire attacks, like mortars and rockets, because we can't really do fuck all to counter them. But when they come at us, we can take our destiny in our own hands and wipe them out as we have been consistently doing in every battle we fought against them.'

On the morning of 11 September it looked as if the epic showdown was about to begin. Sergeant Major Scrivener hurried round the compound ordering extra ammunition supplies to all the positions. An aircraft had reported seeing a crowd of four or five hundred men, only two and a half miles south of Musa Qaleh. There were further sightings throughout the day, in different locations. But as the hours passed and the shadows lengthened, the great attack failed to materialise. There was an exchange of small-arms fire when the Outpost came under attack. The 7 RHA guns out in the desert bombarded a Taliban position. These, as it turned out, were the last shots Easy Company would hear fired in anger in Musa Qaleh.

The first signs that a dramatic change was on the way had come a few days earlier, on 8 September, when the defenders had been told, once again, to prepare to leave. Adam Jowett announced to his men that they could be moving out as early as 13 September and returning to Bastion before redeploying to the relative tranquillity of Gereshk to carry out gentle reconstruction tasks before flying home in mid-October.

What would happen to the base at Musa Qaleh after they departed was unclear. A rumour circulated that it would be abandoned. This story received a mixed reception. Everyone was delighted to be leaving. But no one liked the idea of ceding the place they had fought so hard to defend to their enemies. The soldiers had beaten back over a hundred attacks in forty days. Three of their friends had been killed and fifteen injured. To walk away seemed to negate the value and the purpose of all their effort and sacrifice.

As it turned out, the timetable laid out by Jowett was wildly optimistic. But the episode reflected a profound shift in Britain's strategy in Afghanistan. The incoming chief of the general staff and head of the British Army, General Sir Richard Dannatt, had just made a visit to Afghanistan. Brigadier Ed Butler had spelled out for him, in stark terms, the risks that were being run every time a casevac operation was mounted and the strong possibility that 'an immeasurable strategic shock to the overall campaign' was likely. He outlined the worst case scenario he had gone over many times with Stuart Tootal. It was 'that we'd have a casualty, we'd put a casevac helicopter [out], that would be shot down. We'd then have [to make] the decision: "Do you send in another helicopter into a high-threat area to try and rescue the helicopter that was down, and the casualties?" That got us very close to the decision for me to say, "We're going to have to withdraw from Musa Qaleh."' This, Butler said, was not an admission of defeat. 'It was the fact that pro-fessionally, personally and morally I could not keep my troops in such constant danger without a viable casevac system in place.'

Butler's concerns were deepened by intelligence reports he was getting saying that the 'Tier One' Taliban had identified the platoon houses' reliance on helicopter support as a critical vulnerability and were more determined than ever to shoot one down. In his opinion it was 'very much a matter of when, and that was going to be sooner rather than later'. His professional judgement 'was that to lose a helicopter, with twenty troops on board, would be a significant blow with strategic consequences from an Afghan, a London and a NATO perspective'. He had decided that 'we should come out unless there was a dramatic ... change in the situation'.

He passed this on to Dannatt and to PJHQ in Northwood, which had ultimate operational control of the British effort in Afghanistan. The decision was his own. He would 'make the call when the next casualty came through'. It was a very exposed position to be in for an ambitious officer. But Butler felt that the risk of catastrophe was enormous. He compared it to having 'a loaded revolver pointed to [your troops'] head, and there's a bullet in the breech, the safety catch is off and [you've] taken the first pressure on the trigger'.

Butler's message was taken very seriously in London. He had raised the question of how the British public would react to the sort of disaster he had outlined. The deployment had not been popular. The reasons behind it had never been properly articulated. Few understood what the British were doing in Afghanistan and the scant reports filtering back from the battlefield painted a gloomy picture.

Plans were now made for an immediate withdrawal from Musa Qaleh. Events had moved quickly. Butler's superior General David Richards, the commander of the NATO-led ISAF force in Afghanistan, was opposed to the idea of a swift pull-out. He had inherited the outstation strategy when he took over command from the Americans in August and had made it clear to all that he thought it was mistaken and an inappropriate use of military resources. He believed that Butler should have resisted the Afghan government pressure to ride to the rescue in Musa Qaleh and Now Zad and concentrated on securing the 'Triangle' in central Helmand and establishing the reconstruction programme.

Although Richards was keen to reverse the policy, he believed there were considerable long-term dangers in simply withdrawing. He thought an abrupt retreat would be portrayed by the Taliban as a historic defeat for the British. It would be 'Maiwand revisited' – a reference to the debacle in 1880 when the self-proclaimed sovereign, Ayub Khan, defeated a British brigade near Kandahar and besieged the garrison in the city. That had happened 130 years earlier, but was still fresh in the minds of the insurgents.

The claims the Taliban made mattered. A scramble from the platoon houses would demonstrate to the great army of the undecided in Helmand, the huge swath of the population who yearned for stability and prosperity but above all wanted to survive, that the British could be beaten. The promises of devotion to their well-being and commitment to the long haul were not to be believed. The British had shown that they could not provide protection. Survival, then, would mean living with the Taliban.

Richards spoke urgently to London. He talked to the prime minister's foreign affairs adviser, Sir Nigel Sheinwald, and the Chief of the Defence Staff, Sir Jock Stirrup. He told them that a unilateral withdrawal would count as a defeat. Any pull-out would have to be finessed if the British mission to Helmand was not to go down in history as a disaster.

The Afghan government were also dismayed by the plan. A retreat would mean that, despite all the fighting, the 'black flag of Mullah Omar' would fly over the district centre of Musa Qaleh and the Taliban's dreams of reconquest would take on a little more substance.

A crisis was approaching. But just as a diplomatic and military collision seemed inevitable, an escape route appeared. It was provided by the people in whose name the battle was being fought. The representatives of the long-suffering citizens of Musa Qaleh approached the Afghan authorities with a proposal. The battle of Musa Qaleh had been a disaster for the inhabitants. Much of the town centre was in ruins. They had lost homes and businesses. Most of them had fled to the countryside or the fringes of town. Anyone who ventured into the streets was liable to die. A woman and child had been killed in a pick-up truck in the bazaar to the west of the base during a firefight on 26 August. It was the fate of the powerless to accept the rule of the victors. But it seemed to the people of Musa Qaleh that no one was winning.

A group of local leaders devised a plan by which both sides

would withdraw and they would take responsibility for running the town. 'It was a tribal elders' initiative,' said Governor Daoud. 'They proposed it. They said, "We will be responsible for security. We will ask the Taliban to leave the area, not to fight any more in the town." They came to us. They said, "We have convinced the Taliban, because we told them we have lost property and you are not able to capture Musa Qaleh."' The insurgents had failed to capture the town from the British. But they had kept on trying, nonetheless, bringing continuing destruction and misery to Musa Qaleh. Daoud said the locals had threatened to side with the British unless the Taliban gave up.

Daoud called Butler in on the evening of 12 September to tell him about the offer. According to Butler, the elders had 'turned to the Taliban and said, "You've now caused so much destruction here our people aren't being fed, we haven't got our crops in … winter's approaching, hospitals are being blown apart, no one's in the bazaars, the kids can't go back to school. You created this situation as much as the Coalition. You must stop the fighting."' Daoud told Butler the elders would be phoning later on and asked him what he could do to help. 'I said, this is very easy,' he recalled later. 'If they get the Taliban to stop firing at my troops, I will tell my troops to stop firing at them.' At ten minutes to ten the governor's satellite phone warbled. 'The message came back saying, yup, they're pre-pared to cease fire. And I said, "Well, fine, I will tell my troops to stop firing unless there is a direct attack on a sangar."' There had been some exchanges of fire that evening. At 9.41 p.m. the shooting stopped and Easy Company were given orders to fire only in self-defence.

The elders' intervention was later presented as one of the achievements of the platoon house strategy. It was a triumph of people power over coercion. Whichever way the initiative was spun, the proposal was a sign of desperation. It was not only the civilian population who had reached their limit. Both sides were ready to disengage. The solution the elders offered would never have worked if it had not suited the Taliban and the Coalition alike. The attackers were all but fought to a standstill. The defenders were exhausted.

The elders offered a solution that allowed everyone to draw breath and, as importantly, save face.

Their proposal was snatched up with telling enthusiasm. When Butler told his superiors in PJHQ that they were no longer pulling out because of the changed situation he was told they 'fully understood'. The move fulfilled Richards's conditions for a finessed withdrawal.

It was a peace of exhaustion. It was important to set up a meeting to cement the deal while the mood lasted. There were certain pre- sentational problems that had to be overcome. The Coalition could not be seen to be dealing with the Taliban. The Americans in particular, who were never to accept the Musa Qaleh arrangements, regarded any negotiation as an act of surrender. The understanding would have to be brokered through the elders.

The following day the men of Easy Company, perched on the sangars, saw a surreal sight – a group of robed, bearded men walk- ing from the direction of the bazaar and up to the main gate. It was, as Danny Groves wrote, 'probably the first time in two months that anyone has been allowed to walk up to the base without being pumped full of lead'. The elders of Musa Qaleh had come to see Adam Jowett. He cleared away the rusty junk that had accumulated around the gate during the siege and came out with an interpreter to greet them. 'There were about sixty of them just standing there,' he said. 'And behind them, in black, were the Taliban. Without a shadow of a doubt.' The sight was oddly reas- suring. It told Jowett that the deal was serious. 'These guys had the influence and realising that very quickly made me feel better about the whole thing.'

Later that day, a *shura* was held in the desert west of Musa Qaleh. Butler flew in with the Foreign Office representative, Nick Kay. 3 Para's Patrols Platoon and the Household Cavalry set up a security perimeter. They put up a tent and waited. An hour later, a cloud of dust appeared to the east and a convoy of pick-up trucks emerged from the murk. The elders had arrived. They were seated and given cold drinks and water. Butler started with a spiel he had by now delivered many times. He told them, 'We are not here as occupiers, we are here as your guests. We're here to make a difference. When the job is done and you want us to go home, we will go back home. I have a family like you back in England and I want to go back to them when the job is done.' The elders were 'very respectable, very well spoken, very proud'. In the background sat men in black scarves, the Taliban or their representatives, who took no direct part in the talking. 'You could tell them by their features, their dress and everything else,' Butler said.

The first business was the terms on which the ceasefire would continue. David Richards in Kabul was clear that it would have to hold for a period of up to a month before a withdrawal could begin, leaving security in the hands of the elders. Butler wanted to ensure they would be able to get access to the base, in the event soldiers needed evacuation. The elders promised to provide Easy Company with food and water.

They kept their word. Soon after the meeting, civilians began to appear again on the the streets of Musa Qaleh. Some of the shops and stalls reopened for business. 'We got some potatoes and cooking oil so we could have some chips and – whoosh! Morale went sky high,' said Freddie Kruyer. This was just as well because two days after the start of the ceasefire, Adam Jowett broke the news that they would be staying put for up to two more weeks. That night, Captain Mark Johnson, the senior Royal Irish officer, who had been in Musa Qaleh since the beginning, talked to his men. He emphasised the need to see the mission through. If they left now the base would almost certainly fall into the hands of the Taliban. It would not be fair to their dead and injured comrades. Staying on was 'the right and proper thing to do'.

The message was that if some sort of normality was established and Afghan forces took control of security then their mission was accomplished. Over the next days and weeks, the ceasefire took hold. Governor Daoud had drawn up a fourteen-point plan, which was put into effect gradually. Among the protocols were that the flag of Afghanistan would always fly over the district centre and the chief of police would be chosen by the governor. The Taliban would withdraw from town, leaving the elders with responsibility

260 • PATRICK BISHOP

for security. The elders promised to provide sixty men from their own families to provide the core of a new police force.

Adam Jowett was a natural diplomat. He held regular meetings with the elders, sipping sweet tea and eating flat bread. They talked about their Christian and Muslim faiths. 'We discussed the differences, and more often than not the similarities,' he said. 'The subject came up readily and was important in helping them realise how normal we were and how much we had in common.' They also talked about repairing the town's damaged and destroyed buildings, including the bombed mosque. Initially, there had been plans to send in outside contractors but the community insisted they would do the work themselves. The elders included some returnees from the diaspora who had worked in America and Germany and spoke good English. 'They were professionals,' said Butler. 'They just wanted to return home, to get their lives in order, rebuild their villages, restore their country and keep the Taliban out.' They proposed that the Coalition provide the cash and they would find the labour. The work would provide a constructive alternative to the sort of employment the Taliban could offer.

The soldiers of Easy Company were used to fighting by now. They woke each morning doubting that the ceasefire would survive the day. They used the downtime to build up the base defences. But the remaining weeks they spent there passed with no noise louder than the honking of the traffic in the streets outside.

Easy Company did not leave Musa Qaleh until the middle of October. Jowett and Mark Johnson walked the commander of the newly raised Afghan militia around the base, pointing out where things were and the kit they had left behind for their use. It was, he said, an experience he knew well from his army service, 'as if you were handing over to another unit'.

There was a last duty to be done before they climbed into jingly trucks and drove out into the desert where the helicopters were waiting. Someone had drawn a memorial to Easy Company on one of the walls. It bore the Royal Irish crest and their motto, *Faugh a Ballagh* (Clear the Way), the battle cry of the fighting clans of the west of Ireland. It carried the names of everyone who had served in

Musa Qaleh and those who had died there. Now it was painted over. For better or worse, Musa Qaleh belonged to the Afghans now.

18

Going Home

With the new arrangements in place in Musa Qaleh, the tempo of violence in Helmand slackened for a while. 'A relatively quiet day,' wrote Stuart Tootal in his diary on 14 September. 'The level of activity across the area of operations seems to have reduced over the last few days.' The next day was also 'unusually quiet', with 'no attacks against Now Zad or Musa Qaleh and only one attack against the ANA at FOB Robinson and against our own troops in Sangin'. So it went on. The 18th was 'probably the quietest day we have had since June'. There were 'no contacts anywhere until after 17.00 hours and then only two brief attacks, one against Kajaki and one against Sangin'.

Across the battle group, everyone wondered about the possible causes of the lull. It could reflect the Taliban's battle weariness, after four months of fighting and heavy casualties that had failed to win substantial gains. There was evidence that the insurgents were finding it difficult to recruit locally and were having to draft in more foreign fighters. Seven Pakistani men of fighting age had been arrested in the Sangin area in the second week of September.

It might also be a sign that, as in Musa Qaleh, local people were turning against the Taliban. In Sangin there were indications that prominent figures were also exploring an initiative to exclude both the insurgents and the British from the town and take charge of security themselves. Or it might simply be that winter was coming and the gunmen were calling a seasonal halt to allow the poppy fields to be planted for next spring's harvest. No one believed that the Taliban had given up, and their caution was justified. There were to be another seventy-six shooting incidents between 18 September, the 'quietest day', and the end of the battle group's tour on 6 October.

Soon, though, the fighting would no longer be the responsibility of the Paras and their comrades. New faces were appearing in Bastion. The first elements of 3 Commando Brigade, who were taking over, were trickling, then flooding, in. On 29 September, 'L' Company of 42 Commando, The Royal Marines, flew to Sangin to relieve the Paras' 'C' Company, who had been there for a month. The base was still under regular attack. The day before it had been hit by small-arms fire and RPGs, one of which struck the roof of the FSG building.

The Marines landed just before first light. 'B' Company of the Paras went with them to protect them during the transition. They spent the morning alongside 'C' Company fighting running battles with the Taliban through the dusty cornfields and muddy irrigation ditches south of the district centre, supported by Apaches and A-10s. At least four insurgents were killed. But in the process of clearing the ruins of the JDAM building, two 'B' Company officers, Captain Guy Lock and Captain Jim Berry, were hit by grenade fragments, and Berry was badly hurt. The Household Cavalry were leaving too. Shepherded by the Paras' Patrols Platoon, they forded the Helmand river in their armoured vehicles and headed south to Bastion.

As the last soldiers boarded the helicopters they were seen off with a final salvo of small-arms fire from the Taliban. Despite the danger there was an end-of-term feeling in the air. The Paras and their battle group companions had been in Sangin for ninety-one days. In that time they had clashed with the Taliban 138 times. Sometimes these encounters were brief and lasted only a few minutes. Sometimes they went on for hours. What was constant was the knowledge that violence could erupt at any second. Behind the stoical joking and the wind-ups, a low buzz of anxiety was always present.

And now, for 3 Para, it was over, or nearly so. At the beginning of September, 'A' Company had been sent to Gereshk, back where they started, five very long months before. They had arrived first and set the standard for the battle group. They had also suffered more casualties than the other two rifle companies. By now, though, no one was making any distinctions. Helmand had been equally hard on everyone. 'A' Company started to move out on 2 October, with 'C' Company following them. 'B' Company and Easy Company, which stayed on to observe the cessation of hostilities in Musa Qaleh, were the last Paras to go.

Tootal handed over responsibility for the British battle group to the Marines at twelve noon on 6 October. Before that, there had been one last helicopter mission to fly. The base at Now Zad, which was defended by soldiers of the 2nd Battalion of the Royal Regiment of Fusiliers, had come under attack and two men had been hit by shrapnel from RPGs. Both would recover but both needed surgery. The Fusiliers would have to wait until November, when rain and mist settled on Now Zad and the trenches on ANP Hill filled with mud, before they left.

Hanging around in Kabul, waiting for a flight to Cyprus where the battalion was to enjoy a short break for relaxation and decompression before continuing the journey home, there was plenty of time for reflection. The Paras were returning from a very different mission to the one they had embarked on. Before the British arrived in Helmand there had been virtually no Coalition presence apart from a hundred American soldiers who were concerned only with hunting down Taliban and al-Qaeda leaders. The Paras had gone there to bring stability. Their presence had provoked a reaction. That had been expected, but not on the scale that developed. The battle group had been forced by the Taliban to fight what was known as a 'break-in battle'. That meant establishing the British presence in Helmand and creating the conditions in which they would be able to stay.

This had taken up all their resources and energies. As a result, little progress had been made on reconstruction, the underlying purpose of the deployment. No 'quick-impact projects' had been realised. With nothing to do, the Department for International Development had pulled out of Helmand in August. The inactivity was summed up by the story of the washing machine in Gereshk hospital. The unplumbed appliance had first caught the eye of the

Paras back in April. Fixing it seemed a simple way of declaring their good intentions to the local people. When they left, it was still swaddled in its plastic wrapping.

Instead of construction there had been destruction. Any buildings that the Taliban used as firing points were liable to be bombed flat and the areas around the district centres of Musa Qaleh, Now Zad and Sangin were scarred and battered by the continuous battles. The people of these places had no reason to love the British. All the violence had failed to break the Taliban's grip on the inhabitants. They were still able to carry on intimidating, threatening and extorting.

'What was it all about?' asked an officer who spent nearly two months in a platoon house. 'Well, I flattened the town and I killed a lot of Taliban … did that achieve a good effect? I don't know.' He comforted himself with the thought that 'what you could say is that we held the Taliban in Now Zad, Musa Qaleh and Sangin in order that they didn't get Lashkar Gah and Gereshk'.

That, ultimately, was the justification for the platoon house policy. Almost from the beginning, Governor Daoud had warned Brigadier Butler that if Now Zad and Musa Qaleh went, then Sangin and the hydroelectric dam at Kajaki would follow within a month. Then, the front line would be Highway One, the strategic road that loops through southern Afghanistan, and the Taliban would be inside Helmand's capital Lashkar Gah and neighbouring Gereshk 'before you can blink'. Butler believed him. By answering Daoud's call, the British 'kept the front line deep in northern Helmand and the enemy chose to attack us there and that's where the battles were fought'.

In the course of the fighting the Taliban suffered heavy losses. In all there were 498 engagements. It was impossible to establish exactly how many insurgents were killed but the figure was in the high hundreds, perhaps as many as a thousand. The attrition reduced the Taliban's capacity to expand. It also punctured their claims to have the strength and skill to topple the government and sweep the British out of Afghanistan, as their ancestors had done before them. Their inability to do this damaged their prestige in the eyes of the local people. This was a major setback in what was essentially a struggle for the approval, or at least the acquiescence, of the population of Helmand.

With the insurgents' advance stemmed, the south stayed calm for almost all the time the 3 Para battle group were present. There may have been little reconstruction, but that was not the fault of the military. There was, at least, stability.

In early February 2007, five months after the Paras left, the front line edged a little closer when the Taliban broke the agreement they had made with the elders of Musa Qaleh and stormed in to take over the town. They set about imposing their own brand of authority on the inhabitants. They murdered the leader of the elders, Haji Shah Agha, who had initiated the plan for the Taliban and British withdrawl. There have been reports of public hangings. The reoccupation followed an American air strike that killed a local Taliban leader, his brother and other fighters. The Taliban claimed they were inside the 'exclusion' zone where, under the terms of the agreement, they should have been exempt from attack, though this was disputed. The collapse of the agreement suited the Americans, who had opposed any accommodation with the Taliban all along.

But the fall of Musa Qaleh did not signal the start of a domino conquest southwards. By the summer of 2007, British troops of 12 Mechanised Brigade and their Afghan allies had cleared the Taliban out of large areas of the Sangin Valley. Discussions about security in Now Zad, Kajaki and Sangin did not evolve into formal arrangements but the soldiers were on good terms with large sections of the local people and their leaders, and work had begun on building and rebuilding in Lashkar Gah, Gereshk and Sangin. The engineer presence had been tripled and a full regiment of engineers was at work with local contractors on projects costing more than £3 million.

All progress in Helmand was slow. Daoud, who was recalled to Kabul at the end of 2006, said once that 'pessimists don't realise the amount of time needed' for things to begin to work. The 3 Para battle group had fought and won the vital break in battle that would allow a start to be made.

They had done so with extraordinary courage, resolve and good humour. In the end, the greatest achievement of the deployment lay in the conduct of the soldiers themselves. Everyone in the battle group could feel proud. They had fought a gruelling war bravely and cleanly and stopped the Taliban encroachment. Their achievement was reflected in the haul of medals announced later that year*. Among them were the Victoria Cross awarded to Bryan Budd and the George Cross won by Mark Wright. It was telling that both medals were earned not for killing the enemy but for actions aimed at saving the lives of friends. In the middle of the swirling political and military uncertainties of Helmand, as solid and enduring as the mountains that overlooked the battlefields, stood the ideals that motivated every proper soldier. These were nothing to do with queen or country, religion or political ideology. What sustained them was the determination not to let themselves down, and above all, not to let down their friends.

Pride in the awards was tempered by sadness at the lives that had been lost and damaged. Fourteen members of the battle group, along with one gallant interpreter, had been killed. Then there were the forty-six who suffered serious wounds. Visiting those who had been drastically injured during the Kajaki mine strike, Stuart Tootal noted in his diary that 'long after this tour has ended, the war will go on for them'. Many men would have to spend the rest of their lives struggling to achieve a fraction of the fitness and mobility they once rejoiced in.

The fighting had been hard on minds as well as bodies. The damage was not obvious in the euphoria of survival and home-coming. But over the months, a number of cases of post-traumatic stress disorder were diagnosed among battle group soldiers. Though this number was in single figures, no one was immune. Almost a year after the events, one of the bravest and most opimistic of the senior NCOs could not bear to fall asleep for fear of the flashbacks and the faces of his dead friends that haunted his dreams.

Homecoming was weird for everyone. The ordinariness of

* See Honours and Awards annexe.

Colchester life was startling and unsettling after what the men had been through. 'It was off the scale, what we were seeing and doing in Afghanistan,' said Zac Leong, 'A' Company's sergeant major. 'It was very hard to be in the thick of it one day and having a beer in a beer garden the next.' For a while he found it difficult to readjust to family life. There had been changes while he was away. When he left his daughter had been a 'blonde-haired, blue-eyed, gorgeous little thing. When I came back she was a Goth!'

He found himself 'really short tempered with anything and any-one ... Before I went to Afghanistan I was a really nice, chilled guy. I came back and I couldn't tolerate anything being wrong, and I think that was due to the op.' Leong soon reverted to his genial, chilled self.

Looking back, he reckoned that he and his comrades had written an important new chapter in the history of 3 Para. It was a feeling that everyone shared. The Paras' deep awareness of their antecedents had helped to carry them through. 'You never quite know whether you are going to be able to match the reputation that precedes you,' said 3 Para's RSM, John Hardy. 'But the men lived up to everything we have done in the past, all that and more.' The essential charac-teristic of the war they had been fighting was its repetitiveness. 'You have had a good look at the dragon and he has had a good look at you and you go back again,' Hardy said.

At the time of writing the war in Afghanistan is open-ended. Britain's ambassador in Kabul has said our involvement could last thirty years. In Colchester, preparations are already under way for another deployment. The Paras are approaching it with an enthu-siasm that seems undiminished by their recent ordeal. There are no dramas. They are just cracking on. 'It's what we do,' said John Hardy.

Acronyms and Abbreviations

A-10	A-10 Thunderbolt jet (aka 'Warthog' and 'Tankbuster')
ANA	Afghan National Army
ANP	Afghan National Police
CAP	Company Aid Post
CIMIC	Civil–Military Cooperation
CO	Commanding officer
DfID	Department for International Development
FAC	Forward Air Controller
FAO	Forward Artillery Observer
FCO	Foreign and Commonwealth Office
FLE	Forward Logistic Element
FOB	Forward Operating Base
FSG	Fire Support Group
GPMG	General Purpose Machine Gun
GPS	Global Positioning System
HAHO	High Altitude High Opening jumps
HALO	High Altitude Low Opening jumps
HCR	Household Cavalry Regiment
HE	High Explosive
HLS	Helicopter landing site
IED	Improvised explosive device
IRT	Immediate Response Team
ISAF	International Security Assistance Force in Afghanistan
ISTAR	Intelligence, Signals, Target Acquisition and Reconnaissance
JDAM	Joint Direct Attack Munition
JOC	Joint Operational Command
JTAC	Joint Tactical Air Controller
LAV	Light armoured vehicle

LMG	Light machine gun
MO	Medical Officer
MoD	Ministry of Defence
MOG	Manoeuvre Outreach Group
NATO	North Atlantic Treaty Organisation
NGO	Non-governmental organisation
OC	Officer Commanding
OEF	Operation Enduring Freedom
OMLT	Operational Mentoring Liaison Team
OP	Observation post
OTC	Officer Training Corps
PJHQ	Permanent Joint Headquarters
PKM	The Russian-made equivalent to the British GPMG, often used by the Taliban
PRR	Personal Role Radio
PRT	Provincial Reconstruction Team
QIP	Quick-impact project
R & R	Rest and recreation
RAP	Regimental Aid Post
RHA	Royal Horse Artillery
R IRISH	Royal Irish Regiment
RLC	Royal Logistics Corps
RPG	Rocket-propelled grenade
RSM	Regimental sergeant major
Snatch	Armoured Land Rover
SUSAT	Sight Unit, Small Arms, Trilux
UAV	Unmanned Air Vehicle
UN	United Nations
USAID	United States Agency for International Development
WMIK	Weapons Mount Installation Kit
WP	White phosphorus

Honours and Awards

Victoria Cross
Corporal Bryan James Budd, The Parachute Regiment (killed in action)

George Cross
Corporal Mark William Wright, The Parachute Regiment (killed in action)

Commander of the Order of the British Empire
Brigadier Edward Adam Butler DSO MBE, Late The Royal Green Jackets

Officer of the Order of the British Empire
Lieutenant Colonel Richard Friedrich Patrick Felton MBE, Army Air Corps
Colonel Martin Nicholas Nadin, Late Royal Army Medical Corps

Member of the Order of the British Empire
Lieutenant Colonel Steven Peter Walter Boyd, Corps of Royal Engineers
Major Sean Michael Burke, The Royal Irish Regiment
Captain Marcus James Dicks, The Royal Rifle Volunteers Territorial Army
Major David James Eastman, Corps of Royal Electrical and Mechanical Engineers
Major Huw Spencer Williams, The Parachute Regiment

Distinguished Service Order
Major Paul Alan Blair, The Parachute Regiment
Lieutenant Colonel Stuart John Craig Tootal OBE, The Parachute
  Regiment

Conspicuous Gallantry Cross
Lieutenant Hugo James Edward Farmer, The Parachute Regiment
Acting Captain Timothy Holden Illingworth, The Light Infantry
Lance Corporal of Horse Andrew Geoffrey Radford, The Life
  Guards

Military Cross
Captain Douglas Ricardo Beattie, The Royal Irish Regiment
Flight Lieutenant Matthew Kenneth Carter, Royal Air Force
Second Lieutenant Oliver Dale, The Parachute Regiment
Corporal of Horse Michael John Flynn CGC, The Blues and Royals
Staff Corporal Shaun Keith Fry, The Life Guards
Corporal Stuart James Giles, The Parachute Regiment
Lance Corporal Karl Wayne Jackson, The Parachute Regiment
Private Peter McKinley, The Parachute Regiment
Major Giles Matthew Timms, The Parachute Regiment
Captain Patrick James Williams, The Blues and Royals
Private Mark James Wilson, The Parachute Regiment

Distinguished Flying Cross
Major Mark Christopher Hammond, Royal Marines
Flying Officer Christopher Michael Haslar, Royal Air Force
Squadron Leader John Finbar Monahan, Royal Air Force
Flight Lieutenant Craig Thomas Wilson, Royal Air Force

George Medal
Lance Corporal Paul Hartley, Royal Army Medical Corps

Queen's Gallantry Medal
Corporal Stuart Henry Pearson, The Parachute Regiment

Royal Red Cross 2nd Class
Captain Catherine McWilliam, Queen Alexandra's Royal Army
Nursing Corps

Mention in Despatches
Captain Matthew Anthony William Armstrong, Royal Regiment of
Artillery
Lieutenant Nichol James Emslie Benzie, Royal Navy
Private Johnnie Chad Bevans, The Parachute Regiment
Warrant Officer Class 2 Michael John Bolton, The Parachute
Regiment
Warrant Officer Class 2 Karl Terence Brennan, Royal Regiment of
Artillery
Captain Alexander John Eida, Royal Regiment of Artillery (killed in
action)
Captain Mark Richard Eisler, The Parachute Regiment
Corporal Stephen John Farling, The King's Royal Hussars
Lieutenant Thomas David Fehley, The Parachute Regiment
Rifleman Ganesh Gurung, The Royal Gurkha Rifles
Warrant Officer Class 2 Trilochan Gurung, The Royal Gurkha Rifles
Corporal Benjamin Stephen Hall, Royal Army Medical Corps
Private Stephen James Halton, The Parachute Regiment
Lieutenant Martin Joseph Hewitt, The Parachute Regiment
Lieutenant Paul Ronald Hollingshead, The Royal Gurkha Rifles
Sergeant Daniel Jarvie, The Parachute Regiment
Warrant Officer Class 2 Thomas Heron Johnstone, Army Air Corps
Corporal Kailash Khebang, The Royal Gurkha Rifles
Sergeant Carl Frederick Lane, The Parachute Regiment
Warrant Officer Class 2 Zachary Adam Leong, The Parachute
Regiment
Captain Alexander James Mackenzie, The Parachute Regiment
Lance Corporal Luke Edward Patrick McCulloch, The Royal Irish
Regiment (killed in action)
Warrant Officer Class 1 Christopher Paul Mulhall, Army Air Corps
Rifleman Nabin Rai, The Royal Gurkha Rifles
Staff Sergeant James George Rankine, Corps of Royal Engineers

Warrant Officer Class 2 Andrew Kenneth Schofield, The Parachute
Regiment
Major Toby Patrick Oughtred Till, Coldstream Guards
Sergeant Daniel Cameron Baxter, Royal Air Force
Sergeant Graham Martin Jones, Royal Air Force
Squadron Leader Michael John Woods, Royal Air Force

Queen's Commendation for Bravery
Lance Bombardier Daniel Mark Byrne, Royal Regiment of Artillery
Warrant Officer Class 1 Andrew Steven Gee, The Royal Logistics
Corps
Corporal Nicholas James Grant, Royal Army Medical Corps
Warrant Officer Class 2 Andrew John Stedman, The Royal Logistics
Corps

Queen's Commendation for Bravery in the Air
Senior Airman Jason Broline, United States Air Force
Staff Sergeant Cameron Hystad, United States Air Force

Queen's Commendation for Valuable Service
Colour Sergeant Stuart Bell, The Parachute Regiment
Captain Nigel John Bishop, The Parachute Regiment
Brigadier Nicholas Roy Davies MBE MC, Late The Parachute
Regiment
Lance Corporal Adam Spencer Fear, Royal Corps of Signals
Lieutenant Colonel Martin Andrew Fenn, MBE, Corps of Royal
Engineers
Colonel Charles Peter Huntley Knaggs OBE, Late Irish Guards
Major Piers Guy Beresford Strudwick, The Royal Regiment of
Scotland
Wing Commander Richard Francis John Clifford, Royal Air Force

Acknowledgments

Most of the events in this story were told to me first-hand by the people who took part in them. To everyone who appears in these pages my deep thanks for your recollections, insights and observations. I owe a special debt to Lieutenant Colonel Stuart Tootal of 3 Para for making the project possible. Also to Captain Martin Taylor for his patience and diligence. The team at HarperCollins, led by Annabel Wright, were, as usual, superbly professional. In Kabul, Tom Coghlan kindly provided me with material on Helmand politics. A huge thank you to Cindy Utley for transcribing the interviews. And to Henrietta for everything.

Index

Also available as an audiobook from

HarperCollinsAudioBooks

www.harpercollins.co.uk